THEORY AND PRACTICE OF PUBLIC ADMINISTRATION: SCOPE, OBJECTIVES, AND METHODS

This monograph is the eighth in a series published by The American Academy of Political and Social Science. Monographs previously issued in this series are:

Monograph 1: October 1962   THE LIMITS OF BEHAVIORALISM IN POLITICAL SCIENCE

Monograph 2: June 1963   MATHEMATICS AND THE SOCIAL SCIENCES: THE UTILITY AND INUTILITY OF MATHEMATICS IN THE STUDY OF ECONOMICS, POLITICAL SCIENCE, AND SOCIOLOGY

Monograph 3: August 1963   ACHIEVING EXCELLENCE IN PUBLIC SERVICE

Monograph 4: April 1964   LEISURE IN AMERICA: BLESSING OR CURSE?

Monograph 5: February 1965   FUNCTIONALISM IN THE SOCIAL SCIENCES: THE STRENGTH AND LIMITS OF FUNCTIONALISM IN ANTHROPOLOGY, ECONOMICS, POLITICAL SCIENCE, AND SOCIOLOGY

Monograph 6: December 1966   A DESIGN FOR POLITICAL SCIENCE: SCOPE, OBJECTIVES, AND METHODS

Monograph 7: May 1967   GOVERNING URBAN SOCIETY: NEW SCIENTIFIC APPROACHES

THEORY AND PRACTICE OF PUBLIC ADMINISTRATION: SCOPE, OBJECTIVES, AND METHODS

Monograph 8 in a series sponsored by
The American Academy of Political and Social Science
Cosponsor for this volume:
The American Society for Public Administration

Edited by James C. Charlesworth

© 1968, by
THE AMERICAN ACADEMY OF POLITICAL AND SOCIAL SCIENCE
All rights reserved

PHILADELPHIA
October 1968

Issued by The American Academy of Political and Social Science at Prince and Lemon Sts., Lancaster, Pennsylvania.

Editorial and Business Office, 3937 Chestnut Street, Philadelphia, Pennsylvania 19104.

CONTENTS

	PAGE
FOREWORD .... *James C. Charlesworth*	vii

SCOPE

Scope of the Theory of Public Administration *Dwight Waldo*	1
Commentary on Waldo's Paper ...... *Wallace S. Sayre*	27
Professionalism, Political Science, and the Scope of Public Administration .... *Fred W. Riggs*	32
Conference Discussion	63
Scope of the Practice of Public Administration *Herbert Emmerich*	92
Commentaries on Emmerich's Paper ... *Herman G. Pope*	108
Lennox L. Moak	114
Conference Discussion	119

OBJECTIVES

Objectives of the Theory of Public Administration *Stephen K. Bailey*	128
Commentaries on Bailey's Paper ..... *Albert Lepawsky*	140
Emmette S. Redford	145
Conference Discussion	149
The American Public Executive: New Functions, New Style, New Purpose .... *Harlan Cleveland*	165
Commentaries on Cleveland's Paper ... *Arthur Naftalin*	179
Eugene H. Nickerson	183
Conference Discussion	188

Contents

METHODS

	PAGE
Methodology in the Theory of Public Administration *Lynton K. Caldwell*	205
Commentaries on Caldwell's Paper..*G. Homer Durham*	223
York Willbern	228
Observations on Willbern's Commentary *Lynton K. Caldwell*	234
Conference Discussion	236
Methodology in the Practice of Public Administration *Harvey Sherman*	254
Commentaries on Sherman's Paper ..*John W. Macy, Jr.*	291
Bernard L. Gladieux	297
Conference Discussion	301

* * * * * * *

A Report, and Also Some Projections, Relating to the Present Dimensions and Directions of the Discipline of Public Administration
James C. Charlesworth 322

FOREWORD

Although the officers of this Academy were aware of a number of studies of the adequacy and pertinence of the discipline of public administration, we believed that there have been some rapid developments in the field and that a new synthesis or selective appraisal would be currently useful. Accordingly, we organized a conference, which met in Philadelphia on 28 and 29 December, 1967, and addressed itself to the task of analyzing "The Theory and Practice of Public Administration: Scope, Objectives, and Methods."

Eighteen scholars and public officials accepted our invitation to participate:

Stephen K. Bailey	Syracuse University
Lynton K. Caldwell	University of Indiana
Harlan Cleveland	North Atlantic Treaty Organization (NATO), Brussels
G. Homer Durham	Arizona State University
Herbert Emmerich	University of Virginia
Bernard L. Gladieux	Knight and Gladieux, New York City
Albert Lepawsky	University of California, Berkeley
John W. Macy, Jr.	United States Civil Service Commission
Lennox L. Moak	Pennsylvania Economy League, Eastern Division
Arthur Naftalin	Minneapolis
Eugene H. Nickerson	Nassau County, New York
Herman G. Pope	Public Administration Clearing House, Chicago
Emmette S. Redford	University of Texas, Austin
Fred W. Riggs	University of Hawaii
Wallace S. Sayre	Columbia University
Harvey Sherman	New York Port Authority
Dwight Waldo	Syracuse University
York Willbern	University of Indiana

Unfortunately, Nickerson, Pope, and Redford were prevented

by illness or other imperative from attending, but they, along with all the others, contributed papers.

Also attending, but not contributing papers, were Harold B. Finger and Frank Smith, of the National Aeronautics and Space Administration (NASA).

The chairman was James C. Charlesworth, president of this Academy and professor at the University of Pennsylvania. There were two cochairman: Stephen B. Sweeney, former director of the Fels Institute of Local and State Government and former president of the American Society of Public Administration, and Don L. Bowen, executive director of the Society.

Six principal papers were prepared well in advance of the conference—one on theory and one on practice for each of the main subdivisions of the subject (scope, objectives, and methods). Two critiques of each of these papers were also prepared in advance, and all of the papers were distributed to the participants about a month before the meeting.

As chairman of this conference, after having been chairman of the 1965 meeting on "A Design for Political Science: Scope, Objectives, and Methods," I was able to make the stereoscopic observation that the papers and the discussion in the public administration meeting were better ordered and the participation better structured than in the earlier meeting. One may perhaps conclude that the discipline of public administration rubs off on its practitioners.

The reader may wonder why the discussants of the "Scope" and "Objectives" papers occasionally referred to the "Methods" discussion in the past tense. The reason was that several participants were unable, because of pressing official business, to be present at the times indicated by the sequence of topics in the Table of Contents of this volume, so we scheduled our sessions in the order of Methods, Objectives, and Scope instead of Scope, Objectives, and Methods. Since this rearrangement in no way harms the continuity of the written treatment, and since we wish to adhere to the format established for the political science and sociology monographs, we present the sequence of topics in this volume as originally planned.

Several members of the conference detected an element of

repetition in the discussions, and recommended that the editor make the appropriate excisions. This repetition was not planned, of course, but was the result of the disposition of some discussants to return to a theme which they considered important or basic. One may be reminded of the Probst personnel-rating forms, which were designed to reflect and score as more significant the items which the rater repeated. For this reason, I have not expunged any substantive discussion; I merely asked the participants to polish their oral syntax.

As with the conference on political science, the participants in this meeting evinced a "mood to make a bold and synoptic approach to the discipline" of public administration, and "sought to measure the importance" of public administration "in a broad philosophic context and to consider whether it is an adornment of the mind as well as a practical instrument of government."

This monograph will be distributed free to all members of the American Society for Public Administration and the American Political Science Association.

JAMES C. CHARLESWORTH

Scope of the Theory of Public Administration

By Dwight Waldo

SOME observations on interpretation of the topic to which I have been asked to address myself are a proper beginning.

First, I have not consulted with Steve Bailey on what would appear to be a serious boundary problem. While "objectives" and "scope" are not synonyms, it is certainly not possible to discuss one without reference to the other. I suspect, therefore, that we will have surveyed some of the same territory, however much our reports on that territory may differ. Second, I shall be using "theory" in the loose sense of general or abstract thought, rather than in some single, more restricted sense; that is, I want to talk to the important conceptual or intellectual problems bearing upon the scope of self-conscious public administration,[1] without distinguishing between theory and philosophy on the one hand, or giving theory one of its sharper "scientific" meanings on the other. Third, I shall assume that I have been commissioned not so much to report on what I perceive to be the present scope of the theory of public administration as to discuss problematic aspects of the "scope of the theory."

But to use language suggesting that one has an option between merely reporting present theoretical boundaries and arguing for different ones is misleading. It implies that presently public

[1] Discussions of public administration are plagued by a serious problem because differing meanings may be given to or understood by the phrase. Sometimes in seeking to be clear and precise, I have used upper case to refer to the self-conscious enterprise of study, and the like, and lower case to refer to the practices or processes which are the object of our attention. Unfortunately, while this device has its uses, it does not solve all the problems. For sometimes "public administration" is used to refer to *both;* and, also, one meaning has a disconcerting way of flowing into the other. As I proceed, I shall, of course, try to make clear my meaning, *but the reader should bear the problem in mind throughout. For this semantic problem is not accidental and extraneous to the subject of the essay, but deeply involved with it, as the introduction will indicate.*

administration has discernible boundaries that could be reported straightforwardly, whereas, in fact, there is so little consensus that to discuss the problematical is unavoidable. Similarly—and relatedly—my statement that I would use "theory" in a loose sense was misleading, by implying that I could choose to use the term in some single, narrow sense, which would be understood and agreed upon. To reverse the old jibe about sociology, that it is a discipline in search of a subject matter, and to say that public administration is a subject matter in search of a discipline is pertinent but less than a half-truth, suggesting as it does that our subject matter is a given. But, alas, while certain that we do indeed have a subject matter—public administration *exists*, by evidence as palpable as that by which we accept earth and sea, it *is*—our certainty, or rather our agreement, stops there.

All of this is to suggest the difficulty of addressing oneself to the subject in any obvious and straightforward way. In fact, I have never experienced so much difficulty in trying to find where to "take hold" and how to proceed. If desirable or necessary scope of the theory of public administration is indicated by *problems*, problems that have both practical and theoretical dimensions, then my quandary is understandable. For if one points in any direction, he points at a problem facing us in the conduct of public administration; and each problem intertwines with others in a bewildering and maddening way. Our problems in conducting public affairs would be serious enough if there were a clear and agreed-upon self-conscious enterprise—discipline, profession, ideology, whatever—of "public administration" to which they could be related. But "public administration" itself is problematical, controversial.

This may seem to be an involved, unnecessarily confusing way of saying that our theoretical problems are divisible into two types: those internal in the sense that they relate to the self-conscious enterprise we call public administration for purposes of academic-organization teaching, publishing a review, and the like, and those external in the sense that they are problems of the existential world which are our concern and to which we relate. One *can* make such a distinction for certain purposes. But it is a distinction that is rough and arbitrary at best, and is ultimately unrealistic, misleading. *For the two sides of the dichotomy do not stand independently, but rather each "defines" the other. Further: there are certain crucial matters of the definition of reality and stance toward it—matters involving ideas and values but also institutions and events—that overreach the dichotomy, define both sides, and relate one to the other.*

In attempting to speak relevantly to my subject, I shall address four themes or at least proceed more or less by four stages. I shall first set forth a perspective for viewing our present situation. Then, working from the center to the periphery, from the theoretical problems involved in our self-perception and self-definition to those theoretical problems that importantly challenge us in the practice of public administration, I shall talk about a widening circle of matters that seem to me to be of importance. At some point in this widening circle of attention, I shall make an arbitrary decision that I am moving from "internal" problems to "external" problems: that is, recognizing that to distinguish between problems intrinsic to the self-conscious enterprise and those posed by its practice risks distortion and deception, I shall nevertheless do it as a device for exposition and analysis. Finally, I shall give some attention to what I referred to as "overriding" theoretical matters.

A Perspective: Crisis of Identity

A catalogue of the contributions to the study of public administration since World War II is impressive. Whether made by those *in* public administration or merely adopted or adapted, the contributions are many and varied. We have not been a stagnant backwater of American intellectual life. In what follows, however, I shall be accentuating the negative. For, despite the accomplishments, we confront problems of the most serious nature. To diagnose, to analyze, to explicate, requires that I be critical and candid. Whether I err in this direction is for you to decide.

Let me suggest a perspective or orientation, based on an analogy, that seems to me appropriate and useful. Rapidly changing circumstances, new knowledge—a variety of causes—often bring an individual to the crisis stage. He may collapse; he may readjust and reintegrate, rapidly or slowly, temporarily or permanently, at a "lower" or "higher" level. In a very loose or general way, I propose that we think of public administration analogously. Indulge my fancy for a bit, at least, and judge if any useful insight is gained.

In the 1930's, public administration had emerged from its childhood, perhaps even from its adolescence—not to put too fine a point on my analogy. Anyhow, in its POSDCORB and Principles days, it appeared to be self-confident and healthy. While challenged by its institutional and intellectual environment, youthful energy and perhaps a certain brashness enabled it to meet the situations of the time. But sharper challenges were coming. Intellectually, these were represented by such items as *New Frontiers in Public Administration* and *Federal Departmentalization*. Institutionally and historically, they were represented by World War II and its aftermath of reconstruction and continuing crisis.

To the latter, in the immediate postwar years, were added intellectual challenges that brought public administration to the point of crisis, of possible collapse and disintegration. A groundswell of doubt and dissatisfaction brought about by measuring POSDCORB public administration against the war experience was topped by criticism of the most searching and damaging kind by a new generation of students. Adding to the problem, in this situation of severe intellectual challenge and stress, the environment of public administration became less supportive; in fact, more demanding, indifferent, or hostile. Forwarding reconstruction in Europe, responding to perceived threats to national existence, aiding a developing Third World, and trying to develop and stabilize a new type of international or world life were added to continuing and severe domestic problems. While reaction to war did not, under these circumstances, permit a "return to normalcy" mood of the severity of the 1920's, there was nevertheless a reaction against government; and this, plus highly rewarding opportunities in private employment, hardly fostered a climate conducive to focusing attention upon problems of public administration. At this point in history, the mother discipline of political science became engaged in an emotional and disruptive self-study and reorientation, the effect of which was often to accentuate indifference or hostility toward public administration. Add the fact that, out of disenchantment with the "old" public administration and intrigued by what seemed promising new horizons, foundation support turned decisively in other directions.

The postwar critics of the older public administration did not speak with one voice, but there was nevertheless a remarkable similarity in the indictments. The charges included the following major items: that the claim to science was, with respect to substance, premature and, with respect to method, immature or erroneous; that the "principles" which were the issue of the science were, at best, summary statements of common sense; that economy and efficiency as goals or criteria were either too narrowly conceived or were misconceived; that the separation between politics and administration is arbitrary or false and must be abandoned or thought through on new terms. There is no need to relate in detail a familiar story. But to recall it to mind is a necessary preface to setting forth the perspective that I propose. This perspective may now be stated as follows.

The effect of the complex new tasks plus the critical attacks was to create a crisis of identity for public administration. Both the nature and boundaries of subject matter and the methods of studying and teaching this subject matter became problematical. Now, two decades after the critical attacks, the crisis of identity has not been resolved satisfactorily. Most of the important theoretical problems of public administration relate to this continuing crisis, to ways in which it can be resolved, and to the implications and results of possible resolutions

Various "solutions" or at least approaches to solutions of our disciplinary problem have been offered during the two decades. Perhaps the most devastating of the critics, Herbert Simon, offered formulae for reconstruction and renewal as well. Based on logical positivism, these formulae were in some aspects radically new, but at the same time presented some formal similarities to the "old" public administration—a call to science, a twofold structuring of the "universe," emphasis on efficiency as criterion—which, one might presume, would make them readily acceptable.

For whatever reasons, this did not prove to be true. Simon's formulae and prescriptions did, of course, provide "answers" for some, and their impact through two decades has been large, and perhaps increasingly large. But since this impact is interwoven as cause and effect with some major currents in social science (behavioralism, decision-making, and the like), it is hard to estimate. As to the future, I should guess that whatever happens from this point forward will show a significant Simonian influence, but that the still continuing crisis of identity will not be resolved by any simple "conversion," Simonian or other.

The generalizations about public administration during the past two decades that seem to be the most obvious and certain are at the same time the most significant and profound—whether or not my "crisis of identity" perspective is accepted. After critical attacks that seemed to many to have destroyed its former orienting premises, self-conscious public administration continued, in the main, to follow the paths of subject matter and approach on which it had been set. Even the most cautious and traditional of its adherents, however, recognized a necessity to move with the times; and the more adventurous actively sought to find or develop new areas to address and new methods of addressing them. We have indeed been generous in recognizing and accepting the new in *some* ways, constantly enlarging the perimeter of our interests and concerns, as our publications abundantly witness. The content and treatment of old categorical concerns, such as personnel and budgeting, have evolved swiftly; and many facets, dimensions, and interests—for example, case method, "ecology," comparative administration, decision-making, systems theory—have come to be regarded as our proper concern. But while constantly enlarging the scope of interests and commitments, we have not advanced in understanding of, or at least in agreement on, what we *are*. We cannot say confidently and with one voice: This is what public administration *is*, *this* is why you should study it, and *these* are the methods and tools for that purpose.

Toward Crisis Resolution: Core Problems of Identity and Orientation

The first step in bringing our crisis of identity to an end and in moving decisively into a new phase in public administration is to recognize that *there is no solution to the problem of identity at the level at which it was posed two decades ago after the post-war criticism.* By this I mean that, generally speaking, two decades ago the solution to the problem of identity was viewed as a choice of two alternatives, neither of which was viable. That neither of the alternatives could evoke or sustain the new synthesis that seemed necessary is not, from the vantage point of the late 1960's, so much a matter for puzzlement as an obvious conclusion.

In one of the two perspectives, public administration was viewed as a branch, field, or subdivision of political science: a subdiscipline. This was not an unreasonable view. It is slight exaggeration to say that professors of political science, and *only* professors of political science, were responsible for the development of self-consciousness: for the bringing together, in books, courses, and the like, of concepts and materials from political science and concepts and materials from "management science." In retrospect it seems clear, however, that the bringing together of the concepts and materials from the two areas was *only* a bringing together, and not a real fusion; and the rationale that served to justify and sustain the bringing together was destroyed by the critical attack. To define public administration as "the management of men and materials in the accomplishment of the purposes of the state" will not now do for a number of reasons, one of which is that it implies a separation of means and ends which for a long time now has not been accepted.

My own point of view is that it is now unrealistic and unproductive to regard public administration as a subdivision of political science, however one reads the history upon which I have just put my own construction. This is not to say that there are not, cannot be, and should not be important relationships between the two; it could hardly be otherwise, as the sequel will indicate. But, for the moment, I restrict myself to a brief statement of the reason for my position against a subdisciplinary perspective.

We confront a fact, and not a theory. Or, rather, we confront a number of facts, and the "scope of our theory" must perforce be related to these facts. From one side, public administration as orientation and literature, as research, activities, concepts, and techniques, has grown so large and heterogeneous that to think of accommodating it as a subdiscipline of *anything* is prima facie absurd. From the other side, political science has not only become a much larger and more complex enterprise, but the main directions of its evolution since World War II make the task of trying to "fit in" public administration as a subdiscipline difficult to the point of impossibility. The truth is that the attitude of political scientists (other than those accepting public administration as their "field") is at best one of indifference and is often one of undisguised contempt or hostility. We are now hardly welcome in the house of our youth. It was not due to an oversight in scheduling that public administration disappeared as an organizing category in this year's meetings of the American Political Science Association (APSA).

Whether "ideally" political science and public administration should be closely joined intellectually and institutionally (separable but related matters) is an interesting subject for speculative thought. Perhaps they should. Perhaps the estrangement is unfortunate for one or both, and for society. Certainly, one can imagine lines of development that would have been different (if, for example, the efforts of the APSA Committee on Practical Training for the Public Service, in the Progressive era, had found fruition); and perhaps now-unforeseen developments may bring the two together. But, I repeat, presently we confront facts that are plain and that, short range, simply must be accepted. The strategy must be to make the most of them.

An alternative perspective and proposed approach has been to regard public administration as itself a discipline. This alternative is obviously subject to differing interpretations because "discipline" is not clear from definition or agreed-upon referents; but in general what has been meant and envisaged has been a more or less coherent subject matter studied and taught in an independent academic department coequal with the "other" social sciences.

This point of view is not absurd. At least, in certain cases, independent departmental status might provide the best solution for a complex set of opposing theories and pressures (as, indeed, continued existence within departments of political science will be the only "practical" solution in most cases in the immediate future). But the idea of public-administration-as-discipline suffers from two grave defects: it is at once too ambitious and too little ambitious. It is too ambitious in believing (if it does believe) that it is possible to identify and develop a coherent body of systematic theory which will be substantially independent of other social sciences and will concern itself only with *public* administration. The intellectual difficulties of doing this I judge to be insuperable, given the recent and prospective development of the conceptual-scientific world. I have in mind, for example, the problem of countering the well-formulated and widely held position that administration is a general or generic social process, of which *public* administration is only one variety or aspect.

On the other side, public-administration-as-discipline is not ambitious enough. It looks inward toward neat conceptual boundaries and outward chiefly toward neat departmental boundaries. It does not take adequate account of the contemporary university as an exploding intellectual-organizational universe and of demands upon public-administration-as-process in a chaotic and dangerous world. The argument made above is relevant here also: As we cannot crowd into *sub*discipline the necessary range and variety of present concerns, neither can we crowd them into a *discipline*.

In brief compass, let me now state the case for a professional perspective as the appropriate, indeed necessary, resolution of the crisis of identity. Brevity is necessitated by my larger or different assignment, but it is facilitated by what I have just been arguing: part of the case for a professional perspective is made when the obstacles and inadequacies of the subdisciplinary or disciplinary perspectives are set forth. If my analyses and arguments are substantially valid, what is then indicated? Which way do we turn? My own conclusion is that the most promising, and perhaps, in fact, necessary, line of development is found in adopting a *professional* perspective. This might be described as making a virtue of necessity. In any case, it prescribes a strategy properly adapted to the contemporary development of ideas and institutions.

Some difficulties and objections are obvious. The concepts "profession" and "professional" are not clear and indisputable; the phenomena of professionalism present important negative burdens as well as positive benefits; it is not possible that public administration as a whole can become a profession, or by parts a cluster of professions, in the foreseeable future; nor is it clear that it *ever* can or, more importantly, *should*. Such considerations are not trivial, but of great substance. Fortunately, it is not necessary to my argument and purpose to try to deal with them.

What is necessary, instead, is to discuss the difficulty in terminology and to explain as clearly as possible what is proposed. Regarding terminology, the point is that *profession* and *professional* are used for lack of better terms. They are used by loose analogy, rather than to argue for a strict correspondence with any one existing profession or some Platonic ideal of a profession. *Occupation* and *occupational* might be used instead, but have other and greater difficulties. There is no terminology that precisely fits the situation and the need.

What I propose is that we try to act as a profession without actually being one, and perhaps even without the hope or intention of becoming one in any strict sense. Frankly, it took some courage to say that, as it is patently open to ridicule. But it is what I mean, as clearly as I can state it. The professional perspective or stance is the only one broad and flexible enough to enable us to contain our diverse interests and objectives, yet firm and understandable enough to provide some unity and sense of direction and purpose. It has meaning and contains useful cues and imperatives both in the academic world in which public administration is studied and taught and in the governmental world in which public administration is practiced. In the larger environment in which both these related enterprises are carried on, it gives us more purchase than any other orienting idea.

My favorite analogy is to medicine. By common consent, this is a profession; but it is also a congeries of professions, subprofessions, and occupational specializations, ramifying in fantastic complexity. It is science and art, theory and practice, study and application. It is not based on a single discipline, but utilizes many. It is not united by a single theory, but is justified and given direction by a broad social purpose.

Public administration in contemporary government is not less, but more, complex than caring for and curing the ill (which, in a formal sense, it often embraces). We need a perspective, an orientation, appropriate to the task. In terms of my assigned topic, the scope of our theory should extend as far as the professional challenge and should respond to the needs and opportunities it presents. If the analogy to medicine has any validity, this means that we must be concerned not with a theory but with theories, indeed, with theories of many types, many dimensions and facets. The professional stance does not by a simple coin-in-the-slot procedure provide "answers," nor does it even provide a complete and clear agenda of theoretical problems. It does provide a framework large enough to embrace our theoretical problems; it helps to clarify the problems posed and to define the nature of proper answers; it gives direction on the time at which and the level at which to seek solutions. Above all, it gives unity while permitting diversity.

While thorough exploration and defense of the professional approach are not possible, a few words must be included on an obviously important matter. As is well known, the vast majority of persons now holding middle- and top-level administrative positions in public administration were not trained in courses or schools of public administration, and even if such courses and schools were to multiply rapidly, this situation would not change. There is general agreement—recognized by such phrases as "the second career concept"—that this situation must be accepted and, indeed, much opinion that this situation is healthy and advantageous *if* the strategy of public administration is adapted to it, utilizing its strengths but correcting or compensating for its weaknesses. From my point of view, a professional approach to public administration not only does not run counter to recognition of the large role that persons trained in technical, scientific, and established professional roles play in public administration, but, properly interpreted, affords a philosophy and an institutional base for the necessary task of countering the centrifugal pull of the "other" professions, through a varied strategy beginning with co-operation in such matters as joint courses in the professional schools.

An Agenda of Old Problems in Need of a New Look

Let me confess that to frame this heading was painfully difficult. The matters concerning the scope of our theoretical concerns that I wish to discuss are reasonably clear: they are self-defining and orienting matters at the center of our enterprise. I should like, naturally, not merely to list them but to say something significant regarding approach or solution. Now, I have been touting the professional perspective, and you could reasonably expect that I demonstrate its usefulness; and I would have been greatly pleased to have prefaced: "New Light on Old Problems." However, I confess that (at least in the time and space available) I am unable to demonstrate effectively the relevance and usefulness of the professional stance in providing the needed new light. The confession made, my position is that it is at the professional level that new or further answers should be sought and will be found.

Be that as it may be and will be, my present argument is that we need a new and thorough survey of the theoretical problems posed by the putative destruction of the old "orthodoxy" by the postwar critics. In two decades, much useful theoretical work has, of course, been done, but the intellectual-theoretical landscape is extremely untidy. Feeling some special concern for helping to get the urgent work of government done leads many of us to put aside overt theoretical concerns, and interest in specific theoretical concerns leads others of us to neglect (or depreciate) the theoretical concerns of others. With the advantage of some years to provide a deeper and wider temporal perspective, we ought now to be able to achieve more understanding and order: that is, the argument for a resurvey does not depend necessarily or wholly upon the validity of the "professional" argument above.

Specifically, I urge that it would be useful to review each one of the old Articles of Faith, re-examine the criticism of it, trace its lines of development in recent years, and assess where we now stand with respect to the issues involved. Taking one of these, the separation of politics and administration—which is perhaps the key one—let me explain what I have in mind.

To give meaning and force, I state an orienting thesis: Though we decided two decades ago that a separation of politics and administration is impossible, we have not faced up to the implications of that decision—not really, not systematically and thoroughly. Did we, in fact, "decide" as I indicated? In any case, what was *then* the response, what since have been the main lines of development, where do we stand today—justified by what theoretical statement?

To respond to my thesis and questions would be a substantial task in scholarship and analysis, and I but suggest some aspects of a response.

The proper beginning would be a re-examination of the pre-World War II literature, for it is more complex than some of the "believers" thought or pretended, which means, in turn, that what was "rejected" may have been oversimplified, distorted. I have in mind, for example, that though Woodrow Wilson is often credited with supporting the separation of the study of administration from that of politics, it is little noted that he held that the first object of administrative study is "to discover . . . what government can properly and successfully do." I have in mind also that Willoughby's theory of the constitutional status of administration does not look as naïve to me as it did a quarter of a century ago, and that he might have a contribution to make to a theory appropriate to present circumstances and needs.

Another aspect of the proposed review is obviously to examine not just the criticisms of the politics-administration dichotomy but the attempts to respond consciously and carefully with new theories of necessary or proper relationships. The most important agenda-item here (as I indicated earlier) is Herbert Simon and his critics; more generally, the development of the issues dialectically and as shaped by the evolution of ideas and events.

The central task, however, would not be to trace the history of ideas, but to analyze and explicate, carefully and fully, what it means for the study, teaching, and practice of administration to "reject" the separation of politics and administration. While many of us, at some time and in some fashion, have addressed ourselves to some aspect of this subject, nobody has addressed himself to it frontally and globally. A work which put our own literature in a classificatory-analytical framework, which related our ideas to the "outer" world of developing ideas and events, and concluded with a "position statement" for our reaction and discussion would be of inestimable value.

If the role of public administration is not simply to execute the "will of the State" in the most economical and efficient way, if the view is rejected that public administration is a multipurpose, value-neutral instrument, then we are confronted with a bewildering array of value problems. These range from relatively simple questions of personal behavior in an administrative context to grand and perennial questions about the nature and ends of government. If this is true, why have we not responded in any systematic and determined way?

To engage in a horseback survey, the value problems which we confront include the following:

(1) Problems of personal ethics in and related to administration. These range from matters so slight that they shade into questions of protocol and etiquette to the grim and sickening atmosphere of genocide trials. If anyone has tried even to map this terrain, I am not acquainted with his effort.

(2) Problems of politics and power. Here the need for theory has been recognized: John Gaus's dictum of 1950 that "a theory of public administration means in our time a theory of politics also" has been cited with approbation again and again, and a number of writers have dealt with force or insight with some facet—for example, Norton Long with power and Albert Somit with bureaucratic *realpolitik*. Even so, I think it is correct to say that we lack even a good general map of the terrain, one which will delineate the various varieties of politics—office politics, party politics, issue politics, pressure politics, and the like—one from the other and indicate their relationships. In advancing in this area, we are aided by much that is taking place in the study of politics and organizational behavior. On the other hand, I suspect that we are hindered by a complex of historical-emotional-partisan factors which often lead to self-deception, cant, and dishonesty: we like it both ways, anonymity and neutrality or identity and a cause, as suits our purpose of the moment. (In this connection, I cite as a case study the actions and the literature following the election of President Eisenhower.)

(3) Problems of constitutional status, law, and jurisprudence. Perhaps I have been subverted by two years of association with the Continental administrative-law approach to public administration, but I am of the opinion that we now suffer from lack of attention to constitutional-legal matters. Our early antilegal and antilawyer bias is understandable and forgivable, but it is

now dangerously obsolete and self-defeating; with charity, our present attitude and interests might be described as absurd. Discussing our enterprise more than a decade ago, John Millett stressed the remarkable fact that we lack "an adequate and accurate theory of constitutional status." While such stalwarts as Paul Appleby and Emmette Redford have spoken insightfully and usefully to some of the issues involved, one can hardly say that the problem has been solved. Here the currents of the behavioral studies run against us, reinforcing old prejudices and ignoring our "decision."

Public administration, by definition, functions in a constitutional-legal context. If instrumentalism is abandoned, we must recognize fully and responsibly that public administration is input as well as output, that it helps to create and sustain constitutional-legal norms, and does not simply "apply" them. What we do not do for ourselves in recognizing and responding is not likely to be done for us, but to us.

(4) Problems of public policy. Here our response has been fairly good in a number of ways. Some of us have developed a competence in some policy area; some have contributed to our understanding of what might be called the mechanics of the policy-making process. A great deal of work has, of course, been done in philosophy, in various social sciences—God knows where —which is more or less relevant and has been or could be relevant to our problems. One might be self-praising or optimistic here—except for the obvious fact that the response and the immediate promise is far short of the need, and that the need constantly expands. In this case, what we do not do may not be done by anyone; in some cases, it will be done for us, but less well than if we had at least contributed; and in other cases, it will be done to us by an assortment of economists, mathematicians, and computer experts.

(5) Problems of political theory and philosophy. It is an irony of the old public administration that in its attempt to divorce itself from politics, it articulated a distinctive political theory, and one may judge that this theory served the time and purpose well. But now, a generation after it has been destroyed and abandoned, we have nothing to take its place that is well-argued and generally accepted. Again, it is proper to acknowl-

edge that pertinent and useful work of analysis or reconstruction has been done here and there, in and out of the public administration fraternity. But, again, one must also say that the need so far outruns the accomplishment that it is disturbing and puzzling.

It is disturbing because, by widespread agreement, ours is an organizational, an "administered," civilization, and if it is to survive and flourish, then we need the most serious attention possible to the connection between what used to be called the "ends of the State" and the organizational-administrative apparatus (in and out of formal government) which helps both to define and to realize these ends. Our achievement is far behind our needs in framing and justifying theories to relate administrative means to the objectives of free and democratic government under conditions of the late twentieth century. In fact, "antiorganizational" theories and values may be growing at such a rate as to threaten what Kenneth Boulding called the Organizational Revolution with an Antiorganizational Revolution.

The lack of response is puzzling because of the interest and obvious importance of the problems. Of course, I may but express an interest-based bias: Problems are not problems unless perceived as such, and interest is a response of a perceiver, and not a quality in what is perceived. So I must fall back upon a question: Why are those whose disciplinary specialty is political thought not interested in what seem (to me, but certainly not *only* to me) to be some of the most significant and urgent problems of contemporary government? I think I know the answers to my own question, and if I am correct in my appraisal, then we had better look to other resources, including our own.

A Larger Circle of Theoretical Concerns

Again, I am dissatisfied with the heading: It is banal and not really informative. But, again, it is the best I can do; and it will at least serve to indicate that, as I view things, I am looking at a different order of theoretical concerns. In a temporal sense, the view is more forward; in a spatial sense, the view is more outward. Perhaps this is only an arbitrary ordering of our "universe," seized upon by my mind to save itself from chaos and collapse, but I shall hope to be addressing myself to real and important matters in that universe, whatever your own ordering.

In any case, what follows is an agenda of important and urgent matters for our concern, which call for various types of actions, including the development of appropriate theoretical responses. The items on the agenda will not be new, and the ordering will be more or less arbitrary. For my part, no treatment of the "scope of the theory of public administration" could ignore them, however, and I respectfully suggest that a deeper appreciation of their significance may follow from viewing them in two lights or perspectives. One of these is—of course—the professional. For, clearly, matters of such scope and diversity are not simply "disciplinary." What follows if one adopts the approaches and instruments that are best to deal with them, with the general end in view of good, wise, and effective government (for this is what I mean by urging a professional perspective)? The other perspective is that of political science in a central and historic sense. For, patently, at least the earlier items on the agenda have been central concerns of government and self-conscious political science from their inception, and a sense of depth and an appreciation of significance follows from this recognition. To recur to an earlier point: To argue that public administration is not a subdiscipline of political science is not to argue that "historic" political science is irrelevant to our concerns. How could it be? The point is rather (and in part) that contemporary political science is often indifferent to the urgent and overwhelming problems of contemporary government and that, in part and in degree, therefore, we must be our own political scientists.

Some would argue, I suspect, that these two perspectives are not really two, only one: that I have made the "professional perspective" so broad, so loose, that it is simply another way of putting the historic (or today "necessary") concerns of political science. I would not be disturbed by this charge; I think it worth a discussion. But to get to the agenda:

(1) *External and internal security.* This broad terminology is used to emphasize the connection between "historic" political science and the more specific categories and terms (for example, defense, the military establishment, riots) of contemporary attention. It is hardly too much to say that government originated in

and evolved as an enterprise of collective security against aggression, both external and internal; certainly, the history of the modern nation-state cannot be written without putting this fact at the center of the narrative. How, then, could public administration be ignorant of and indifferent to the main issues and activities of contemporary external and internal security? The sad fact is that, to a remarkable degree, we have been, and *are*.

Respecting external security, history (isolation) and ideology (isolationism and liberal idealism) worked together with the strategy of achieving identity and status (instrumentalism) to effect a lack of concern or "engagement"; and until World War II, it did not much matter. But this event marked a national turning point: thereafter, defense was to be a continuous major concern and a large military force was to be maintained on a permanent basis. The issues were great—at the extreme, life or death; the effects of a large, permanent military-industrial complex on our national life have been enormous; the implications and ramifications are almost endless. But public administration has responded only weakly and marginally to this new historic situation. As in so many cases in this essay, it would require an essay in itself to explicate what I think could and should be done by "us," to propose a program of theoretical development and professional action appropriate to the situation. I must content myself with brief sermons and strident exhortations. Let me just add that, for all that is gained by the current frantic drive towards rational decision-making (Planning-Programming-Budgeting Systems and All That) there is also something lost and much risked through premature closure, through too narrow premises and false parameters. It is not unreasonable to conclude that some of our difficulties in Vietnam have such an origin. It is not necessary to deny the usefulness of cost-effectiveness analyses to question whether they lead to oversimplification, if not systematic blindness in some situations.

When we turn to internal security, the story is similar: although public administration in its early days paid a fair amount of attention to the administration of justice, with the passage of time this attention tended to dwindle, became sporadic and marginal. Patently, some of our most important current national problems are posed by organized and unorganized crime, endemic and epidemic lawlessness, and delay and disorganization, often approaching chaos, in the courts. Yet, for the most part, we act as though these phenomena did not exist, or existed in the Congo; the attention given them in our books, journals, and courses is miniscule. There is even an element of priggishness and hypocrisy: we often snidely depreciate what is being done in these areas and freely criticize and gratuitously advise those who do it. But we would not soil our hands by actually helping.

How can public administration *not* be concerned with and involved in matters of internal security, which inevitably are a major concern of government? How can we afford not to be concerned with the several bodies of theory (for example, theories of crime and penology) relevant to internal security, ideally contributing to them, and certainly "joining" them with our own distinctive contribution?

(2) Justice. Justice in many ways is the "other side" of external and internal security; the essence of both is the formulation and execution of group norms. As considerations of internal and external security shade imperceptibly into each other, so do considerations of security and justice. This is perhaps so obvious that it could be taken for granted, but I make a point of it to underscore the connection with the historic concerns of political science and to emphasize again that if we are serious about abandoning simple instrumentalism, the implications are far-reaching.

The close connection between security and justice is illustrated by a matter that would deserve some comment, in any case, in any present survey of areas in which we must think seriously about policy—and policy implies theory. This is the matter of increasing unionization in public administration and increasing militancy of union action. From the viewpoint of government, the central issues are those of security; from the viewpoint of unions, the central issues are those of justice. Both views are right and both are wrong, of course; the tangle of issues is incredibly complex and troublesome. We are now moving rapidly into a crisis period; injuries to "both parties," to groups of citizens, to the polity, appear inevitable. We who are formally identified with public administration need not accept all the responsibility, of course. But is part of it ours, in failing to have thought seriously enough, early enough?

If we accept even a partial responsibility for policy-making, we will inevitably find ourselves participating, somewhere and somehow, in the never-ending inquiry into the origins, nature, and dictates of justice. The scope of our theory must extend even this far.

(3) Education. One of the central and enduring concerns of government and political philosophy is the education of the young, more generally, of the citizenry. In the United States, a concern for and commitment to education has been a notable characteristic from the beginning; our present educational enterprise—most of it under a "public" label—is the greatest in history. As external defense takes the largest slice of our national budget, education accounts for the largest slice of our subnational public expenditures. One might reasonably expect, therefore, to find that public administration is deeply concerned with the development of educational policy and with the way an enterprise of such scope and so vital to the future of the polity is carried on.

In fact, we *are* sometimes and increasingly concerned, if for no other reason that, since many of us "live" in educational enterprises, we can scarcely avoid being Where the Action Is. The central fact is, however, that educational administration (as did police administration and some other "public" areas) developed essentially as an independent enterprise, with which "general" public administration had no substantial connections, however much the concepts of the two drew from the same sources and ended in similar prescriptions. I do not pause to examine how this situation arose or whether it was justified in the past, but proceed to the exhortation: It is absurd and dangerous for us *now* not to take an active interest in education. If we are to survive, prosper, and move toward solution of radical national problems, the public educational effort cannot but increase in size and intensity; and the scope of our theory must extend as far as necessary to make our participation wise and effective. Situational and strategic factors urge us along this road, which both duty and self-interest indicate that we should follow. Educational administration is experiencing a rejuvenation, and increasingly it will become a source and center of significant research and new theory. Also—let us be frank—educational administration is increasingly not only where the action and the ideas are: it is where the money is.

(4) Government by osmosis and symbiosis. I use these terms to designate two parallel and more or less related developments which have now received a fair amount of attention. These are the development of a network of relationships between government and private enterprise of such scope, depth, and complexity as to make the delineation in some areas of any clear line between "public" and "private" impossible; and the development of a network of intergovernmental relationships of such scope, depth, and complexity as to make conventional or simple theories of the "federal" nature of our government quite obsolete.

Our publications and other activities witness a mounting interest and response, and I shall not, in this case, scold. However, it is proper to note that the interest and response from any and all quarters is not on a scale—of resources *or* time—commensurate with the phenomena. And I add my regrets that the most incisive and imaginative attempts to explain the meaning of such present developments and to project and interpret the future—certainly those most widely read and noted—are not by persons identified with public administration (or, for that matter, with political science).

(5) Science and technology. That I might say something new about science and technology in a few paragraphs is as unlikely as my saying something new about God or Reality. On the other hand, any discussion of the scope of the theory of public administration that failed to touch on this subject would be incomplete, even absurd.

The essential facts are that the contemporary human condition is without precedent, in important respects because of science and technology; that science and technology are constantly and rapidly accelerating in scope and impact; and that there is a widely diffused and plausible feeling about that science and technology are "in control," or have created such a situation that human affairs cannot *be* controlled. One need not be convinced by the arguments of Jacques Ellul to have this sense of loss of control; I confess that it chills me in my unguarded moments. Certainly—to take an example—it is worth pondering how much, not simply of our "life style," but of our *public policy* (national, state, and local, to use the quaint old terminology) is made in Detroit, not in our capital cities.

Now, some of us (witness the recent symposium in the *Public Administration Review*) are addressing themselves to questions posed by the interconnections between science and technology, and government and society, and at least one of us, Don Price, is acknowledged to be an outstanding figure in "explorations of the interface." But my plea must still be: more and, if possible, even better. The need is not for a global policy on science and technology. At least, if one assumed or argued for the *need*, the possibility does not exist for the present. But there is a vast range of policy questions, from the amount of money to be spent on a space program to the conditions under which new pesticides shall be used, to which we might reasonably be expected to make some contribution. And beyond and in addition to such policy questions, there are many other matters that should excite our efforts: for example, the conditions of creativity in laboratories, as related to organization and administration. In sum, to avoid being ruled by what Lapp calls the "New Priesthood," we should move quickly and think sharply.

(6) Urbanism. This is another alarm bell you have heard so many times that you have perhaps lost all emotional capacity to respond. (As you know, the number ninety rings the alarm bell in both cases: 90 per cent of the scientists who ever lived are still living; 90 per cent of our population will soon be living in cities.) I will not further depress your capacity to respond with yet another recitation of the facts and figures. My assignment nevertheless requires that I remind you that the city is *there*, and growing at a stunning rate into a sprawling, often noisome and dangerous, God-knows-what; and that this, too, creates a new Condition of Man for which we have not received any rules from the past and concerning which there is little agreement in the present.

In fact, the nub of the matter is not that we lack theories or philosophies concerning the city or urbanism, but that we have such a profuse growth of them and so much difficulty in deciding which one to choose. If one were to select an area of public policy and action characterized by milling confusion, he might well choose this—over strong contenders. Are we, perhaps, asking the wrong questions, when we ask: What should the city be? Or even: What is the ideal city of the future? Does introduction of the word "city" (which some of the theories hold to be an obsolete concept) pose an unanswerable question or guarantee futile answers? Are we trying to solve the problem in the wrong way, at the wrong level?

In any case, if public administration is to be relevant, and to become *more* relevant, it cannot avoid confronting the urban fact and artifact. This assignment is inevitably included in the "scope of our theory."

(7) Development. In a number of instances above, one or the other of us had a suspicion that I did not know what I was talking about. In this case, I openly confess it: I don't know what I mean by "development." However, it is a frequently used term and apparently a key concept, not just in our own circles (in which case we might in self-depreciation judge it nonsensical) but in social science generally and, indeed, in respectable circles beyond. I conclude, therefore, that an important item on our agenda of theoretical concerns is to inquire as closely as we can to see what sense can be made of it, what use it can serve. The list of pertinent questions includes the following:

Does it make sense to talk about "development administration" or "the administration of development" (either of which makes *some* of our colleagues wroth)? If these two expressions mean something different, what and why? Is development administration the "applied side" of comparative administration, or simply a term from another realm of discourse? Is it true, as some (including myself) have argued, that a generalized concept of development administration solves the psychological and strategic problem posed by such terms as "underdeveloped countries," since all countries can be or should be perceived as "developing"?. Is "developing" just another way of positing Western values as superior and as the proper goal of administrative change or activity? Have the students of comparative politics reached agreement on *political* development and, if so, does their solution aid us? Do we use the word and the concept in lieu of "progress," about which we are now uneasy? Can the word and concept be given any agreed *substantive* content? Can we, at least, give the word a set of conventional, instrumental goals as "meaning"? or, at bare minimum, some "procedural" meaning?

This list of theoretical concerns in the "larger circle" could obviously be extended. I did not, for example, touch upon the subject of inter- and supra-national administration. Obviously, also, a somewhat different list could be presented; or the same matters could be presented in a listing of another kind. But perhaps I have in rough fashion indicated important items within the "scope of our theory." I beg to be exempt only from one line of criticism, namely, that I failed to recognize connections between the problems and areas discussed. I was, in fact, keenly aware of the connection, say, between the rise of science and technology and the spread of urbanism. But to have recognized, much less to have explored, all the interconnections would have been a book-length task.

Some Concluding Thoughts

In concluding, I return to the subject of a professional perspective or stance. I shall try to draw together some thoughts in the presentation. I shall also touch upon some implications and aspects of the "professional" thesis not yet recognized.

My argument is that for public administration a professional perspective is appropriate, and indeed necessary, at the point which we have now reached in the evolution of ideas and events, and that a realistic and fruitful canvassing of the scope of the theory of public administration reflects this fact. The argument for a professional perspective rests on the contentions (1) that our crisis of identity, created two decades ago by a challenge to the essential orienting concepts that had served up to that time, *was not and cannot be* solved at the level of subdiscipline or discipline, and (2) that the set of concepts and attitudes designated by the word "profession," properly qualified and appropriately used, will enable us to resolve our crisis of identity at the proper level. I recognize many difficulties in this way of looking at things, and I do not argue that public administration can or should in any simple sense become "a" profession. I do argue that only the professional approach or perspective is broad enough and flexible enough to contain the many and diverse interests we now present, while at the same time giving a feeling of unity and a sense of direction. Incidentally—and as a caution—I do not rush from the position I have myself adopted to easy or firm conclusions about many practical problems. For example, while I believe that the professional perspective is a useful one for justifying and guiding the development of graduate programs in public administration or public affairs, it affords no easy answers to what should be done about public administration in curricula below the graduate level.

A serious dilemma or contradiction in the professional approach to public administration has, at most, only been suggested. It must be openly recognized; and if it cannot be successfully countered or resolved, it will prove to be fatal. The danger is that the professional idea, if it proves strong enough to give coherence and a sense of identity and mission, may by that very result prove to be too strong a unifying agency.

Professions tend toward group egoism and group selfishness because this is the nature of groups. By common definition, a profession has as a distinguishing characteristic the rendering of a service to society, and in the case of the "regular" professions, there is always an uneasy balance between the phenomena of inward-facing selfishness and the phenomena of outward-facing public service. If one seeks to apply the professional approach to public administration, he obviously "takes on" this problem of achieving an equilibrium between self-interest and altruism.

But, for good or ill, he does not take it on in any strict sense, for the argument is not that public administration can or should become a profession in any strict sense. Rather, the argument is that we seek to extract from the complex of ideas, attitudes, and institutions represented by professionalism those aspects which are relevant and useful to our purpose, and try to avoid or counter those which are not. That this is a heroic task is obvious, and the outcome of an attempt is unpredictable. But, for my part, I do not know a reasonable alternative strategy. Indeed, I do not know of an alternative, other than quitting the game. In academia we face what Professor R. S. Parker calls "The End of Public Administration": that is, the "old" public administration has been so eroded by ideas and events that it cannot survive without change.

There are two further related matters—related to each other and to the success of the professional strategy. One of these is the idea that administration is a general or generic process, that "administration is administration is administration," and that therefore public administration is but one aspect or instance of the *general* phenomenon, which can be taught, learned, and practiced "as such." Who would deny that there is much truth and force in this view? It is one of the concepts that brought public administration into being, that is, as a self-conscious enterprise. Such is its force today, however, that it threatens what it helped to create, at least if we take as sign and evidence the creation of Schools of Administration—without qualifying adjective.

As indicated, I think there is much validity in the idea that administration, wherever found, tends to have common aspects. Indeed, I have argued elsewhere that we ought to recognize that ours is an administrative *culture* and, so recognizing, take action to extend and improve this culture. But I have argued elsewhere also that we who are identified with public administration should take as a first order of business the development of a "public philosophy," the development of a distinctively *public* point of view.

As I view it, these two positions are not incompatible. On the contrary, both of them are necessary to the success of a strategy of approaching public administration as a profession. One pertains to noun, one to adjective. That administration is a general phenomenon gives us a firm base of science and technology, and *part* of a necessary professional philosophy. That public administration, often and characteristically, is different from other forms of administration (and often should be, *needs* to be different) dictates a somewhat differentiated science and technology, and supplies the other part of our professional philosophy.

Finally—I have no illusions about the difficulties of developing and sustaining a public philosophy adequate for our purpose and strong enough to survive and grow. But is not a philosophy of the public interest essential to the existence and survival, to the very *idea*, of government—however much such a philosophy appears, in the light of much current philosophy, impossible?

When Woodrow Wilson said, in 1910, "a new era has come upon us like a sudden vision of things unprophesied, and for which no polity has been prepared," he did not know the half of it.

Comment on Waldo's Paper

By WALLACE S. SAYRE

IT is invariably instructive to read Dwight Waldo on any subject that he chooses to confront, even if one does not share in full his youthful pessimism about the complexities of the matter he is addressing. In the instant case of his concern with the scope of the theory of public administration, my first (and, for this occasion, my only) response is to simplify his problems, although I can anticipate his probable reaction that I have grossly oversimplified them. And, regrettably, I must begin by saying that I do not find persuasive his conclusion that "the most promising, and perhaps, in fact, necessary, line of development is found in adopting a *professional* perspective." My initial difficulty is in grasping satisfactorily what is meant by the statement; my continuing one, to the extent that I think I understand what is meant, is a feeling that present ambiguities are merely being exchanged for new and larger ones. This is not an indefensible intellectual strategy, as all who deal with theory recognize, but one of its necessary defenses is that the strategy has a demonstrable payoff in disposing of the present burdens and/or enriching the perspectives of those wrestling with current ambiguities. These virtues may be latent in the concept of "profession," but, if so, they are not made sufficiently explicit to this reader.

These uncharitable comments on a significant and provocative paper impose an obligation to risk some generalizations in turn.

To begin: In the interest of simplification we may take the title of the paper as suggesting some boundaries for our problem. The word "scope" implies boundaries. The word "theory" is presumably not used casually; accordingly, we may assume that our concern begins with the problems of those who aspire to develop general and partial theory about a finite body of phenomena. That is to say: one indicated boundary is the recorded striving of a group of identifiable authors who have attempted, or are attempting, to make generalizations that have explanatory power about a phenomenon called "public administration." The authors and their recorded efforts may be numerous and perplexing, but the number of writers is finite, and their records are not wholly impenetrable. The word "public" is also presumably not an accidental choice, but is apparently intended to exclude something thought of as "not public." This particular boundary is, no doubt, arbitrary in most societies, including our own, but arbitrariness seems characteristic of all boundaries in theory-construction, and less troublesome in this case than in many others. The word "administration" is also presumably selected deliberately instead of, say, "government" or "politics." The word can, of course, be tortured into complexity and ambiguity without end, but most of those who encounter it validly assume that it is meant to exclude some phenomena—for example, the act of voting in a general election. In fact, the boundary problems for both "public" and "administration," even for the purposes of theory-construction, can easily be exaggerated, and often are. At the present stage of theory-development, we know with sufficient certainty the parameters of our concern: in the United States, for example, the data that we are trying to explain are centered in and around the "executive branch" agencies of the national, state, local, and intermediate governments. Exotic boundary questions about these phenomena may sensibly and decently await the refinement stages in a general explanatory theory, of which we now possess only rudimentary beginnings.

In sum, these simple-minded observations lead to the unsurprising conclusion that, rather than an irreducible mystery, we face merely a difficult task. Not to put too fine a point on the matter, and to state it in the vocabulary of the scene in the United States, the subject of our deliberations is: What might be the agreed priorities of those theory-constructionists, anchored in but not confined to academia, who wish to offer generalizations about "executive branch" governmental units? Should these priorities be the conditions under which such units are conceived and brought into being, the ways in which they manage their external relations, the ways in which they order their internal life, and the consequences of their activities for themselves and all others in the society?

It is important to note, as Dwight Waldo does with catholicity and emphasis, that much valuable partial theory-construction has already been accomplished and that rich deposits of relevant data have also been the subject of preliminary sifting and analysis. The theory of public administration in these respects has no major dilemma of scope not shared by other social sciences, and is therefore under no necessary compulsion to flee from its present disciplinary base to seek a new home in some more vaguely bounded half-world called "profession."

In the postwar decades, three major trends are discernible in the literature of public administration. Each of these three categories of description and analysis contains significant contributions to partial theories of public administration. It is a general theory which is lacking—a gap shared by all social sciences, and thus suggesting that, in the absence of a great synthesizer in its ranks, the society of those concerned with public administration must rely upon the gradual accumulation of satisfactory partial theories until the burden of synthesis into a general theory is no longer too great for the boldest of its members.

The first set of partial theories about public administration is to be found in the writings of those interested in what may be called the "politics of public administration." The ICP series of case studies was the trail-blazer in this approach. But the partial theory that the administrator and his staff are themselves actors in a political system which embraces in a bargaining or similar relation a wide range of other actors, governmental and nongovernmental, is now extensively assimilated into the literature of public administration, as well as into the more general literature of political science. It may be that this situation reflects the greatest (although unpublicized) accomplishment of the students of public administration: that is, the disappearance of the rubric of public administration from the American Political Science Association's annual-meeting agenda may represent a conquest, a deep penetration into all political science concerns, not the defeat or separation seen by Waldo. It is clear that this political-system approach to public administration is one of the strongest ties to political science and one likely to endure; even if public administration were to become separatist, the political scientists have no choice about their necessary concern with the roles and functions of administrators and bureaucrats in the world of theory to which they are committed.

The second set of partial theories in public administration has its focus upon the internal organizational life, or dynamics, of the bureaucratic world—which is to say that it attempts to explain in greater detail the characteristics of one set of the actors in a political system, those actors who are of greatest interest to public administration students. In this body of research and partial theory, political science has been less directly relevant than have some other social sciences, notably social psychology and sociology. It would seem self-defeating, however, for this dependence to become a long-run affair; in the end, public administration theory must return to its preoccupation with explaining, albeit from a specialized perspective, the nature and consequences of the political system. The alternative would appear to be to erase the word "public" from its franchise.

The third set of partial theories to be found in the postwar literature is concerned with explaining the cross-cultural, more ambitiously the universal, characteristics of public administration. In part, this effort was at first an exercise in humility and apology for the self-confidence with which the United States exported, in the 1940's and 1950's, the assumed universal principles of our prewar public administration, but, that apologetic task having been duly performed, the more recent efforts have been vigorous, imaginative and multivocabular. In varying degrees, the literature in this set has borrowed from the two United States-oriented sets described above, but has naturally been expressed at a higher level of abstraction, occasionally with possibly premature aspirations toward a general theory of public administration. In this third set, the relations to political science seem close and mutually rewarding.

There are signs, too, of an emerging fourth set of partial theories. These are concerned with what David Easton calls the outputs and outcomes in political systems—the policies and consequences of the workings of the system. Such concerns have never been prominent in the literature of public administration in terms of systematic inquiry and appraisal, a tendency shared with most social sciences except, perhaps, economics. There are substantial reasons for caution here, but Dwight Waldo is no doubt wise in suggesting that the effort is now an overdue obligation.

In closing this commentary it is appropriate to return more directly to the concerns of the paper which inspired the comments. I do so by asking whether the several sets of partial theories so briefly and superficially described above do not, in fact, embrace most, if not all, of the perplexities identified by Dwight Waldo? If they do, however primitive they may still be as theory, the students of public administration are apparently aware of their research and theory priorities. And if that is so, the problem is how to maximize the incremental gains now in hand or in sight, and how to encourage the convergence of the four sets of partial theory without overstrain upon their individual vigor. Only when the construction of a general theory of public administration is within the range of the possible do the esoteric questions about the outer boundaries, or "scope" pushed to the uttermost, become highly relevant to theory-constructionists. Until then, which is a quite distant date, those concerned with the theory of public administration have all the scope they need.

Professionalism, Political Science, and the Scope of Public Administration

By Fred W. Riggs

PROFESSOR Waldo's paper is so stimulating and interesting in the wide range of ideas suspended tantalizingly before us that one is tempted to respond only with hand-clapping and a loud amen! However, the conventional role of a discussant is to hunt for some points of disagreement, or at least to pick out a peg on which to hang an argument that he has previously been hankering to make. Let me, therefore, take off from one of Waldo's central propositions, namely the need for a "professional" perspective as a means to cope with the "crisis of identity" so widely felt in our field. As a related proposition, he suggests that it is no longer realistic or productive to consider public administration a field within political science.

As to the crisis of identity, I could not more fully agree. Public administration as a "science," as a field of academic research and teaching, is indeed in a parlous state. Professor Parker's strictures on "The End of Public Administration" may, indeed, be not far from the truth. As to Waldo's solution, I confess to some reservations. I agree that professionalism may be a good long-run perspective for public administration—but for the "art," for the teaching and practice of administration, not for the theoretical, scholarly, and research side. Indeed, I see the relation between professionalism and the emergence of a valid "science" of public administration as being the reverse of the sequence proposed by Waldo.

There are risks, I suspect, in premature professionalism. Indeed, one could well argue that it was precisely because public administration during the prewar years did acquire a strong tinge of professionalism that it became suspect in political science departments, and that leading political scientists tended to ignore it. The legitimate teaching needs of future administrators tended to obscure the theoretical problems whose solution was a prerequisite for the emergence of a valid science of public administration. To use the medical analogy (Waldo, p. 10) in a different way, I think that we can well argue that it was not until anatomy and physiology had become established as part of natural science that they could be effectively used in schools of medicine as the foundation on which a changing profession could become "scientific." Had natural science been induced at an early stage to reject anatomy and physiology and turn it over to the doctors, I suspect that it might well have remained in the prescientific stage of humors, of phlegm, choler, melancholy, and other vapors thought in early physiology to determine health and illness. Concentrating on the practical problems of medicine as "art" and the urgent needs of the sick, doctors would have found little time for such "theoretical" concerns as the nature of cells and organs, or the circulation of the blood. Yet, it was precisely on discoveries concerning these esoteric subjects that the whole edifice of scientific medicine was later built. Moreover, the teaching of anatomy and physiology in schools of medicine has not meant the elimination of these subjects from natural science.

The point of the analogy is that, I believe, political science is uniquely capable of contributing a scientific understanding of public administration and that, although other disciplines can, indeed must, contribute to the training of professional administrators, none can or will make the crucial contribution which is still needed for the crisis of identity to be resolved. Moreover, I think political science can and should lay the foundation for professional education in public administration. On the other hand, I doubt that political science departments are the appropriate places in our universities for the training of public administrators.

There is another side to this coin. Not only would it be fatal for the theory of public administration to remove it from political science, but it would be equally fatal for political science to permit public administration to be withdrawn from the discipline. The fact that public administration was, "not due to an oversight," dropped from the program of the American Political Science Association (APSA) for its 1967 conferences need not prove a "wave of the future." Indeed, the APSA program for 1968 already shows a change of mood, for it not only reinstates public administration but adds a new face: there will be a companion set of panels on "comparative public administration." To paraphrase the statement by John Gaus quoted by Waldo, "A theory of politics means in our time a theory of public administration also."

But perhaps this is to jump the gun. The truth of this remark is scarcely obvious today to most political scientists, but I believe it can and will become apparent within the next decade. We may then look back to the year 1968 as the first year of a major new trend in political science.

For it to become apparent, however, we will have to point out why. To give but one clue, Waldo devotes much of his paper to a discussion of the problem of the "separation of politics and administration." We have not, he writes, yet faced up to the implications of the "decision" that a separation of politics and administration is impossible. He points to the implications of this decision for the study of administration and suggests that if political scientists ignore administration, we will have to be our own political scientists to inject political and public policy content in administrative analysis.

But if this be valid, then is not the reverse equally true? If politics and administration are inseparable, then can political scientists study politics without administration? And if specialists in administration withdraw from political science, then will not political scientists have to become their own experts on administration?

Actually, I think that the proposition that politics and administration are inseparable is an ambiguous one, true in some senses but untrue in others. Unfortunately, we tend to base conclusions on the senses in which it is untrue rather than on those in which it is true. I propose to devote the rest of this paper to an analysis, avowedly "theoretical," of reasons which have led me to these views.

Administration as a Function, Not a Process

Despite the popularity of the term, "structural-functional," and the vogue of "system theory," I suggest that an underlying reason for our present difficulties, not only in public administration but more broadly in political science as a whole, rests on our failure to distinguish clearly between structures of government and government functions. Perhaps this failure is reflected in the very terminology that we use to name our discipline, for we have substituted "politics" as the core of *political* science for the more old-fashioned idea of "government." Somehow "politics" sounds more dynamic, more behavioral, more functional, than the static, formal, and structural term, "government."

Let me explain what I see as the crucial difference. I view structures as patterns of action, and in political science I draw attention to the patterns of action which form the basic components of government: political parties, elections, elected assemblies, executives, courts, bureaucracies. The words are so familiar. It is astonishing that we pay so little systematic attention to their meanings. By contrast, let us use the word "function," as in mathematics and economics, to refer to system-relevant consequences of interactions between structures. This meaning contrasts with a common usage in political science, including public administration, where the word "function" frequently means purpose, program, or intention.

Consider what is meant when we say that "administration is a general or generic process" (Waldo, p. 26). It has never been clear to me what people have in mind when they say "process." The dictionary defines the word as an act of proceeding or advancing, as a series of actions or operations definitely conducing to an end, a continuous operation or treatment. It has other technical meanings, but I read the word to mean an intentional pattern of action. If so, then we can say that administration is a "pattern of action," and this is the same thing as saying it is a "process." But structures have been defined as "patterns of action," which leads to the conclusion that administration is a "structure."

Now this conclusion will, no doubt, be resisted because it sounds undynamic, and we want administration these days to be dynamic, even developmental! But there is a more serious objection to this conclusion. Patterns of human action are frequently, perhaps usually, purposive in some sense. The dictionary definition of "process" specifies that it means a pattern of action "conducing to an end." It is easy enough to jump from the assertion of a goal to the assumption that the goal has been accomplished. We tend, in common-sense usage, to jump back and forth between intentions and consequences. An agricultural "program," for example, is normally thought to include not only the intention to modify agricultural practices but the actual modification of such practices. A statute law is taken as evidence not only of an intent to shape behavior but also of the actual accomplishment of such behaviors.

Now, it is no doubt true, in the best of all possible worlds, that intentions are realized, laws enforced, and programs implemented. But in our imperfect world, we would do well to suspend judgment on this point. Although we may hypothesize that purposes are often fulfilled, we are surely wise to consider also the possibility of unfilled purposes.

How does this relate to our conception of what we mean by administration? An old definition of public administration (quoted by Waldo, p. 7) says that it is "the management of men and materials in the accomplishment of the purposes of the state." Waldo thinks that this will not do because it implies an unacceptable separation of means and ends. But it also implies a function, namely, the *accomplishment* of intended consequences, not just the activities *thought to lead* to intended results.

It is notable that other sciences have progressed by making a sharp conceptual distinction between structures and functions. Linguistics may be taken as an example. Traditional grammar confused structural forms of speech with the purposes to which words were put. Thus, it mixed structure and function in its definitions of such familiar words as nouns, verbs, and adjectives. Leonard Bloomfield was among the linguists who pioneered a vigorous and explosive revolution in thinking about language, primarily through the apparently simple device of using only structural criteria to describe and classify words and speech patterns. He was then free to hypothesize about the uses to which these structures were typically, but not always, put. As a result, linguistics has emerged as a true science to replace the set of muddy and incoherent doctrines propounded by traditional grammarians. "Principles" of grammar were replaced by empirical laws about language and linguistic change.

There is no reason why a similar revolution should not take

place in our thinking about government, politics, and administration. But we have to start with fundamentals, and we have yet to take this step.

Let me illustrate, hopefully demonstrate, what I have in mind by making a distinction between "bureaucracy" as a structure and "administration" as a function. No doubt, there are many usages and precedents for treating administration as a structure, as a process, as a type of action. When we talk about an "administrative system," we typically have a structure in mind, but I propose to call that structure, "bureaucracy." Then the meaning of administration can be limited to a functional concept, namely, the *consequence* of action, not the intention, or the action itself.

The meaning of the word "bureaucracy" is almost as ambiguous and controversial as the meaning of administration. But let us establish a structural concept to which the term "bureaucracy" can, without too much strain, be applied. Let us define a pattern of action which contains a set of offices, hierarchically arranged, under the authority of an executive. I wish to call this pattern of action a bureaucracy. An "executive," for this purpose, may be defined as an office asserting authority over an organization. Since we are concerned with governments, we can limit the term to governmental executives.

Right away, we can see that this structural definition brings together a wide range of activities, activities which are likely to have both political and administrative functions. Such a hierarchy includes cabinet members at the highest levels of government as well as lowly clerks far down the pyramid of authority. It includes political appointees and spoilsmen as well as career officers under a merit system. It includes military officers in uniform as well as civilian officials out of uniform. It includes "line" activities as well as "staff." I refer here to the positions, the roles, occupied by such people, not to the personal characteristics of the incumbents. A government's bureaucracy, however, does not include other bureaucracies found in the same country, such as those of private organizations, political parties, free churches, and even the bureaucracies of other governmental jurisdictions, such as autonomous cities and states, school boards, and development authorities. Any one of these other bureaucracies could, of course, be studied separately, and is so studied, for example, in schools of business administration. But our concern here is with *public* administration, and hence I limit myself to governmental or state bureaucracies.

It will become apparent, I think, that this concept differs markedly from what is normally brought to mind when we hear of a "public administration system." Thinking in a confused way of both structure and function, we try to identify offices and officeholders engaged in programs designed to implement public policies. This leads us to think of professional career men in the bureaucracy, and particularly those who come for training to our classrooms. Here is where professionalism tends to confuse the science. We do not have a chance to teach future politicians who will become cabinet members, nor businessmen, engineers, and lawyers who may become political appointees of government. Nor do we teach cadets who become military officers of government, and even most of the program specialists in the various departments of government, in "line" activities, escape our net as specialists in public administration. We are left, then, primarily with people entering civilian-staff career services, augmented by a few administrative assistants, management analysts, and junior executives.

Our picture of bureaucracy, consequently, tends to be screened selectively to include primarily the offices filled by a miscellaneous residual category of people who are not pre-empted by some other professional school or academy. Naturally, given this combination of selected offices and trainees, our view of administration tends to focus on the activities of incumbents of these offices. Moreover, as in medicine, we become interested in providing trainees with the tools they require for positions in bureaucracy, naturally a wide assortment of skills and knowledge from many fields. This distracts us from trying to understand the administrative *function* in government, admittedly a theoretical and scientific subject with little immediate pay-off for practitioners. It is no wonder that we begin to see administration as bureaucratic activity, a process, a structure, rather than as a function, the achievement of intended consequences.

We find ourselves in a trap, I believe, because we lack the conceptual apparatus required to escape the trap. Yet, as with the monkey trapped by his own greed, we have only to relax, to open our hands and give up some pet preconceptions, in order to find a solution to our identity crisis. I shall not pretend that I can offer *the* solution, but I think that I can suggest lines along which a solution will be found.

Functions as Relations within a System

Such a solution, I believe, will be found only when we learn to think about government as a total system. Structural and functional categories of analysis presuppose a system framework. Within that framework, we discern component structures, and analyze how they are related to each other and to the operations of the system, that is, their functions. In such a context, we can also think more clearly about these functions, notably the administrative and political functions.

How are these functions related to the debate about the separation of politics and administration? I said that I thought the statement to be ambiguous. Let us add here that the reason for this ambiguity lies in the failure to specify whether one is speaking analytically about functions, or concretely about structures. The functions are, I believe, distinctively different and analytically separate, but the structures which perform these functions are never separate and distinct. However, in relatively differentiated societies, such as our own, we do see the emergence of some structures which are predominantly administrative in function, notably in the bureaucracy—though not the bureaucracy as a whole—and we also find structures, such as those of political parties, which are predominantly political in function.

What is meant by function in this context perhaps requires further clarification. Let me say first that no action can be characterized intrinsically in terms of a functional category, by definition, since we have defined structures in terms of action, and functions in terms of system-relevant relationships between structures. Following these definitions, therefore, actions are never either administrative or political as such. Yet much of the literature of public administration is couched in terms of "administrative activity" and behavior, usually conceived of in terms of the activities engaged in by professional administrators. Here is where the premature professional orientation of public administration has misled us, for it has turned our attention to the activities of career officials as though these actions were equal to the administrative function. I believe that a professional orientation will not be damaging at a later stage, after the science of government (including politics and administration) has matured, for then the nature of functions will be well understood and the relation between politics and administration can be incorporated fruitfully in the instruction offered to future officials.

To explain more clearly just how the concepts of administration and politics, as functions, can be applied, let us think of the relation between two structures, A and B, each a component of government. If A prescribes norms which are accepted by B as authoritative premises for action, then A performs a political function for B, and B an administrative function for A. In this set of relations, clearly the political and administrative functions are inseparably intertwined yet distinct. If B, in the process of implementing the norms prescribed by A, were to formulate instrumental norms which it, in turn, prescribed as a guide to the behavior of C, then B's actions might be treated as simultaneously "administrative" and "political" in the sense that they accomplish an administrative function with reference to A and a political function with reference to C. This illustrates my proposition that the activity of any unit, such as B, is not intrinsically either political or administrative, but can be assessed in these terms only functionally, in relation to other structures, such as A and C.

To illustrate more concretely, a very rough analogy can be made with market behavior. Buying and selling can be thought of as analogues of administration and politics; a merchant, as comparable to a bureaucrat. Clearly, any market transaction involves both buying and selling, but from the point of view of a purchaser, it is a purchase, whereas from the point of view of the seller, the same transaction is a sale. Moreover, let us visualize the operations of an agent B who buys from A on behalf of a client C. In this case a given transaction by B may simultaneously involve buying from A and selling to C. These economic relations are readily understood in common-sense terms, but when we think of the analogous relations in government between those who prescribe and those who implement norms, we immediately fall into difficulties. It is as though we always referred to merchants as "sellers" and citizens as "buyers." We would then find it paradoxical that sellers (that is, merchants) also buy, and buyers (that is, citizens) also sell.

This analogy helps us understand the ambiguity of the usual statements about the separation of politics and administration. Let us make a similar statement about the separation of buying and selling. If, by this, one were to mean that buyers should be separated from sellers in the sense that one category, for example, citizens, would only buy and another category, for example, merchants, would only sell, the result would be patent nonsense. However, if one were to interpret the statement functionally, that in any market transaction one could analytically distinguish the buying aspect from the selling aspect, then the statement would be true, and the distinction important. In the same way, the separation of politics and administration cannot apply structurally, in terms of action or process, but it does apply functionally, in terms of relationships, of aspects of system-relevant interactions in any polity.

In real polities, relationships are far more complex than in our primitive A-B-C model. There are a large number of structures, and functional relationships are rarely unidirectional. There are normally feedback functions, in the sense that B not only may have an administrative relationship to A, but may also, in turn, set norms which become premises for the behavior of A. Thus, the relation between A and B may simultaneously involve both administrative and political functions. This further illustrates the point made above that the inherent separation of politics and administration does not apply to concrete structures. It is logically absurd to think that any action could be classified as administrative or political—if we accept the functional definition of these terms. However, analytically speaking, the two concepts are always separate, insofar as it is possible to determine, in any pattern of relationships between two structures, the extent to which one prescribes norms accepted as authoritative premises for action by another structure.

Interactions between separate structures need not, of course, involve such relationships. Structures may be autonomous in their relations with each other such that no one of them prescribes or accepts norms set by another as authoritative for its own behavior. A set of families in a community, all in communication with each other, but never accepting each others' decisions as legitimately binding, illustrates such a system. This shows, I think, the misleading implications of the familiar example of two men moving a stone as a prototype of administration, since the two men may be co-operating as a result of a bargain struck between them, in which case we see a collegial or consensual relationship, but not one involving an administrative function. The situation becomes administrative if the men moving the stone are responding to instructions given by a third person, or if one of them is acting on orders of the other.

Bargaining and consensual action is, of course, always involved in collective activity, whether in political parties, legislatures, bureaucracies, or trade unions and churches. Political and administrative functions emerge in addition to these more basic functions. Indeed, it is a sign of development if component structures in a social system begin to accept the legitimacy of prescribing and internalizing norms in their mutual relationships.[1]

Having defined the functional relationships of administration and politics, we must move on to identify the structural components which engage in these functions. Clearly, we cannot define any structures in terms of the functions which they perform if they always perform a variety of functions in relation to other structures, and if these functions change. This is why it is nonsensical to talk of an "administrative system" as though it were a structure of action, and it is particularly misleading to conceive of bureaucracy, or of professional officeholders, as an administrative system.

Actually, much contemporary political science has been guilty, at this point, of a misleading kind of reductionism. We often hear that a system is "nothing but" the sum of its components. If follows that if the components of government are a set of structures, such as bureaucracies, parties, legislatures, and courts,

[1] Elsewhere, I have used the terms "introjection" and "extrojection" to characterize these processes, and to relate them to the phenomena of administrative and political development. See Fred W. Riggs, "Administrative Development: An Elusive Concept," *Approaches to Development: Politics, Administration, and Change,* ed. John D. Montgomery and William J. Siffin (New York: McGraw-Hill, 1966), pp. 225–255.

then we should be able to understand government by looking separately at each of these parts. Moreover, if each component, in turn, has a set of subcomponents, we should gain further clarity by looking at each subcomponent, such as the bureaus, divisions, sections, and offices of which a bureaucracy is composed. Eventually reductionism brings us to the minimal component of any social system, the individual role or office, and then we make one more fatal jump: we equate the role with its incumbent and assume that if we can learn about officeholders, we will understand the offices they fill.

This form of reductionism is reinforced by the current vogue for behavioralism and quantitative methods of research, especially the survey method. I am not criticizing these methods, as such, because they do give us tremendously powerful means for dealing with some political and administrative problems. But they have to be used appropriately, and they are not so used when they buttress a reductionist philosophy.

As currently popularized, functionalism reinforces the same error. If one starts from the premise that there are "functional requisites" of any political system, one may then proceed to enumerate a variety of types of action or process as though they were functions. The next step is to identify concrete structures thought to carry out these functions—not realizing that one is simply using a new set of terms for an old set of ideas which always combined structural and functional properties. What comes out of this procedure is a new list of structural components defined in terms of their assumed functions, and the reductionist process continues. One simply tries to determine the characteristics of more ingeniously named component structures as though they could be added up to generate an understanding of the total system of which they are a part.

Viewing Government as a Whole System

You may well be asking at this point whether there is, indeed, any way to look at governments or polities as a whole. Perhaps we cannot do so, and reductionism, although not the most desirable approach, may, at any rate, be the only one that is currently available. To answer this challenge, I must try to present a framework for looking at governments as a whole.[2]

Actually, I think one reason that we have not been able to view governments as a whole is precisely because of the effects of reductionism. Our tendency has been to look ever more closely at smaller and smaller components of government, ending with detailed studies of the individual persons whose activities make up a political system. Amidst the welter of data thus secured, the basic patterns of government as a whole are lost to view. It is another case of being unable to see the forest for the trees.

Moreover, insofar as governments have been viewed as wholes, our perception has been selective in terms of a single component. For example, the ancient distinction between monarchy and republic is simply a classification based on the way in which the chief of state is recruited, whether by hereditary means or election. The distinction persists into modern states, and is one of the oldest in political thought, but it is largely irrelevant to an understanding of contemporary polities.

The distinction between democratic and totalitarian political systems is one of the most popular in use today, but it is not a structural distinction. Diverse functional characteristics are usually built into definitions, although the distinction corresponds essentially to the difference between polities with competitive and noncompetitive party systems. However, this distinction applies only to certain kinds of "developed" or "modern" polities, and it becomes anachronistic when extended to other types of political systems, just as the monarchic-republican distinction—which was highly relevant in Aristotle's times to governments with few structures besides the office of chief of state—becomes anachronistic when applied to contemporary polities.

In order to have a viable and useful framework for classifying governments, we need to discern the major component structures and understand how they fit together. Then we can examine

[2] I have done this already in several earlier essays, notably "The Comparison of Whole Political Systems" (Bloomington, Ind.: CAG Occasional Paper, 1966), and "Governmental Structures Affecting Administrative Reform," in Ralph Braibanti (ed.), *Theoretical Problems of Administrative Reform* (Durham, N. C.: Duke University Press, in preparation). Here I shall merely summarize a few salient points from these papers.

each of these component structures, in turn, in the light of the role they play in the total system of government. We may also find the study of governmental components intrinsically interesting, and helpful in gaining a picture of the whole.

Let us construct a simplified model of a system containing three primary components, A, B, and C. Each of these components, in turn, is composed of secondary subcomponents, for example, A-1, A-2, and A-3; B-1, B-2, and B-3. Each of the subcomponents in turn may be assumed to consist of tertiary subcomponents, for example, A-1a, A-1b, A-1c and A-2a, A-2b, A-2c. The process could be continued indefinitely until one arrives at the individual role—not the role incumbent—which then constitutes the smallest unit within the system, like a cell in the human body. Anatomists do this when they identify a skeletal system, muscular system, nervous system, circulatory system, and work on down to the organs in each system, eventually reaching the cell as a basic component.

Anatomists would be lost, for example, if they jumped from the body as a whole to the heart, veins, arteries, and capillaries, without recognizing the circulatory system as a larger component of which these organs or parts are subcomponents. But we in political science have made precisely this error. Modern governments contain a relatively small number of primary components, but each of them can be divided into more subcomponents, and we tend to jump over this first level completely, going directly to the second or third or nth (individual) level.

The functional relations of subcomponents are not directly with the whole, but with the components of which they are a part. If we do not think about these components, we will always be mystified by what we see, just as an anatomist would be who failed to see that the heart was part of a circulatory system. Indeed, it was precisely this difficulty which was overcome with the discovery, or rather the proof, of the circulation of the blood, for with the naked eye, one cannot see the capillaries which link arteries with veins. Thus, early anatomists had a picture in their mind of two blood systems, one red and another blue, both somehow connected by the heart, but otherwise not linked into a circuit. I think that we in political science will be in the same predicament so long as we do not see how the various parts of government are linked together, and fail to recognize the major components through which they are linked.

In a literal sense, the growth of governmental structures has been an evolutionary process. New structures have been added to old ones, but the old ones persist. What changes most is their functional relationships, for clearly the addition of new structures to old necessitates readjustments in the functions of the old structures to accommodate their changed relationships to the new ones.

Although the distinction between monarchy and republic has lost its relevance as a basic criterion for classifying governments, the distinction is one of the oldest, precisely because it relates to the first major component of government, the "executive." It is not kingship *per se* that is ancient, and many contemporary governments lack kings, just as many archaic governments also lacked kings. What is ancient, and what persists everywhere, is the "executive" as a major component of government. The term is artificial reflecting the fact that it has not been recognized as a component. We could use other words—head, chief, monocrat, pooh-bah—if preferred. Only the various kinds of "executive" have been recognized and given familiar names. The lack of a name for the general concept reveals a gap in our conceptualization.

It will certainly be objected that the word "executive" carries many other meanings, and this is no doubt true. What is important is the concept, the idea of an office which asserts authority over a polity as a whole. It is the activity of asserting authority which shows the existence of an "executive" structure, not the effective exercise of power, which is a functional relationship. The functions of "executives" change, but the structure persists. Modern "executives" (monocrats, heads, pooh-bahs) typically do not exercise much power, but we should not overlook the persistence and importance of the role as a primary component of government.

HIERARCHIC AND POLYARCHIC STRUCTURES OF GOVERNMENT

What other components need to be recognized? Let us turn to a second one, which is also very old, though not as old as the "executive" office. It was discovered in ancient times, but continues today as a major, perhaps the most important, component of government.

I have already suggested above that we need a concept for all the offices which are hierarchically subject to the authority of an executive. However, it is rare that this set of elements is viewed as a whole. Typically, it is thought of as having at least three separate components: the cabinet, the civil services, and the military services. Additional elements, such as commissions, intelligence services, the police, and sometimes tribunals in civil-law countries, are viewed as unrelated to any single structure within government, or as first-level components of government. Normally, one of these subcomponents, the civil service, is viewed as the "bureaucracy." It may be stretching the normal meaning of the word to call this whole set of components the bureaucracy, but if we cannot do this, we will have to coin a new term for the set, because, I think, we lack any better word for the whole primary component, and we do need to be able to think of the total set of offices under the authority of an "executive" as a single component of government.

Perhaps one reason we have not formulated a single term for this component is because we have tried to attach functional labels to describe patterns of action which have multifunctional relationships to other structures. Thus, we equate bureaucracy with an "administrative system," and then we see that parts of the bureaucracy, for example, the cabinet, have more political than administrative functions, and so we exclude these offices from the bureaucracy. If we look at the bureaucracy as a whole, however, we readily perceive that it performs political and administrative functions for government, and that the higher offices, especially at the cabinet level, perform particularly crucial political functions.

The underlying principle of the second component of government is its hierarchic structure, the derivation of the authority of subordinate offices from the authority of superiors. Such authorization from above institutionalizes political and administrative functions from the top down. In other words, the political function is exercised from above toward offices which are more numerous and lie below, as visualized on an organization chart. (We could change the imagery by using a set of concentric circles, in which case, authority flows from the center out.) The important point is that the political function is polarized to flow in one direction, the administrative function in the other, and many do (administratively) what the few (politically) decide.

There is an opposite principle of organization which may be called "polyarchic," in which a few do (administratively) what many (politically) decide. Using a vertical organization chart, authority flows up, not down. (On a circular chart, authority flows from the periphery toward the center, not from the center out.) The institutional device which makes polyarchic organizations possible is the vote. When there is agreement on a method of voting, and consensus on the legitimacy of the outcome, it becomes possible for the many to register their wishes on particular questions and to arrive at a decision which may, and typically does, involve naming someone (by election) to make other decisions. Substantive decisions on policy questions, on norms and rules, may, of course, also be made by vote at any level of a polyarchic structure.

There has, no doubt, always been polyarchic decision-making in government, as there has been hierarchic decision-making, but the large-scale institutionalization of a structure for polyarchic decision-making is a modern phenomenon, not an ancient one. Thus, the process of modernization in the twentieth century has involved the spread throughout the world of a structure for polyarchic decision-making as a primary component of government. Just as there is no generally accepted term for the concept of a primary component of government which is hierarchic in structure, so there is no term for a primary component which is essentially polyarchic in character, but there are names for the various subcomponents of this primary component. These subcomponents go by such names as legislatures, political parties, and electoral systems. If one looks at them as a single concrete structure of action, one readily sees that they are as integrally related to each other as are the various parts of the biological circulatory system. One can trace through the stages of interaction just as one identifies the parts through which blood flows.

In this polyarchic system, the core structure is an elected assembly, a collegial body of offices whose members are peers, who make decisions by voting, and who are elected to hold these offices. In order to be elected, there clearly must be a mechanism for holding elections and for constituting a body of voters, plus rules for the conduct of the voting. Among the structures needed for the holding of elections is machinery for nominating candidates, and we find political parties performing this role.

Each of the component parts of this major government structure may be defined by the part it plays in the whole. Thus, a political party can be defined structurally, not in terms of its political or administrative functions, but as an organ which nominates candidates for elections to an assembly; an electoral system, as a procedure whereby voters carry out such elections; and an elected assembly, as a college of offices filled by these elections.

What shall we call the primary component, this total concrete system? We cannot call it a "polyarchic system" because other systems are polyarchic, and its components are also polyarchic. In the same sense, the components of a bureaucracy are as hierarchic as the whole. Properties of components of a system can scarcely be used as defining characteristics for the whole system.

Nor can we call it a "political system," since this would attribute a single function to a structure which is multifunctional. Moreover, we have political systems which lack this particular polyarchic structure—ancient polities, for example—and we have seen that executives and bureaucracies also exercise political functions.

Whereas for the second (hierarchic) component of modern governments, I used a familiar term but gave it an extended meaning, I cannot find a comparable term which could readily be redefined to cover the third component. We need to reserve such terms as "party system" and "electoral system" for the subcomponents of this third major (polyarchic) component. Consequently, I think that the best solution is to coin a phrase, and I propose therefore to call this third component of government a *constitutive system*. No doubt, a better term may be found by someone, but meanwhile it is the best that I can do. It seems to be relatively easy to remember and use, and does not already have another meaning which clearly interferes with this one.

FUNCTIONAL RELATIONS BETWEEN PRIMARY COMPONENTS

How shall we now relate these various components of government to each other, and can these mutual relationships be used to characterize governmental systems? More particularly, will these relations help us to understand the scope of public administration?

I believe that they will. Let us recall that these components have been defined structurally, not functionally. It follows that any functional relationship is possible among the components. For example, the bureaucracy may internalize and carry out norms prescribed by the constitutive system, so that the constitutive system exercises a political function in relation to the bureaucracy and the bureaucracy, an administration function in relation to the constitutive system. However, this is only one possibility—although the normal one, as we conceive the operations of modern government.

Alternatively, however, a bureaucracy may be dominant, exercising a political function with reference to the constitutive system, while the constitutive system serves an administrative function in relation to the bureaucracy. This, indeed, is the situation in a number of countries where military officers, members of the bureaucracy, rule. Clearly, theories of public administration which assume that the bureaucracy is the "administrative system" are turned upside down in such a context.

There are, of course, other possibilities. There may be a struggle for power between bureaucracy and constitutive system such that each influences (or fails to influence) the other in approximately equal measure.

It may be argued that the concept of polyarchic and hierarchic authority in itself tells us how governmental power is exercised. But this is to confuse formal authority with effective control. In fact, those in authority may not rule, and those without authority may dictate. We must clearly separate the consequences of action, the function of effective control, from the action itself. Statements of intent to control, that is, authority, characterize a structure of action, not a function. We cannot assume, in other words, that formal structures of authority correspond to effective functions of control.

This brings us back to our starting point. We can understand the scope of public administration only in a context which tells us how the political function is exercised, and, reciprocally, we can understand politics only if we know how governmental decisions are implemented. In this sense, the attempt to detach the study of politics from administration, or administration from politics, is like trying to separate a man from his shadow, or to snap your fingers with only one finger.

Can the administrative and political functions be clarified any farther in the light of the foregoing discussion? Consider Figure 1.

FIGURE 1. FUNCTIONAL RELATIONSHIPS BETWEEN STRUCTURES

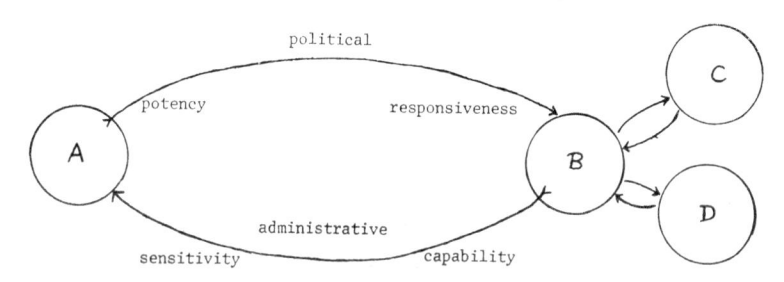

Let us think of A and B as any two structures of government which are so related that A sets premises for the guidance of the behavior of B. Such relationships might be found between higher and lower offices within a bureaucracy, between an executive and a bureaucracy, between a constitutive system and a bureaucracy, or a bureaucracy and a constitutive system. Although the relationships consist of a single set of concrete actions, they may be looked upon analytically in terms of two functions, political and administrative. Of course, these relationships can also be analyzed in terms of other functional categories, such as co-operation, conflict, communication, adaptation, system-maintenance, and the like, but our interest here is just in the political and administrative functions.

The upper line symbolizes a political function, an output from A which becomes an input for B. The output consists of the authoritative prescription of norms intended to serve as premises for B's actions; the input consists of the internalization by B of these norms. Clearly, the extent to which A's prescriptions are enforced or enforceable can vary, as can the degree to which B internalizes or introjects these norms. Let us call the degree to which A's prescriptions are capable of enforcement "political potency" and the degree to which B accepts these prescriptions "political responsiveness."

The degree of political potency and responsiveness of A and B, respectively, are much affected by another aspect of their relationship which can be symbolized by the second, feedback line from B to A, which represents the administrative function. The output from B represents the extent to which B can carry out effectively the prescriptions of A. For a variety of reasons, such as lack of human and material resources, the impracticability of A's demands, inappropriate organizational structure, inability to secure co-operation from other units (C, D, and the like), B may be unable to implement premises which it has fully accepted. The input to A represented by the second line is the degree to which A becomes aware of B's performance and of the obstacles to implementation of A's prescriptions. A measure of this awareness is the extent to which A uses this knowledge to modify A's prescriptions, to provide additional resources, or in other ways to enable B to carry out its mandates more effectively. Let us call this output from B "administrative capability" and the corresponding input to A "administrative sensitivity."

To summarize, the political and administrative functions are not characteristics of A or B considered as patterns of action, but consist of relationships between A and B. The political function is an output from A and an input to B, characterized as degrees of potency and responsiveness, respectively. The administrative function is an output from B and an input to A, characterized as degrees of capability and sensitivity, respectively.

This simplified model assumes an asymmetrical relationship, but, of course, B may also prescribe norms for A, so there may simultaneously be political and administrative functions between B and A in the opposite direction, creating symmetrical politico-administrative functions. Moreover, B may have similar relationships with C, D, and other structures. Thus B's relation to A may be primarily administrative, in the sense that it is asymmetrical and B accepts A's premises for action, but B's relations to C may be primarily political, in the sense that B authoritatively prescribes norms governing C's behavior.

Figure 2 illustrates the additional point that political and administrative functions *within* a structure, A, should be distinguished from the political and administrative functions occurring *between* A and such other structures as B, C, and D.

FIGURE 2. Functional Relationships within Components

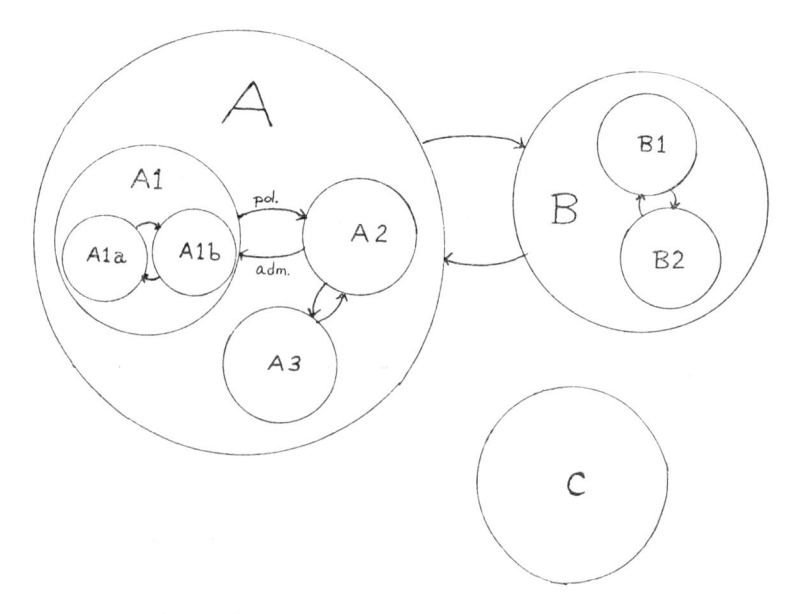

Thus, if A's activities result from interactions between A-1, A-2, A-3, and other components of A, we examine political and administrative functions between these subcomponents at a different level of analysis from the political and administrative functions which A exercises with respect to such other structures as B, and C. Thus, just as a constitutive system may be in politico-administrative relations with a bureaucracy, so there are politico-administrative relations between parties (A-1) and elected assemblies (A-2) within a constitutive system, and between committees (A-2a) and other component bodies, including a parliamentary or congressional bureaucracy (A-2b), within the elected assembly.

We may thus analyze A's actions administratively only at its own level, that is, in relation to B, C, and similar structures, where A is regarded as a "partial" system. However, we may also analyze political functions *within* (but not *of*) A, that is, between its components, A-1, A-2, and similar structures, where A is treated as a whole system. In this sense any structure, A, is neither a "whole" system nor a "partial" system in any intrinsic sense, but may be treated as both a whole and a partial system, but at different levels of analysis. Similarly A's actions are never intrinsically political or administrative. They may involve these functions in relation to other structures, and A's actions may reflect the outcome of politico-administrative function occurring between its subcomponents, A-1, A-2, and similar structures.

To avoid misunderstanding, let us be clear that these concepts refer to formal organization, and we are treating government as a formal organization. Social action occurs in many unorganized contexts, and through collectivities which are not organizations, such as markets, campaigns, riots, and wars. Moreover, actual behavior is affected by ecological constraints and by deliberate choices of human actors, all formally outside the structures of governmental action considered here. This is not, in other words, a framework for explaining any social action, but only a framework for analyzing political and administrative functions as they occur in organization (governmental) contexts.

Types of Bureaucracy and Types of Government

Let us apply these concepts to our earlier discussion by relating them to bureaucracy and constitutive system as primary components of modern governments. Let us consider first the normal case, the case which we expect to prevail on the basis of American and European governmental practice. Here we expect norms generated by the constitutive system to be introjected and acted upon by the bureaucracy, in other words we expect the bureaucracy, B, in Figure 1, to be *politically responsive* to the constitutive system, and *administratively capable* of implementing the norms authoritatively prescribed by that system. Conversely, we expect the constitutive system to be *politically potent* and *administratively sensitive*.

Yet we know that in underdeveloped countries, these relationships do not always prevail. Indeed, we know that in some countries, notably those with military dictatorships and rubber-stamp parliaments, it is the bureaucracy, or segments thereof, which is politically potent and the constitutive system which is responsive. We also know situations, as under party rule with rampant spoils in the appointment of public officials, where a bureaucracy may be politically responsive but not administratively capable.

Are there any structural characteristics of a constitutive system which affect its political potency and administrative sensitivity, and of a bureaucracy which affect its political responsiveness and administrative capability? I shall try to deal with the latter half of this question, not the first, because it bears more directly on the scope of public administration.

Let us first make a distinction between several levels of bureaucratic office. Remember that we have defined bureaucracy structurally, not functionally. We are not imputing any particular functions, political or administrative, to bureaucratic offices, and we extend the hierarchy to the very top, excluding only the executive office. Let us then define the *first level* of a complex bureaucracy as including all cabinet members, the formal heads of ministries. The *third level* may be defined to include all the offices which direct the major organizational components within a ministry, such as bureaus and departments. *Second-level* offices can then be defined residually as those which lie hierarchically between the first and the third levels.

Let us next make a structural distinction between two patterns of recruitment of persons to fill these offices. If incumbents are career men whose primary experience has been gained within a given bureaucracy, they may be called *insiders*; if their experience has been primarily outside that bureaucracy, they are *outsiders*.

Let us then hypothesize that a bureaucracy whose *first-level* offices are filled predominantly by outsiders drawn from the constitutive system will be far more *politically responsive* to that system than will a bureaucracy whose first-level posts are filled by insiders. Let us further hypothesize that a bureaucracy whose *third-level* offices are filled predominantly by insiders will be far more *administratively capable* than one in which these posts are predominantly filled by outsiders.

We can now recognize two major types of bureaucracy. One type will consist of those in which the first level is filled predominantly by outsiders, and the third level by insiders. Using the word "compensate" in its mechanical sense of correcting for opposed tendencies, we can refer to any bureaucracy of this type as a *compensated bureaucracy*. By constrast, bureaucracies in which both first- and third-level posts are filled by insiders, or by outsiders, may be called *noncompensated bureaucracies*. The term is clearly not used here in the sense of payment for services.

Let us now add a second distinction. If most positions up to the second level are filled by insiders, a bureaucracy may be regarded as a *closed bureaucracy*. However, if most positions at the third level, or at the second level, are filled by outsiders, a bureaucracy will be called an *open bureaucracy*.

Using these two sets of criteria, we arrive at a fourfold classification of bureaucracies as *compensated and open*, as *compensated and closed*, as *uncompensated and open*, and as *uncompensated and closed*. Figures 3 and 4 may help us to visualize these possibilities.

FIGURE 3. TYPES OF BUREAUCRACY

	Uncompensated	Compensated
Closed	I	II
Open	IV	III

FIGURE 4. ANALYSIS OF TYPES OF BUREAUCRACY

	I	II	III	IV
First Level	+	—	—	—
Second Level	+	+	—	—
Third Level	+	+	+	—

+ = predominantly insiders
— = predominantly outsiders

Can we now relate these bureaucratic structures to political and administrative functions? Let me hypothesize that the degree of political responsiveness and administrative capability will tend to be considerably higher in governments with compensated than with uncompensated bureaucracies. Moreover, we can hypothesize that governments with uncompensated bureaucracies will rank lower in both functions, but that those with uncompensated closed bureaucracies will tend to be particularly low on political responsiveness, and those with uncompensated open bureaucracies will be particularly low on administrative capability.

A similar approach can be used to study relations between *executives* and the other primary components of government. If an executive is formally subject to replacement by a constitutive system, or if he cannot name persons to first-level positions in the bureaucracy without the endorsement of the constitutive system, then the executive office is *accountable*. If one of these conditions is not met, the office is *nonaccountable*. We find nonaccountable executives today in a few monarchies and in some countries where elected presidents have been able to secure lifetenure in office for themselves. Governments in countries under colonial rule where the appointed governor is not accountable, even though a constitutive system has been established in that country, also satisfy the criteria for a polity with a nonaccountable executive. I think that the political and administrative relations between constitutive system and bureaucracy outlined above have to be reformulated to apply to conditions in polities with nonaccountable executives. This gives us new types of bureaucracy in addition to the four described above.

We can now formulate a basic fourfold structural classification of the types of government found in most contemporary societies. There are polities with nonaccountable executives, polities with accountable executives and compensated bureaucracies, polities with accountable executives and uncompensated closed bureaucracies, and polities with accountable executives and uncompensated open bureaucracies.[3]

Implications for the Scope of Public Administration

If there be any value to the framework of analysis presented above, then certain implications follow for the scope of the theory of public administration. We have, essentially, a basic subject with unity and coherence, namely, the study of government, a

[3] In "Governmental Structures Affecting Administrative Reform," *loc. cit.*, I suggested that we call all polities having a constitutive system, executive, and bureaucracy, *tonic polities*. The four types of polity identified here might then be called, respectively, *protonic, orthotonic, homotonic,* and *syntonic*. Polities lacking a constitutive system, of which only a few remain in the world today, are *pretonic* polities, by this definition.

study which includes, on the structural side, an analysis of three primary components, executives, bureaucracies, and constitutive systems. Historically speaking, political science also includes the study of governments lacking constitutive systems, and governments lacking bureaucracies. There may be very primitive societies lacking an executive, and the social structures of such societies are, perhaps, not appropriate subjects for political science.

Within the context of a structural approach, political scientists still have more than enough to do. They can study not only the various types of government and how they work as a whole, but they may also specialize in the study of selected components and their subcomponents at the secondary, tertiary, and other levels. The minimal component of any social system is the role occupied by an individual. Behavioral and survey methods are particularly appropriate for the analysis of these tiniest components of government, but it should be clear, I think, that these methods do not enable us to understand government at the level of primary and even secondary components of government.

One of the possible specializations-by-components-of-government would be the study of bureaucracy. However, if one took bureaucracy as a primary component, one would want to include not only the civil services as subcomponents of bureaucracy, but also the military and intelligence services, the cabinet, and the "political" offices of government. In this sense, the study of bureaucracy covers much more than what has traditionally been thought of as "administration." Certainly, offices at the first, and frequently at the second, level of bureaucracy, are thought of as "politics." Thus, the study of bureaucracy involves the political function as much as the administrative function.

Let me note here, without further discussion, that I think it is probably true that second-level offices in a "presidential" system have to be staffed predominantly by outsiders, and in a "parliamentary" system, predominantly by insiders. This leads to the hypothesis that parliamentary systems tend to have compensated closed bureaucracies, and presidential systems, compensated open bureaucracies. Thus, two subtypes of compensated bureaucracy correlate with two types of constitutive system.

Assuming that the United States has a presidential system,

with a compensated open bureaucracy, we note an important consequence for the scope of public administration. Professionalism in the academic study of public administration has led to a concentration on the problems of bureaucracy at the *third* level and below, excluding the first two levels, for the most part, and also excluding those services, including the military, for which university students do not prepare. By contrast, in Great Britain, where a parliamentary system with a compensated closed bureaucracy prevails, professionalism in relation to the study of public administration leads to an interest in the problems of officials at the second (administrative-class) rather than the third (executive-class) level. But positions at this level are much more concerned with public-policy issues than they are with questions of management and implementation. Accordingly, we may expect the scope of "public administration" theory in the United Kingdom to be public-policy-oriented, and interested in humanistic education more than in training for what they refer to as "executive" officer positions, at the third level and below.

If we were to make bureaucracy the organizing principle for studies in public administration, in a word, we would have to expand its scope to include the "political" functions carried out by offices at the first and second levels of bureaucracy. From this "bureaucratic" perspective, the study of public administration could scarcely progress without a major input of political science to establish its foundations.

The converse is also true, of course, for the study of politics. Students of politics have apparently assumed that constitutive systems, or the subcomponents and sub-subcomponents of such systems, could be politically potent without examining their relation to bureaucracy, and without considering the extent to which they were administratively sensitive. Nor have they examined the structural conditions in constitutive systems which affect their ability to be both politically potent and administratively sensitive. This is why I believe that the study of administration is as crucial for the study of politics as the reverse.

Let us consider an alternative way of dividing political science. Instead of looking separately at the component structures of government, we might concentrate on the functions, the relationships between these components. Suppose we were to focus on the administrative function as an organizing principle for determining the scope of public administration theory. We would then want to study the administrative feedbacks from bureaucracy to constitutive system, the relation between bureaucratic outputs, and inputs to the constitutive system, evaluated in terms of capability and sensitivity. I think that we find in the literature on administration much discussion of the problem of control over bureaucratic action by extrabureaucratic institutions, but very little on the conditions within constitutive systems which affect their administrative sensitivity, and hence their ability to change conditions so as to make possible increased administrative capability.

If the study of public administration, in other words, were to focus on the *administrative function* rather than *bureaucratic structures,* it would need to devote about as much attention to characteristics of constitutive systems as to properties of bureaucracy. Yet very little attention has been devoted within the field of public administration to this aspect of the subject, functionally considered. If we wish to enlarge the field to make a comprehensive study of the administrative function possible, we will need the help of political scientists who have focused their attention on behavior in constitutive systems.

Note the corresponding implications for the study of politics. If attention is to be directed to the *political function* rather than *constitutive systems,* as much thought needs to be given to the political role of bureaucracies as to those of parties, elections, and legislative bodies. In other words, we can study the administrative function or the political function only by looking at both constitutive systems and bureaucracies. If we study bureaucracies only, we must look at their political as well as their administrative functions; and if we study constitutive systems only, we must look at their administrative as well as their political functions. To separate the study of administration from politics (or of politics from administration), therefore, is like studying buying without selling, up without down, fronts without backs, black without white, or arteries without veins.

Conclusion: The Professional Perspective

This brings us back to professionalism, the separation of

politics and administration. The relevant distinction within the university, it seems to me, is not between subject matters, but between training programs. Political science as a discipline has a proper focus on government, including both its political and administrative functions. The impact of functionalism has been harmful to political science insofar as it has led to the false inference that politics could be studied separately from administration, and administration separately from politics.

Behavioralism, while making a major contribution to our understanding of the sub-subcomponents of government, has also had a harmful impact by drawing attention away from the wholeness of government as an integrated system. In administrative studies, behavioralism led to the analysis of behavior in individual offices, just as in political studies it led to a concentration on the voter, the politician, the legislator, and the socialization of citizens. To strengthen political science, I believe, we must try to recapture the sense of the wholeness of government which our forebears, from Aristotle to the Federalists, so clearly felt, without losing, of course, our new-found ability to examine sub-subcomponents of government and to utilize newly discovered high-powered methods. Attempts to separate politics and administration as subjects of study, then, are doomed to failure and frustration.

But there is a different kind of separation which is probably necessary and desirable, and this is a separation of academic programs by the training needs of the students. Let us assume that some graduate students wish to make careers for themselves in government as public officials and others wish to become teachers and scholars. The former should study some political science, and acquire an understanding both of bureaucratic structures and of political and administrative functions. They should also be sensitized to a wide range of public policy issues of the type described in the last portion of Waldo's paper. They will undoubtedly also need statistical skills, language competences, and education in history, law, psychology, sociology, economics, and other subjects. The training of a highly qualified public servant is indeed an arduous and complicated task, but it is one which, I believe, should be performed in the professional school, not in a disciplinary department. This is also true for public servants who prepare for their careers in military academies, law schools, and colleges of medicine.

The lack of professional schools for the public service, except in a few universities, has thrown responsibility for offering this kind of training to political science departments. There it has proved disruptive to the discipline because scholars primarily interested in the study of government do not want to teach these students. Moreover, these departments cannot provide the varied offerings needed by candidates for the public service, so the students emerge ill prepared for their career roles.

By contrast, scholars in political science need to study bureaucracy and the administrative function just as much as they need to study constitutive systems and the political function if they are going to understand modern government as an operating system. Accordingly, it would be disastrous for political science to transfer the study of public administration to a professional school, just as it is harmful for effective public service training to try to do it in a political science department. Public administration needs to be taught and studied both in political science departments and professional schools, though for different reasons.

The best solution, it seems to me, is to establish professional schools for the public service, and perhaps also for persons planning careers as politicians and as administrators of philanthropic and social service organizations. They will need to be taught by political scientists and by sociologists, statisticians, historians, economists, and others, just as are their counterparts in schools of business administration. But meanwhile the study of public administration as a part of the science of government needs to be carried forward within the discipline of political science.

Conference Discussion on the Scope of the Theory of Public Administration

CHARLESWORTH: When I was a shiny pants colonel in the Pentagon during World War II, ten o'clock meant five minutes to ten but now that I am again a professor, ten o'clock means five minutes after ten. We had better begin; we have a lot of ground to cover.

Naturally, I am proud to welcome such an impressive group. A political science symposium was held in this hotel in this same manner two years ago, and presently there is a symposium on sociology going on on the other side of the hotel. The sociology symposium will result in another monograph similar to the one that we got out in December 1966. In case you have forgotten what I said in my letter, the papers you wrote and the discussion that is about to take place will be published in a monograph which will be distributed free to the members of the American Society for Public Administration and the American Political Science Association.

Gentlemen, let us follow the order of inviting the author of the principal paper on the scope of the theory of public administration to tell us what he thinks of the comments on his paper.

WALDO: I would like to back up, if I may, and spend about five minutes on the paper itself. I assume that most of you read it some time ago, but I think a review is in order to set the stage for discussion. In reviewing it myself, and listening to the discussion, I was impressed with the fact that it was an *untidy* paper. This I knew when I was writing it, but the extent of the untidiness I did not fully appreciate. It would be a classic example of one's reach having exceeded his grasp, I presume. At the same time, I remain of the opinion that the direction of the reach was correct.

The paper began with some preliminary head-scratching on the nature of the subject and the task. I decided to talk about public administration in the academic, disciplinary, intellectual sense on the one hand, and on the existential, activity side on the other hand; and then try to relate the two. This, of course, got me into deep and rough water. Art Naftalin said that he perceived three centers of interest, three foci, and ended his statement by saying that he was confused: he thought that these three matters were quite separate and that we ought not to mix them.

The paper took as its base what I called a crisis of identity, and I spent some time exploring the dimensions of this. I discussed its origins in terms of doctrine and history, and argued that, for a generation now, we have lacked the certainty on scope and mission which we once had. Then I had a section titled, "Toward Crisis Resolution—Core Problems of Identity and Orientation," in which I discussed the possibility of integration and orientation that might be obtained from conceiving of public administration as a subdiscipline of political science—given the necessity of taking political science as it now is. I concluded that this is unrealistic. I concluded also that to regard it as a discipline in itself, in the sense of being a separate social science equivalent to economics or anthropology, makes somewhat more sense—but not enough. I argued that something further is needed, and that this is a *professional* approach, perspective, or stance. I appreciated that I did not know exactly what this means. I confess it again now. But I think that this is the direction which we should take, the line of development that we should explore. This *is* the direction in which we are going, at least in some senses. I think that it is quite clear that there are going to be more schools, separate curricula, and training programs. There will, for sure, be more of a professional approach on the training side.

I want to underscore the *nots* here. I was *not* saying that public administration has no relation to political science. This would be absurd. It has extremely important relations to political science. The point is that political science is not giving us aid and support at this point in its history and, as a matter of fact, is often positively hostile. The argument is that, in default, we must become our own political scientists, or get into an organizational position in which we can contract for the services of political scientists.

I proceeded in the paper to what I called "An Agenda of Old Problems in Need of a New Look," and I reverted to the problems created by the repudiation and abandonment of the old ideology:

the separation of politics from administration, the idea that administration is or can become a science—generally, the cluster of ideas which a number of persons attacked with a great deal of force after World War II. I argued that these ideas need a new look in terms of the events and the developments of the past twenty years. I took one of them as an example and drew it out in some length to illustrate what I had in mind.

I proceeded then to what I called "A Larger Circle of Theoretical Concerns." These are: external and internal security, justice, education, government by osmosis and symbiosis, science and technology, urbanism, and the idea of development. There is a concluding section labeled simply, "Some Concluding Thoughts," in which I revert to the subject of professionalism. Here I take the position that the idea of administration as a generic process gives us half of a sound professional base; but that we need to explore and emphasize the *public* aspect of public administration to provide the other half.

Now, proceeding to the critiques, and addressing first Wally Sayre's. When I met Wally I called him "The Old Optimist," since he had found my argument filled with "youthful pessimism." I had not thought of it as "pessimistic," but certainly I had thought of the world as full of problems. Now, Wally plays an important role in conferences such as this. This role is to restrain nonsense. By turns skeptic, optimist, philosopher, or simply historian, he plays the role superbly well. I might say that one Wally Sayre is indispensable for a conference such as this, but two or more would be simply intolerable, since the rationale for a conference is that there are problems! The reservations that Wally had against the word "profession" and, more generally, the professional approach, I must confess, may be well taken. I have reservations myself, and I frankly confess that I do not know exactly what I mean. To me, it is a search for a strategy for dealing with what I perceive to be problems and difficulties.

Rather surprisingly to me, there has been no reference in the discussion so far to the report prepared by Jack Honey for the Council on Graduate Education in Public Administration, which I know many of you have seen, and which is the *pièce de résistance* in the issue of the *Public Administration Review* for November. As many of you know, Jack's premise is that public administration is "the process of government in all branches and at all levels." Now, if Wally thinks that pushing toward "profession" is a little too wide, I hesitate to think what he would conclude with regard to Jack's definition. As a matter of fact, it disturbs me, and Jack and I have exchanged about three memorandums apiece trying to understand and educate each other. I am willing enough to admit that public administration has to be *concerned* with government in all branches at all levels, but to say this *is* public administration seems to me not to define, but to abandon the attempt to define.

Focusing on Wally's comments, and just picking up some "points," on page 27, he said, "Present ambiguities are merely exchanged for newer or larger ones." God knows, there are ambiguities in what I propose. But I would prefer to talk about *problems* rather than *ambiguities*. That is, to me, the objective is not to escape from ambiguities, but to find a better situation in which to deal with the problems. To me, the use of the word "professionalism" implies a search for a strategy to deal with problems rather than a search for verbal or even conceptual clarity. At the bottom of page 27 and extending to the bottom of page 28, Wally engaged in a series of remarks which at the bottom of page 28 he called "simple-minded." This is puckishness, of course: Dwight was making complexity out of simplicity. Perhaps—it is hardly for me to decide.

Wally's pages 29–31 are a much needed contribution to the conference. There is nothing in my paper, and, as I recall, nothing in the other papers, which records the very substantial record of achievement in public administration in the last two decades. I only *refer* to it, and go on; and the record needs to be redressed by recognition of the fact that very important developments have taken place in public administration. As you recall, he called attention to three sets—they turned out to be four sets—of partial theories. The first is found in the writings of those interested in what might be called the politics of administration. The second set focuses on the internal organizational life of public administration, on the dynamics of a bureaucratic world. I thought, when I read that far, that Wally was talking about what I would call "theory of organization," and it seems he was, because he referred to the social psychologists and sociologists. But he talked about it in more or less *political* terms, and this made it difficult for me to distinguish it from his first category.

The third set of partial theories to be found in the postwar literature is concerned with exploring the cross-cultural or, more ambitiously, the universal characteristics of public administration —the comparative administration movement, development administration, and that sort of thing. Finally, there are signs of an emerging fourth set of partial theories, concerned with inputs and outcomes of political systems. The last has not involved public administration people extensively, at least until recently, but the first three certainly have had a great deal to do with them.

Coming to the last page: Wally asked whether the several sets of partial theories that I have just briefly and superficially described, did not, in fact, embrace most, if not all, of my "perplexities." This suggestion that I have not understood the meaning of these developments was one reason that I began by reviewing my paper. Again: recall that I mentioned that I think it would be desirable to have a theory with respect to such matters as education, defense, and justice. Now, everyone must answer Wally's question for himself. But my answer would be: not on any reasonable construction of words, or on any calculation of probabilities that is acceptable, and certainly not on any tolerable time scale.

Turning to Fred Riggs' comments—Fred has reservations about professionalism, too. As a matter of fact, he is specific about what it is that he is against and what he fears, and I cannot argue for the things that he is against or for those which he fears. I think that they are real. To me, it is a matter of recognizing dangers and devising strategies to avoid or nullify them. I do have some arguments with specific points. For instance, we differ on the sequential relationship between professionalism and the emergence of a "science." While I share Fred's reservations of the dangers of a premature professionalism, I do not know any reason in logic, history, or experience why his observation on this point holds true. Often the emergence of a profession leads to stimulating processes which result in more science, not less. It is a very complicated interaction, certainly, if we take medicine or engineering as examples. I do not accept the proposition that if we start to think of public administration in professional terms we assume we already have all of the "science" we need.

I doubt that political science departments are the appropriate places in our universities for the training of public administrators. Fred expresses the willingness, indeed the desire, I suppose, to have training for people in public administration separated from certain types of academic pursuits. In that sense, we are in agreement, though there might be disagreement on the fine points. Certainly, I am not proposing to abolish the departments of political science. Let them be bigger and better. But my concern is that preparation for public administration is hampered and depressed and, in some cases, killed and suppressed in departments of political science. I propose that, where feasible, it be given freedom from such departments. We shall leave it at that.

I shall not try to deal here with Fred's very substantial positive argument. As you appreciate, and as Fred knows, this is a paper in itself. The argument is complex, and my responses toward it are complicated. But I have already taken more time than I should for an opening statement. Since I am not dealing with it, Fred ought to have an opportunity to present it briefly and defend it if we have the time, and an interest in doing so.

Back to professionalism and its relevance: As a result of the criticism of my paper and of the discussion, I see a connection between two sets of my concerns. This connection is by way of the sociology of knowledge. Ideas, in some sense, come from wherever they will—they are unpredictable. But, in some sense, they are predictable, and they depend upon a set of historical circumstances and a keying and motivation of people by institutions and problems. The relevance that I see is this. One can continue to work on the problems which I talked about, and which Wally and Fred talked about, in a disciplinary setting. This is not absurd. It gets results of a sort. On the other hand, to put the problems into the milieu of a professional school, into a professional setting, changes the rules of the game. It changes the way in which problems are viewed. It changes the way in which priorities are assigned, and it changes the answers that people come to when they pursue the problems. I think that we are likely to get quicker answers, and better answers, for our problems in a professional context than in a strictly academic-department context. I repeat, still again, that I am not for stopping any inquiry in the political science departments. But I find wildly unrealistic Wally's idea that there has been a silent conquest of political science by public administration and that a lot of our problems presently are being fruitfully addressed.

SAYRE: I feel a little boxed in. I think that almost anything I say will be held against me. But the main argument that I was trying to make in my paper—which had only one virtue, its brevity—was that I think efforts to construct a general theory of public administration are, for the field as a whole, premature. I think that we can expend some manpower on it. If Keith Caldwell wanted to pursue this line, I do not see any reason why he should not—and I am sure that he will, whatever I think, do what he wants to do. That is one of the virtues of the profession.

But, in terms of a priority for those who study public administration, striving for a general theory (that is, striving for boundaries so theoretically comprehensive that they make the boundaries exotic) is a mistake. This is, for us now, a misplaced priority. So I was really arguing substantially along the lines that Robert Merton argues for sociology: that what we need most is middle-range theory, or to put it in public administration terms, what we need is not general systems theory applied to public administration (except on the part of those who wish to play the role of the lonely pioneers), but theory-construction at the partial-theory level. Now, with my characteristic optimism, as Dwight has put it, I argued that we have accomplished a great deal here in the postwar years, that it seems to me that I can see, in the literature at least, three sets (or categories) of partial theories, a phenomenon which does not seem to be too difficult to describe for purposes of priority research. I have described those three sets, and I have added as a possible fourth this concern with *consequences,* the long-range consequences of actions taken by government and therefore involving public administration.

I may not have spelled out that fourth set sufficiently. I

would regard the graduated income tax, for example, as an output which is a product of our political system, in which the public administrators did play, and have continued to play, a key part. But with the redistribution of income that results from the long-range impact of this graduated income tax, its long-range social consequences, the students and writers about public administration have not been very much concerned. Recently, I would judge, this kind of policy consequence has become one of the main concerns of Emmette Redford and others.

I am suggesting that a high priority in the study of public administration is to fill out these four sets of partial theories, and not to give high priority to the construction of some general theory to embrace all four of them—but this is simply a subjective judgment as to what our priorities are.

Just by way of a footnote, Dwight's first reaction about my second set of partial theories was correct: what I did mean there was the internal life of bureaucracy, that is, organization theory. I did mean the things that concern James March and Victor Thompson, though they are concerned with the first set also, politics in administration. As a matter of fact, the boundaries between these three sets are quite permeable; almost everybody acknowledges the existence of the other two sets of partial theory when he is expounding his own set. A question which I did not raise in my paper, and which I might have raised, is whether—if we think of these four sets of partial theories as four different horses that students of public administration are riding—the tracks these horses are following are converging or diverging. I would guess that there is some sentiment around this table that they are diverging: that is, the feeling shared by some that there is an impending divorce between political science and public administration which has already reached the stage of a not very amicable separation.

This seems to be a suggestion that at least one of these horses is going off in a divergent direction. But, though it is difficult to tell about that fourth horse (since he is still so near the starting line), I believe that there is a convergence here. It would be premature, however, to insist upon any timetable for complete convergence, or for the development of any all-embracing theory. I do have a persistent feeling, despite the derision with which my position is regarded by Jim and Dwight, that the political science departments which I know are not hostile to public administration. A more accurate picture would be one of silent conquest, and I base this on what I think is a fairly wide acquaintance with the market of Ph.D.'s in political science. As chairman of a department producing Ph.D.'s, I get almost every day, from all parts of the United States, requests to fill posts, and I do not see any secular decline in the demand from political science departments for people trained in public administration. Though I know that there are problems on certain campuses in these relationships, particularly between professional training for public administrators and political science departments' interest in other objectives, this seems to me to be a very small percentage or sample of the general status of the profession. What may be misleading to some of us is that the request for public administration personnel in the teaching departments of political science around the country are frequently accompanied with a hope that this prospect, this young Ph.D., will be trained in the behavioral approach. I think that this simply means that they want someone trained broadly as a political scientist as well as a public administration specialist. So I would like to reiterate that I believe there is a misreading of the evidence here on the relationship between the great majority of political science departments and the teaching of public administration.

RIGGS: Let me say that although I picked out the question of professionalism as handled in Dwight's paper to criticize, my admiration for the paper as a whole is very great. I think that it contains many subjects which are important for us to consider and which the field of public administration needs to study. Some, Wally, certainly relate to your fourth category, the impact of administration on the general environment. This is surely part of Dwight's public-policy emphasis.

May I take up here a different point, namely, Dwight's view about the hostility of political science to public administration, a theme to which Wally has also just responded. Are there not, perhaps, two different issues which ought to be separated? *The first issue*—and this relates to what Mr. Naftalin was saying about different levels of issues—has to do with how people are trained for the public service. On this point, I agree with Dwight, if I understand his view. Political science departments do not want—at least in most instances—to undertake responsibility for training people whose main career will be in the public service. Certainly, for these people, as Dwight clearly shows, professionalism is the answer. We need professional schools.

But this answer is not a simple one. If a school tries to prepare candidates for public service careers by teaching only courses in public administration, then such a curriculum is too narrow. This is the main thrust of Jack Honey's report on preparation for public administration, and Harvey and others have also pointed out that most top administrators in government have come up through a variety of professional schools oriented to different program fields, usually not public administration as such. I recall that the first time I met Paul Appleby at Syracuse, he raised this very question: How could a school of public administration make a useful impact on the curriculum of other professional schools? In other words: How does the study of public administration get introduced most effectively into the teaching of agricultural administration or educational administration or public health administration?

I think that this is still one of the most challenging problems confronting public administration as a professional field. On this point, the experiments being carried on in California, at Davis, Riverside, Irvine, and now at Berkeley, are worth our attention. They are not trying to combine business and public administration, but, rather, leaving out the private sector, they are trying to combine the administrative component of all those professional schools whose graduates, in large numbers, enter public service careers.

The problem, in other words, is how to enrich the training of students preparing for a variety of professional careers by adding, as an essential component, some study, not only of public administration but also of politics. I fail to see how anyone can serve the government well, whether in public health or agriculture or education or social welfare, who lacks insight into the political and administrative aspects of government. In addition, of course, he also needs to know some economics and sociology and psychology and to have an adequate command of logical, semantic, and statistical tools of analysis. This means only that we want public servants who are well-educated men, and the study of public administration should be a part of their education. While it should not be omitted, it is also far from the whole content required for the education of a "Compleat Public Servant."

Although this issue is an important one, and one on which I think Dwight and I would be in pretty close agreement, it is not the issue on which I would like to focus my attention here. Rather, there is *a second issue*, and this has to do with theoretical questions about what is the proper subject matter of public administration as a science, as a field of study. Here, I feel, the answer places public administration squarely in political science rather than in professional schools. Perhaps this is because I stress the *public* aspect more than the *administrative* aspect of the term, because I feel that administration can only be understood in its political context and that politics becomes meaningful only when seen in its administrative context.

On this point, I think that I agree with Wally, but perhaps I agree in a somewhat different way. If public administration has made a conquest in political science, as Wally claims, it is not by way of the terminology and the classical principles of public administration, for these, I think, have been rudely rejected. Rather, some of the key problems of public administration, formulated in different terms, have become part of the central concerns of political science.

Perhaps I can best illustrate my point by using the word "bureaucracy." Most political scientists respond much more positively to a discussion of the role of bureaucracy in government than they do to talk about public administration. But the word has not been used here. It is a kind of taboo word among specialists in public administration, like showing the skeleton in one's closet. This reticence stems from the ambiguities of the word. It carries unpleasant connotations. Especially in its adjectival form, to be "bureaucratic" is to indulge in red tape, delay, obscurantism, rigidity, and the like. Victor Thompson has made the useful distinction between bureaucracy as a form of organization, neutral in connotation, and "bureaupathology" as a kind of sickness or disease that sometimes afflicts bureaucracies.

For many people, unfortunately, the word "bureaucracy" seems to convey, inescapably, the meaning "bureaupathology." For those of us concerned with the study of public administration in the less developed countries, the problem is particularly acute, for here we find many of the pathologies of bureaucracy in their most disturbing form. Yet, if we are to clarify our analysis, we must be able to distinguish between the type of structure and characteristics which may or may not be associated with it.

The advantage of the term "bureaucracy" is that it enables us to refer to a structure of government, the executive branch if you wish, but excluding the head, the president or king, while including all offices in a hierarchy of authority under this head. Thus, the word "bureaucracy" is not a substitute for the term "public administration." Indeed, it is clear that this governmental structure, bureaucracy, is very much a part of the political process, more so overseas even than in the United States, but, certainly, bureaucrats participate politically in every government. Certainly, it was clear in what Bailey and Moak said yesterday that public officials play an important part in our political process.

Not only is this true, but I see no reason, in principle, why it should not be true. Consequently, our theoretical framework, our terminology, should be so chosen as to make it easy to view the matter in this light. Unfortunately, our choice of words interferes with clarity of thought and forces a normative bias on us. This is why we must see bureaucracy as intrinsically and necessarily involved in the political and administrative functions of any government.

My point can be illustrated by the term, "public administrator." It was used quite often in our discussion yesterday. Yet, the expression is highly ambiguous and gives rise to a serious contradiction of ideas. We would not have this difficulty if we understood that the term was a short-cut for a more complicated expression, like saying the "sun rises" instead of, "the horizon of the earth is dipping so that the sun becomes visible." Having learned Copernican astronomy we are content to keep the picturesque phrase, "the sun rises," and are not confuesd by its implicit imagery of a sun swinging around the earth.

However, we are still trapped by the phrase "public administrator" because we have not experienced a similar Copernican revolution in our way of thinking about government. The confusion arises, I believe, because we mix together two different ways of looking at things, one structural and the other functional. In much of our discussion here, we have used the word "administration" to stand for a function, a relation between the making and implementing of policy. We have also talked about civil servants and public offices, clearly referring to a role or structure in government.

The term "public administrator" confuses these two perspectives. It implies a public official who is a part of a bureaucracy, and hence a structure. It also implies a specific function, the administrative as distinct from the political function. If we now say that a "public administrator" exercises a political function, it sounds like a contradiction in terms, or at least something improper.

By using the word "bureaucrat" we can very simply overcome this confusion. We can say that the role of a bureaucrat, a public official, entails the exercise of a variety of functions, among which are political and administrative functions. One can then raise empirical questions about the conditions under which the administrative functions of bureaucrats prevail over their political functions, or the reverse, and one can ask what the consequences may be for government under a variety of circumstances.

Political science has become increasingly self-conscious and careful about semantics, about the precise meanings of terms and logical relationships. It has been greatly influenced also by structural-functional analysis and system theory. Consequently, if you talk to political scientists about the political functions of bureaucracy, they see it as a legitimate part of their concern with the political process. They can also see quite readily how the administrative function arises not only out of the activities of bureaucrats, but also from the roles of party leaders, legislators, chief executives, citizens, and interest groups. In other words, they not only recognize the political significance of bureaucracy, but they can see the administrative significance of governmental structures outside the bureaucracy.

However, if you talk to them about "public administrators"

they may well say—if they pay careful attention, which they may not do: "Well, look here, aren't you attributing a functional consequence to a particular governmental role which is just not valid?" This leads them to turn away from administrative studies when it is the terminology that they find confused, rather than the subject matter, which they find interesting and relevant —when couched in analytically precise forms. This is the main point that I was trying to make in my written comment on Dwight's paper.

I think that I would now like to go beyond the point that Wally was making about the receptivity of political science to public administration. While agreeing that public administration, in restated forms, has penetrated political science, I claim that public administration has a message for political science which it has not yet heard, and this is a message which can enrich and strengthen political science itself.

The need for this message grows out of the preoccupation of political science, especially as expressed in comparative politics, but also in some other branches, with functionalism and behavioralism. Let me talk particularly about functionalism, which has, I think, been carried to ludicrous extremes. Historically, no doubt, functional analysis played a salutary role by raising questions about some weaknesses in the way institutional, legal, and historical models had been employed. Particularly when we began to look carefully at the governments of new states in Asia, Africa, and Latin America, we became aware that, although there were parallels between their institutions and ours, the performance of these institutions was quite different. This led most of us to ignore institutions of these countries. An influential response in political science was to say that it was the functions of politics that needed to be examined, and that the diversity of institutional patterns did not matter. This has been the prevailing mood in comparative politics—at least until quite recently.

Much of public administration theory has taken a different tack. It has essentially said, as has been clearly asserted several times at this meeting, that all we can really do is study American administration, or at most administration in Western democracies: if the resulting theories and principles have any relevance for other countries, well and good, but that is not our concern.

Well, I do not think that either response is good enough. We must be concerned with the institutions of government, including bureaucracy, in many countries, authoritarian and Communistic as well as democratic. The morass into which we have fallen in Vietnam grows in large part, I believe, out of our inability to comprehend the dynamics of this kind of government. If we understood it better, we would see that all our efforts to help it can only lead to undermining whatever popular support it has, and hence to strengthening the Viet Cong and the insurgency movement. Unless we understand how such governments work, the same thing will happen in other countries, such as Thailand, where the same pathologies are already apparent.

We must, in other words, find a way to examine the concrete structures of government in non-Western as well as Western societies, and this will enable us to understand how administrative as well as political functions are performed (or not performed) under varying circumstances. One of the main thrusts of the movement for comparative public administration has, accordingly, been to find a theoretical framework within which to explain differing structures of government and how they perform.

Perhaps the value of this approach, and its integral link with political science as well as with American public administration, can best be illustrated by reverting to Bailey's definition of public administration in which he stressed the constitutional framework of action by public officials. Some people, of course, argue that what is defined as constitutional in one culture may not be accepted as constitutional in another. This cultural relativism prevents clear thinking. Take the Greek case as an example. I submit that most Greeks do not consider what the present Greek government is doing to be constitutional. The very fact that the military regime wants the king to return after he tried to stage a revolution gives us an important clue. The new power-holders feel threatened and insecure, and they are willing to swallow their pride if only the king will return and thereby help to enhance the legitimacy of their regime. This would make it easier for civil servants and the public to agree to follow the policies set by a regime which most Greeks probably consider unconstitutional.

If the administrative function occurs only under constitutional government, then there is no public administration in Greece today. But I cannot accept this view. Rather, I would say that Greek bureaucrats engage in political and administrative functions as do the bureaucrats of every other government. However, under the conditions of unconstitutional government, their activities become highly politicized, and the difficulties they experience in trying to accomplish administrative functions is greatly increased.

One conclusion to which this type of analysis drives me is that the way to increase the effectiveness of administration in Greece is not to try to apply any so-called principles of public administration but rather to seek to enhance the legitimacy of government, to transform it into a constitutional regime. Paradoxically, externally mediated efforts to strengthen administrative efficiency and effectiveness in an unconstitutional government are more likely to reduce the legitimacy of the regime than to enhance it, and hence to lower the level of administrative performance of the government. The politicization of bureaucratic action in unconstitutional regimes constitutes, in fact, a recognition of this paradoxical relationship. In general, I think that the more politically oriented a bureaucrat becomes, the less administratively effective will be he. And the more illegitimate a regime, the more politicized will its bureaucrats become.

To return to the way in which we think about administration, I believe that this example illustrates why we cannot equate public administration with whatever public officials (bureaucrats) do. Rather, we must see public administration as an aspect of relationships between structures of government. If, in a government, we find some units able and willing to carry out mandates given them by other units, then the level of administrative effectiveness is high. But if most units consistently refuse to co-operate with other units, then clearly the level of effectiveness is low. The more legitimate, or the greater the degree of constitutionalism in, a polity, the easier it is to co-ordinate, to achieve administrative capability. Conversely, the more illegitimate a regime, the worse the administrative performance.

These propositions lead me to a restatement of Bailey's definition in the form of a hypothesis. Administrative functions occur whether or not public officials act in terms of constitutional mandates, but the effectiveness with which these functions are performed varies directly with the degree of legitimacy (or constitutionalism) of government.

By limiting our perceptions of public administration to *American* public administration, we make it very difficult to think about such propositions. The degree of constitutionalism and legitimacy in American government—and it may be reasonably high, giving ourselves the benefit of the doubt—is relatively constant (although the Vietnam war and race riots signalize a dangerous decline in the last few years). Consequently, our theories of public administration arise within restricted parameters. They tell us only how administrative performance may be enhanced under conditions of governmental legitimacy. But they fail to warn us that similar efforts may cause a decline of administrative performance under conditions of governmental illegitimacy, nor do they suggest how performance could be raised by increasing the degree of constitutionalism of a government.

If we were not so deeply involved in world affairs, I might say that this limited perspective was not dangerous, but we are in fact inescapably entangled with the problems of other governments.

UNIDENTIFIED VOICE: I would like to say something about some things that have cropped up a number of times—but most directly in the exchange between Dwight and Wally—about what Dwight has stated about this divorce between public administration and political science. What Wally views as a trial separation may culminate in an even happier marriage———

SAYRE: I even doubt if there is any separation.

UNIDENTIFIED VOICE: The principal bit of evidence that Wally submits is the great demand there is for political scientists to teach public administration. I submit that that demand is the function of other things as well, including the unprecedented manpower shortage, which tends to make even a warm body pass for anything that you want to label it.

SAYRE: I am aware of these things. I know that they will take the Ph.D.'s, but I know that on the totem pole of demand, international relations is at the bottom.

UNIDENTIFIED VOICE: Well, that is only part of a set of facts. The other is what I would call gross ignorance. We must have in that little office of ours more than 100 earnest legitimate requests for university teachers in public administration. Every once in a whlie, we get to talking to somebody who is in a public administration program. These are not those from the Maxwell School, or from the University of South Carolina, or from the University of Michigan. When we ask how they are doing, they are doing fine. Every Master's degree in Public Administration (MPA) that we turn out has ten offers. It is one of the strongest programs we have. The fact is that anybody who can attach any kind of public administration label to himself is immediately picked up. Many schools operating under MPA's, or perhaps established twenty-five or thirty years ago, have been devoid ever since of any power or self-evaluation or self-criticism. They really have no notion of what they are preparing people for, of the relationship of their curriculum to the outside world, and so I would say that it is a lot more than a trial separation. There really is a divergence.

UNIDENTIFIED VOICE: I do not see that your evidence leads to your conclusion. Your second point does not seem to me to have anything to do with the case. That there is a market for every MPA does not seem to me to point in any direction relevant to the separation of political science and public administration.

SAYRE: I think that what we may very well see in operation here is a self-fulfilling prophecy: that is, if the leaders of the American Society for Public Administration (ASPA) want this divorce, they can manage it.

SHERMAN: I would like to ask Fred Riggs and/or Wally Sayre a question. It seems to me that both of these gentlemen are using the term "bureaucracy" as either equivalent to public administration or equivalent to the executive branch. My question has two parts. First, is not the postman, for example, a member of the bureaucracy but not a public administrator in any reasonable sense of the term? Second, would not the staffs of the congressional committees and congressmen be part of the bureaucracy but not part of the executive branch?

SAYRE: Let me respond to Harvey's question this way, as I

tried to do in my paper. I regard this kind of question as an exotic boundary question. I can make out a case that the staff of an interest group, for example, the United States Chamber of Commerce in Washington, D.C., is a bureaucracy, and I can make out a case that the staff of the Joint Committee on Atomic Energy is a bureaucracy, or that the staff of the National Democratic Committee is a bureaucracy. I am simply saying—I think that it is stated on page 28 of my paper—that these exotic boundary questions, that is, just where we should now draw the line, are not priority questions for us.

SHERMAN: I think that page 28 of your paper is great. But I do not think that this is an exotic boundary question. It seems to me that you and Fred Riggs are proposing that the concept "bureaucracy" is a better concept than "public administration," and I have all kinds of problems with that, because, to me, "bureaucracy" is a very different concept, broader in some respects and narrower in others. I do not see what we have to gain by substituting "bureaucracy" for "public administration." To oversimplify a little, bureaucracy, to me, is civil service, and civil service is not administration.

RIGGS: I cannot agree with Wally that this is an exotic boundary question. I think that it is fundamental. It is certainly not a matter of substituting "bureaucracy" for "public administration." The two concepts are absolutely different. Until we understand the difference, we cannot make significant statements about how they are related to each other, about which bureaucrats, at what levels, under what conditions, serve administrative functions or perform political functions. Moreover, in a country like the United States, there are a large number of bureaucracies, some in private organizations, some in the Congress, in state governments, even in autonomous agencies like the Port of New York Authority. It makes no sense to generalize about bureaucracy if, in fact, you are talking about a particular bureaucracy, like the United States federal bureaucracy, the Thai government bureaucracy, or the bureaucracy of the United States Chamber of Commerce.

May I protest against our habit of substituting euphemisms for words with unpleasant connotations. We never gain clarity of thought by this practice, but only obscure the subject more.

Our problem is to identify the various structures of government, then to figure out how they behave and how they are related to each other, and out of this analysis to understand what makes the difference between more and less effective public administration. Now, one of the major structures of our government, and of every independent state in the world today, is a hierarchy of offices under the authority of a chief executive. This may be called the government bureaucracy, or "the bureaucracy" for short—while recognizing that there are many other bureaucracies in the United States and other societies.

It is a mistake to equate a term like "civil service" with "bureaucracy." Certainly, the American federal civil service is a part of the federal bureaucracy, but only a part. So is the military a part. And cabinet officials form part of this bureaucratic hierarchy, as do mail clerks. Clearly, it is difficult to generalize about all bureaucrats, for the functions performed by a mailman differ radically from those performed by the Secretary of Defense. But this is precisely the importance of substituting the word "bureaucrat" for "public administrator." If we can get away from simple-minded assumptions about what bureaucrats do, we could begin to ask operational questions. We could ask what levels in a given bureaucracy are most administratively oriented, or what determines how politically oriented bureaucrats are.

Certainly, some officeholders in any bureaucracy are more politically minded than others, and some more managerial, while others do quite routine tasks. We can investigate the conditions under which different bureaucrats act in these ways more easily if we do not prejudge the case by calling them all "public administrators," or if we try to think of administrators as those officials who administer and somehow separate them from public officials who do not administer! The more significant issue is what determines when and how well bureaucrats administer, as compared with when and how well they do other things. Thus, a bureaucracy is more than a civil service, and it is not public administration. Let us stop looking for euphemisms and concentrate on the key issues, such as when and how government bureaucracies can administer public policies effectively and efficiently.

CHARLESWORTH: Well, this illustrates the growing alienation

between political science and public administration—this word "bureaucracy." In political science, we have words like "timocracy," "ochlocracy," "plutocracy," "democracy," and "bureaucracy," this last being a term of denigration, like the others except democracy.

CLEVELAND: I would like to go off on a quite different track, taking Dwight's main idea that we should think of public administration as a profession. I find this idea of public administration as everybody's second profession, everybody's second career, immensely clarifying. Administration is not just another professional or academic specialty; it is a different kind of cut at society. It only makes sense as an overlay on all subjects, as an infiltration of all subjects—not as another way of looking at the moon from the same forest but as a way of looking at the moonlit forest as a whole.

There is no doubt in my mind that there is a profession of public administration. That probably is not as glamorous a term as one would like, but if I have a profession, it is as a public administrator. That is what I have done most of my life, but on a variety of subjects. My value to each next subject I take to be the common factors of administrative thinking and experience —what I have learned about how to make things happen on other subjects. If this profession does not exist, then I do not have a profession, and that would be a terrible thing to discover two weeks before my fiftieth birthday.

Related to these comments is a subject that really has not been discussed yet in this circle: Dwight's category of science and technology, where I think he is less successful than he is in the rest of his absolutely first-rate paper. In describing this category, one is not likely to say anything very new, any more than one can say something new about God or Reality. But I think that there is something to be said about how the public administration field or profession ought to *look* at science and technology: that is, we must try to derive from our understanding of the march of science and technology the institution-building tasks that lie ahead. My impression, at least in the international area, is that we have a tendency to let science and technology get quite far ahead before anybody starts asking: "What kind of institution are we going to have to wrap around these new perceptions to control them, to channel them, to make them socially useful?" I understand that the Manhattan Project, for example, did not include any social scientists; it did not think really very hard about what you do with this energy after you succeed. That is probably the extreme dreadful case in our lifetime. A more recent case: we already knew that it was going to be technically possible to get to the moon a number of years before anybody really started working on the law of Outer Space. I went to what I think was the first serious academic meeting on that subject at Rand—organized by the Corporation—and it was already the late 1950's by that time.

It is very hard to extract the social implications of science and technology, but that is one of the modern administrator's main jobs. I took a cut at this in several different fields while I was in the international organization business in the State Department. We had to try to figure out what kinds of international organizations needed to be built—and the United States is always chief builder and chief financier of new international agencies. It seems to take a minimum of seven years to develop a major international program, get it financed, and get it accepted and understood politically in all the member-countries. Seven years is also the normal lead-time of a major breakthrough in a scientific field. It would be nice if we could do the institution-building in parallel with the scientific engineering, both starting from the original perception.

For example: I spent quite a lot of time several years ago on an enterprise that came to be known as the World Weather Watch. I kept badgering about where we should be going with the World Meteorological Organization—a United Nations agency with headquarters in Geneva. At the time, nations were exchanging ground observations on their national weather; but what does it do to the situation when we can look at the sky from above the clouds instead of below the clouds—and take pictures? What happens when we have fast computers? What happens when we have communication satellites? It is very clear that when we can look at the weather in the way made possible by by the space program, we can, for the first time in the history of mankind, look at the weather as a system, as the envelope around the world that it has always really been. With fast computers and fast communications, we can now collect data about that system, transmit it, and correlate it, and get it into the hands of a forecaster before the weather changes. When that is the case, mankind has a world weather system which we never had before. If we have the elements of a world weather system, what kind of a world organization is needed to manage it? This leads into the political problem. Who controls that system? As man gets beyond the forecasting of world weather and into the modification of world weather, so that somebody will have the technical capacity to change the weather in Philadelphia by operating on it, somewhere else in the world, then we all want to be sure that we have our share of influence in the organization responsible for the decisions about weather-modification. We will want to know how many votes other countries have and how many votes we have and the name and nationality of the chief executive and the other details.

I have the impression that very few people—Don Price's is the only literature on the subject which I have really had a chance to read—have interested themselves in what you might call the administration and politics of science. We are very delinquent about dragging out of the scientists and technologists a long-range view which enables us to project the kinds of institutions that need to be built and permits us to begin building them before it is too late, before things are already in a mess. At one time, it might have been possible to predict the mess that the cities are in today. We might have done something then, and have prevented the morass that plagues us now. But we missed the boat. Fortunately, we have not yet missed the boat in the weather field, but only because a certain amount of vigorous action was taken by the United States government to develop the type of international organization which was required. We must recognize that the accelerating kind of change produced by science and technology makes organization-building and institutional development increasingly more imperative.

This leads, in most cases, into international affairs, international politics, and international administration. It leads into the politics of administration in international organizations. And here we have a field which several of us have said is not in this package, perhaps cannot be, but, nonetheless, a field which should be mentioned in the lists of tasks to be thought hard about, the inventories of the type outlined in the papers by Dwight and Harvey. The chief issues of which the politics of international organizations consist are issues of scope, function, and control. How much should the United Nations do about peacekeeping—and who keeps the peacekeepers? Those are the kinds of issues that we have in every field. Of course, most of the fields are not that hot or that productive of newspaper headlines, but they may be equally important—population, agriculture, and many of the so-called technical fields are politically explosive, too. These types of issues represent a piece of international business that should be tackled by the public administration fraternity, by both practitioners and academics.

When it comes to trying to develop an internationally valid general theory about public administration, I think that we are in for real intellectual trouble. We have made a start—albeit narrowly defined—in our work on development administration. A great deal of attention has been given to the problems of how to make things happen in societies where the people are not used to doing things on a large scale. It is evident that many individuals in these societies are unaccustomed to serving a public function; they still believe that their chief function is to be themselves, not to be the Assistant Deputy Administrator of such and such. It it fatal to effective large-scale administration for everybody to be completely subjective about what he does. This can be generalized into a proposition about administration: the capacity to pretend that you are in the job that you are in is really what makes it go. When I am an Ambassador at NATO in Brussels, for example, I am naturally supposed to play a different role from the one I played in the State Department in Washington. If I were to act in Brussels as I would act in Washington, my part of the machine would not work.

How to do things on a large scale in an administratively primitive environment is one aspect of our theoretical problem. I think, however, that we will get farthest in developing general theory about the nature of our business, public administration, if we concentrate particularly on the experience of the most developed, most industrialized, most complex society—which is the one we happen to be in. The more we learn and articulate about our own American experience, the more we can be helpful in setting forth a model of administrative development for those societies which are still administratively impoverished. Other nations might get more out of watching us at work than from hearing us talk about their problems, simply because we do not know how to talk about their problems but we do know something about our own. Many of these nations are still discussing planning, which was a big fad a generation ago with us. They are not yet talking about improvisation on a general sense of direction, which I think is what we have discovered as the key to the enormous accomplishments of our own society. There is no general prescription that tells us how loose administration should be in order to fit each society's growing complexities. That is a formula which the developing nations must devise for themselves, and, perhaps, observing our success, they may find a sense of direction for their own progress—and some warning signs, too.

In summary, I would not think in terms of tackling the international aspects of public administration by Fred Riggs' route of trying to develop a universally general theory. I would concentrate instead on the phenomena with which we are most familiar—the phenomena of extreme complexity, the most complex end of the administrative spectrum. And as far as international affairs are concerned, I would concentrate on pushing more students—and mid-career administrators—into conceiving and developing the kinds of international institutions that are going to be required to channel and control scientific inventions and the technological innovations that are already perceptible at any moment in time.

DURHAM: I would like to ask Dwight a question. It pertains to the medical analogy and the question as to whether public administration is a "discipline" or a "profession." Dwight, is "public school administration and supervision" a discipline or a profession? Is law a discipline or a profession? Perhaps you would care to answer first with respect to law.

WALDO: Yes, it is a profession.

DURHAM: Is it a discipline or something else besides a profession?

WALDO: It is more a discipline than public administration is.

DURHAM: In what way is law more a discipline than public administration is?

WALDO: What I have in mind is that there is more agreement on and uniformity of curriculum—though I grant the wide differences between "Harvard Law" and the night-study "trade school." In the sense that there is more agreement and uniformity, there is more "discipline."

SMITH: When Dr. Charlesworth invited me here, I agreed to accept a "listener only" permit, and so I shall make just this one comment. In most of these discussions, I am struck mainly by the gulf between the kind of introspective discussions that are going on here—relative to definition and identification and whether public administration is a profession or a discipline—between that and the fact that, on the other hand, as Harlan Cleveland mentioned, there *are* professionals working at public administration without regard to how they got there. There are people who are spending their lives at it. The pertinent question, I believe, is: What are the schools of public administration contributing toward helping these people to do their jobs, particularly in the area of the administration of science and technology?

I have a feeling here that is somewhat like driving along a highway that is parallel to an interstate highway; you think that if you could just get over there, you could really make progress. The difficulty is that you often drive miles and miles and cannot find an access to get on the other highway to get any mileage out of it. I have a little bit of the same feeling here: we are greatly concerned with definitions and that sort of thing, whereas there are in view some fairly clear and profitable courses of action that could be taken regardless of the answers to these questions. The practice of public administration—whether a profession or discipline—is, of necessity, going on, even though we are often unable to separate clearly what is policy and what is practice, what is structure and what is function. Nevertheless, there are many things which could be, and I think should be, given attention—the kinds of things that Harvey Sherman mentioned in his paper and that John Macy mentioned yesterday, for example, the matter of the federal government's contracting out some of the functions that might otherwise be performed by government civil service. These kinds of decisions are being made in the absence of a theory and without having made an in-depth study of the long-term implications of the decisions.

You would hardly want to blame Henry Ford for not having considered the problems of air pollution before he invented the first Model-T. But, on the other hand, I think that today we certainly must hold ourselves and the scientists and technologists more responsible for the social and economic consequences of the science and technology that they are advancing. I feel that this is one area where some of the professionals in public administration could really move in and study some of the problems that are being generated, problems that are standing there almost demanding to be looked at and considered. These need to be studied and looked at now. I believe we could, for the moment, bypass the more esoteric questions and move ahead with study of these vital practical problems. Chances are that if we do this, maybe five years from now the answers to many of the questions which we have been discussing these last two days will have become much clearer.

LEPAWSKY: If we look back to begin with, we will find that we in public administration have been phenomonologically bound, though less so than have other applied social science disciplines. Less excusable is the fact that we have been timebound, too. As one looks through our treatises and papers of the past, it is clear that we did not adequately anticipate ensuing developments. If we should try now to identify the emerging future trends, I would suggest that we might anticipate the following kinds of eventualities.

First, we might estimate the possibilities of an upgrading of the general political and administrative intelligence, or at least political and administrative awareness, in our society, and not merely a greater sophistication among administrators and leaders. To put it differently, the gulf between the level of the general public and the professional specialist is narrowing. I realize that there are interpretations in the other direction and that our communications media may confuse as well as enlighten us on this point. But all one has to do is to sample well the discussions and discourses of the members of the most disfranchised and depressed groups in our society in order to realize that, despite some evidence to the contrary, there is much greater articulation and understanding.

Secondly, there is a movement toward a more participatory democracy which is beginning to transcend or outflank the political professionals and administrative technologists. I hope that we shall be able to evaluate the actuality and, if it seems worth-while, the significance of these trends.

WALDO: There are many points, obviously, that could be pursued. A few: To me, it is reasonable to think that a society which is heavily governmentalized, in which the need for people to do urgent government jobs is obvious, to have professional schools in which to train people for the jobs. I hope and expect that there will be a large development in this direction, experimenting with different combinations of the disciplines and approaches. If there is a "narrowing down," the development of a guild or caste spirit, this will, of course, be bad, not good. But I think that this is a small risk, given the counterforces. For one thing, I foresee a great deal of interaction with other professional schools. I think schools of administration, or whatever they are called, are going to help solve the problem of the "second career" or the "overlay." In the two environments that I have experienced recently, other professional schools are reaching out avidly to find what they can in the way of help, realizing that the "second career" in administration is very important for the people whom they are training. I think that giving aid in this direction can be done much more strategically and efficiently from the base of a professional school than it can from the base of a political science department.

I did not find much in the oral presentations of Wally or Fred with which I disagreed. The sharpest disagreement, I suppose, concerns Wally's "silent conquest" thesis, and the attitude of political scientists in the political science departments. A point also with regard to recruitment and the demand for teachers of public administration: I accept Wally's statement of facts in this connection. My observations and experiences match his. For the past fifteen years, the demand for new political scientists with a specialization in public administration has continued to be high, and for the past five years or more, the request is usually for someone in public administration who has some of the new "behavioral" skills. (It is fashionable, and we have to be fashionable in this department!) However, I do not conclude from this that political scientists just love public administration. It is quite another sort of conclusion that I reach. It has to do with supply and demand. It is better understood in economic terms than in psychological terms.

I found Harlan's remarks very interesting, and to use the cliché, I could not agree with him more. We simply do not respond as much as we should, as intelligently as we should, to Big Science and mushrooming technology. I can make my point again about political science in this connection. About three years ago, I decided that people in political science and public administration ought to be thinking more about the impact of science and technology. I made the argument in my, then, department of political science, that in a table of organization of about fifty, one position ought to be thought of as focusing on the intersection of science-technology and government. I got two lines of resistance. One was the "liberal arts" response that this was ungentlemanly, that the business of the political scientist is to think about Higher Things, not to get into mechanics. The other was the "behavioral" response. I was challenged to demonstrate that "laws of politics" would result! It did not make any difference that life and death may depend upon our success in connecting science-technology and government. How scholastic can you get?

The Scope of the Practice of Public Administration

By Herbert Emmerich

IS there such a thing as can be called "the practice of public administration"? What are its limits? Where does it begin and end?

Public Administration: Everything or Nothing?

As a practitioner, only late in life assimilated as a professor, it does not comfort me that the universities are increasingly abandoning the use of the words "public administration" and are embracing such euphemisms as "public affairs." Nor is the term too popular in government circles. Government officials like to say that they are engaged in public health, education, welfare, defense, agriculture, conservation, science, works, foreign affairs, and the like, but seldom identify themselves with "public administration."

That this is also true at the international level was brought home to me five years ago, when the Secretary General of the United Nations asked Pierre Juvigny (France) and me to visit all the specialized agencies and the substantive divisions of the Department of Economic and Social Affairs and report on the "administrative aspects" of their activities. The results of the inquiry were surprising as to the extent of the ingredient of public administration that ran through their work. The international agencies were advising major ministries of sovereign states on matters having to do with structure, method, staffing, pay plans, budgeting, training, and planning as well as on substantive techniques and policies. They were scarcely aware that they had been advising on public administration, and even less aware of the need for co-ordination and consultation with other United Nations agencies advising the same government. Why is there this resistance to identify with public administration? It is less marked in Britain, India, and France where identification with the "civil service" or the "fonction publique" prevails and is a mark of a certain prestige. Must we conclude that in most countries, including the United States, generally speaking, the term has no recognized "Gestalt" or common "construct"?

At the other extreme, one might pose the question whether in the "organizational society" almost everything could not be characterized as coming under the scope of public administration? Some writers even contend that much of large-scale private endeavor falls in this category, a notion which seems to me to verge on sophistry. I will not venture too far into the maze of political ideology except to express my profound sympathy for the political theorists who have to rationalize contemporary governmental systems. Certainly, even in the land of the free, it is increasingly hard to think of anything that is not subject to public laws, regulations, and officials. Their power reaches from before the cradle (for example, the regulation of the pill) to beyond the grave (for example, the taxation of estates). Our government does not operate the economy, but government's influence on the economy is enormous, and government is required by law to manipulate fiscal and monetary policy to assure the economy's stability and growth and to limit its excesses. In the field of social or way-of-life problems, there seems to be a growing general assumption that deep-rooted problems are soluble by crash programs if only enough money is voted and as long as they are not placed in the hands of an agency that has had any previous experience whatever.

Administration and Ideologies

It would be a sterile exercise to talk of the scope of public administration in our time without admitting an awareness of the existence of widely different and antipathetic systems of political and economic ideologies. A Soviet official at a United Nations seminar asked what this thing called "public administration" was anyhow. When it was explained, he replied: "I guess that would include just about everything that is done in my country." But would it any longer? The Communist countries are deviating markedly from Marxian dogma. The growing separation of trade and state is among their latest heresies. They even talk about managerial incentives. The socialist Labour Government of

England appears to impose fewer state controls over its nationalized industries than does the capitalist United States over its private ones. During the Eisenhower administration, a witty colleague at "1313" referred to the movement for municipal cemeteries as "sleeping socialism."

To top this paradox, A. A. Berle, J. K. Galbraith, and others make a strong case that the great increase of government intervention has strengthened the viability of democratic capitalism, while Professor von Hayek views with alarm every new statute as another step on the road to serfdom. Meanwhile, in their several ways, Professors Friedman and Lindblom want to introduce more market mechanism into public operations, while other economists and computer-programmers want to measure all public activities on an input-output or "cost-benefit" basis, giving government operations, at long last, the amoral equivalent of the profit-and-loss statement, free of irrelevant considerations like value judgments.

As we considered the question of what this thing called public administration is, I did not get too much aid and comfort from my friends in academia. In the early days of attempting to found a discipline and a profession, they prematurely set narrow boundaries to their field. They gave undue emphasis to staff functions such as personnel, budgets and accounting, and organization and methods, thus creating a new series of specialties and ignoring the major public administrators (except, possibly, for the city manager), the generalists in the line who must look at performance of a substantive program as a whole. The pioneers, to whom we owe much, tried, I fear, to emulate existing disciplines instead of recognizing that they were dealing with a field which was interdisciplinary and essentially eclectic and which had to become a synthesis of many arts and sciences.

I am slightly consoled to find that public administration is not the only field which has difficulty in outlining its intellectual perimeters. In *A Design for Political Science,* published by this Academy, I tried to find a model for a definition which did not use the word "model." But, alas, our forefathers, the political scientists (who seem to be disowning their child), appeared to conclude that their own field embraced any form of public action, provided only it had not already been pre-empted by the other social sciences. What would Aristotle, Locke, and Mill have said to this? I prefer the bolder type of definition which the late William F. Ogburn applied to sociology: "anything taught under that name by a reputable scholar at a reputable university." If these academic reflections seem to go beyond my assigned topic, it is only because I believe that what has been happening in the field of theory has had a profound effect on the world of practice. But I insist that public administration is something, albeit not everything, and am inspired in this thought by Arthur E. Morgan's book on More's *Utopia* which bears the happy title *Nowhere is Somewhere*.

PUBLIC ADMINISTRATION IS ADMINISTRATION THAT IS PUBLIC

Perhaps this does it, but then it is, of course, too easy, and the problem requires a closer examination than a mere phrase can convey. And just precisely what is "public"? We no longer can rely upon the Supreme Court to forbid public intervention into any field of human activity whatsoever, whether at the federal or state (including the local) levels. I like to ask my students to dream up an activity in which the Court would forbid governments to engage, but I am not certain of the answer myself. If all else fails, there are always the national defense, general welfare, commerce, and fiscal-agency clauses of the Constitution on which to fall back. If the act is carefully drawn, and takes care about such things as due process and equal protection, our legislatures can continue to enlarge the scope of public administration indefinitely, ubiquitous as it already appears to be. The brakes on public action on which the Court relied up to 1937 no longer seem to be working, and the Court is now preoccupied with the procedures of public administration rather than with its content. In certain areas, such as school desegregation, as a matter of fact, the Court seems to have plummeted the legislative and executive into thickets which they would have preferred not to enter. But I do not wish to create the impression that I am against progress. I rejoice that we are free of judicial bars to experimentation, but very much fear that we are trying to launch things too fast, with too many small, specialized programs, and that we are raising false expectations of impossible quick results on hard-core social problems.

In its broadest context, the practice of public administration embraces all executive acts, subject to political control, performed by public agencies, officials, or employees. It would exclude purely political acts such as running for office, collegial action in debate, and voting in legislative assemblies. With few exceptions, administration is the work of the executive branch in our form of government, even though we do not always stick to a clear-cut distinction in the separation of powers, as, for example, in the case of a county board of supervisors.

The tendency in American government has been to reduce greatly the number of elected officials which characterized us in the pioneer stages of democracy and greatly to increase the number and quality of officials appointed on some kind of merit basis. The functions of a President, governor, or mayor are not, of course, exclusively administrative, but there is a large ingredient of administration in almost his every act. We refer to the government of the day in our country as "the administration." But one can easily think of examples of administrative acts performed by judges and legislators. Even political acts, except those confined to parliamentary maneuver and running for office, have a high administrative content. While we have been repenting that it took us so long to perceive the political aspects of administration, we still have to explore the high administrative content of politics. And it begins to look as if, pretty soon, even political campaigns would be increasingly financed and monitored by public agencies.

Quasi-Autonomous Agencies as Public Administration

There are certain areas of public activity which have achieved *de facto* or *de jure* a certain measure of autonomy from conventional executive and legislative controls. These sacred white cows of public administration are (1) the government corporation, (2) the independent regulatory agency, (3) the local school board, and (4) the scientific estate. But they are certainly all within the scope of public administration.

The government corporation or authority usually performs a revenue-producing service, and exempting it from the usual executive and political controls presents special problems. The drive for revenues by an aggressive management may distort its programs and cause it to neglect needed services which are less profitable. Its autonomy may render the corporation immune to policies and programs of elected officials. Sometimes the public corporation is so circumscribed by minute controls that it might as well have been made a bureau. These considerations make one pause before supporting the proposal for incorporating the American post office system, as the British have begun to do with theirs. It is inconceivable that Congress would authorize the delegation to a corporate board of the essential powers, the fixing of postal rates and salaries, and the location of new post offices. But even if corporate in form, the post office would still be within the scope of public administration, for its overriding objective would be the rendering of a national service, and not that of profit-making.

The so-called independent regulatory commissions should be considered as public administration. The body politic would have been less confused and Montesquieu would have rested more easily in his grave if these agencies had been defined from the outset as executive ones. Surely there is no function that they perform that does not have its exact counterpart throughout the regular executive establishment, including those of rule-making, investigation, enforcement, and adjudication. The growing movement to judicialize public administration tends further to wipe out any important differences between the essential nature of these bodies and the regular executive departments that may have been thought to exist when they began to spring up in the 1880's. These functions are the normal by-products of the complexity of modern legislation and the world-wide tendency, based on necessity and convenience, of delegation by legislatures of considerable areas of discretion to the executive. Such delegation inevitably produces functions that might be called quasi-legislative and quasi-judicial, a characteristic of all public administration, and not a reason for giving independent commissions a special status. The limitation of agencies to regulatory duties fails to encourage a developmental attitude, and it was not until the American railroad system, beset by obsolescence and by unco-ordinated subsidy of competing road, air, and water transport, approached operating and financial breakdowns that a Department of Transportation was created. It is still something of a paper dragon, for it had to be pieced together to avoid impairing the authority of the continuing commissions.

American public administration is becoming increasingly law-ridden and judicialized. It is infinitely more so than that of Britain and probably no longer can yield first place to that of France. It is too early to assess the results of the coming into effect on July 4, 1967, of the Administrative Procedures Act of 1966, which was intended to compel disclosure but is more likely to judicialize administrative management still further, increase the cost of administration, encourage duplicating procedures and two sets of records, and further formalize the administrative process. In the face of these trends, it is hard to understand why students and practitioners of public administration continue to ignore the subject of administrative law.

Another area of separatism in American public administration is the local school board. The schoolmen, under the attractive cover of keeping the teaching of children out of politics, have created their own political and administrative apparatus and network of powerful and uninhibited associations. School boards have thus obtained a large measure of autonomy, and independent taxing, borrowing, and spending powers. But I find myself less dogmatically outraged by this separatism from the rest of local government than I was twenty-five years ago. It seems to me that the movement for consolidated school districts in both rural and suburban communities has shown an exceptional ability to enlarge their areas which other units of local government have failed to do. Better roads and four generations of school-busing of children have given us larger, more modern, and better secondary schools, and have made good education available to more children in the countryside. The biggest reduction in the number of local governments in the United States has been in the number of school districts. Furthermore, the concerted attack on poverty and the intervention into the field of education at state and federal levels is tending to co-ordinate public education with the rest of the body politic. Though separate, I nevertheless classify the management of public education as equal to public administration.

The scientists in the last twenty-five years, as Don K. Price has told us so perceptively, have established a new form of separatism. This may be based partly on the inherent mysteries of their calling and partly on the fact that much of their work is defense-connected and wrapped in the cradle of security. They have done this by the activism and ability of the powerful Sanhedrins of their professional societies, which become the inner advisers and often the determiners of governmental policy. The sum available for governmental grants to scientific research and development is now assuming the proportions of something like sixteen billion dollars a year, depending on which budgetary tables you prefer to read; and the influence of the organized scientific community in the allocation of these funds is very great. The trend has been assisted by the great extension of governmental activity through the use of the contractual device, by means of which the government gives large grants and loans to universities and industries for these purposes. In spite of the problems to which this disquieting love-hate relationship between government and science has given rise, the tangible results in scientific and technological advance have been formidable. I know of no simple solutions to the improvement of this relationship except, perhaps, by better grounding in scientific fields of those entering politics and administration and by exposing young scientists to modern concepts in these fields.

On the subject of abstract and theoretical research, the government will probably be compelled to continue to place great faith and trust in, and to accord much delegation to, the organized scientific communities. In the field of applied research and development, public administration is beginning to achieve a certain degree of sophistication and experience. A new breed of scientist-administrator, and even of scientist-politician, is arising, and these are hopeful signs.

In considering all these areas of autonomy and separatism, we must continue to strive to keep public activities public in nature, to insist that they be harnessed to that intangible thing called the public interest, and, in respect to program and finance, even if not in respect to detailed procedures, that they be accountable to political authority, and responsive to changing public policies.

Scope of Public Administration by Types of Programs

At the closing session of the 1966 conference of the American Society for Public Administration, I suggested a number of typologies of nonmilitary public administration which might lead to insightful study, as they had elements in common. I now list a few of these, as they also indicate the variety and scope of contemporary public administration:

(1) *External Programs*: Foreign Affairs, Foreign Aid, Information, Intelligence, International Organizations, Trade, Communication, and Cultural Exchanges, functions which are found almost entirely at the federal level.

(2) *Regulatory Programs*: In which the government has regulatory powers over a given activity or industry: Food and Drug Administration, Interstate Commerce Commission, Securities and Exchange Commission, Federal Trade Commission, and state regulatory bodies, for example.

(3) *Directly Administered Service Programs*: In which the federal government has direct contact with the citizens, such as: Post Office, Internal Revenue, Social Security, and Medicare, involving great masses of transactions. (Law enforcement and public welfare at the local level might be added here.)

(4) *Directly Administered Development Programs*: These may be regional such as Tennessee Valley Authority (TVA), Appalachia, and the District of Columbia, in which case they tend to be multipurpose. They may be functional, such as the resource and development programs of the Forest Service, the Reclamation Service, the Soil Conservation Service, and the Corps of Engineers.

(5) *Programs Administered by Grants-in-aid to States*: Public Assistance, Public Roads, and Public Health, for example, and their effect on state administration.

(6) *Programs Administered by Grants-in-aid to Local Authorities*: Airports, Community Facilities, Housing and Urban Redevelopment, portions of the Education and Poverty Programs, for example, and their effect on local administration.

(7) *Programs Administered by Voluntary Local Groups*: County Agricultural and Soil Conservation Committees, Rural Electrification, Co-operative Credit and Marketing, and Community Groups in the Poverty Program.

(8) *Programs of Loans, Insurance, and Grants to Private Industries and Banks*: Federal Reserve, Farm Credit, Home Loan Banks, Federal Deposit Insurance, Federal Housing Administration (FHA) Insurance, Aviation, Merchant Marine, Railroads and Rapid Transit, Agricultural Price Support Programs, Small Business, and the like.

(9) *Administration by States and Localities, Particularly of Federally Aided Programs and Problems of their Financing*:

(10) *Programs of Government by Contract*: In education, science, research, development, and production with private enterprise, universities, and research bodies.

(11) *Programs of Over-all Management of the Government and the Economy*: Co-ordination of related programs at the center and at regional levels; relation of discrete financial agency programs to general fiscal and monetary policy, business cycle, and employment; co-ordination of programs in the fields of science, conservation of manpower, and conservation of physical resources; and central control and service agencies in regard to budgetary, personnel, management, material, and records administration.

THE MAGNITUDES OF THE SCOPE OF PUBLIC ADMINISTRATION

The following selected excerpts from *Budget in Brief—Fiscal Year 1968* are cited to illustrate the magnitude of the scope of public administration.

From United States Budget in Brief—Fiscal Year 1968

Over the last decade alone, the Nation's population increased by more than 27 million. Changes in the age distribution and location of our people increase public service demands over and above what this total growth alone would require. First, population has increased markedly in age groups under 18 or 65 and over which have greater need for such public services as education or social security. These groups have increased by 20% over the past 10 years and now constitute 45% of our population. Second, the number of people of all ages living in urban areas has increased in this same decade more than 25%, and now makes up more than 70% of the population.

The growing workloads of Federal agencies stem directly from these steadily increasing requirements for more and better public services. For example, between 1958 and 1968:

The number of active urban renewal projects will have risen by over 250%.

Visitors to our national parks will have increased 150%.

The number of occupied federally assisted public housing units will have grown by nearly 70%.

Enrollees in vocational education programs will have increased by almost 80%.

The volume of mail delivered will have risen by nearly 40%.

The number of passports issued will have increased 175%.

The number of Federal grants and loans to college students will increase more than fourfold, to 2.2 million.

Also, the 1968 budget includes many programs which did not exist in 1958. For instance, by 1968:

Medicare will cover over 40% of the medical costs incurred by 20 million aged people.

The education of $8\frac{1}{2}$ million disadvantaged school children will be strengthened.

The number of medical schools improved or constructed with Federal support will total 71.

Federal funds will have assisted in making about 117,000 low and moderate income housing units available under private sponsorship.

For more than a decade, Federal expenditures (NIA basis) have constituted a remarkably stable proportion of gross national product (GNP)—approximately one-fifth. Considering only the administrative budget, which excludes the rapidly growing trust funds, the ratio of Federal spending to GNP will be under 17% in 1968. Excluding special spending for Vietnam operations, Federal expenditures drop to about 14% of GNP in 1968—the lowest in recent years.

State and local governments, in trying to meet their rapidly growing responsibilities, will have increased their purchases of current output by two-thirds in the past 10 years—much more rapidly than the Federal Government. A part of this increase has been financed by Federal grant-in-aid programs. Private spending will have increased by about 50% during the period.

The same trends are evident for Government employment. While Federal civilian employment will increase 22% from 1958–1968, State and local governments will find it necessary to increase employment by more than 70%. Federal employment, therefore, is a declining portion of all governmental civilian employment, 23% estimated for 1968, compared to 29% in 1958.

Federal expenditures to aid State and local Governments (including shared revenue, as well as grants) will have grown from about

$4.9 billion in 1958 to an estimated $17.4 billion in 1968—an increase of 255%. These aids cover a wide variety of activities ranging from airport construction to urban renewal. In 1968, about half of the funds will be spent for highways and public assistance.

The Content of Public Administration

Perhaps the most revealing way to look at the scope of the practice of public administration is from the standpoint of the content of the job of the top administrator, from a look at the summit rather than at the base. This will help to identify quickly some of its special managerial characteristics, for when we say "administration" we mean running something, managing an organization, not just doing an individual job. Much of my terminology relates to the federal level, but I believe that many of the ingredients and characteristics of contemporary administration apply equally at top levels of state and local administration. A look at the content of the duties of the man directly in charge of large operating programs will also help to personify the special qualities needed by him and by his principal subordinates, who aid him in these tasks and who may eventually be candidates to assume his post.

The top American operating official, to an increasing degree, tends to be promoted from the career services. I am talking, of course, of the man who used to be called a bureau chief and now is often the head of an "administration," embracing a number of bureaus. In the cities and states, he may be a head of a large department. Usually, he has entered the service as a specialist, and very often as a technical specialist. At some point, he has indicated aptitudes which we call "administrative" and has, more often than not, assimilated administrative know-how by experience. The American system of recruitment has been for a post rather than for the lower rungs of a career ladder, and technical qualifications usually determine initial recruitment. The military and foreign services are different in this respect, and the lines of promotion are more clearly indicated. But we have no exact counterpart of the British "administrative class" or of the French "grands corps." R. V. Presthus thinks that this is a good thing and that the British have paid too heavily for their preference for the nontechnically oriented generalist. There is still a good deal of lateral transfer in the American service to and from government and the professions, the universities, and industry and commerce, so that we remain an open civil service to a greater extent than the closed civil services abroad. But these transfers are usually for short terms, and are often to the political executive level, or to a post in some important but highly specialized project. The top operating administrator tends to be a professional who has a long-term identification both with government service and with his field of interest and has been able to fuse this with administrative and managerial insights. He has shown the stamina to withstand the hard knocks and frustrations of one of the most exacting of occupations.

The administrative content of the public job gets bigger as a man rises in the hierarchy and the technical content tends to get smaller. There is a vast difference between the scope and content of the jobs of a public administrator and of a person in the more technical echelons of public administration. Hundreds of occupations in government and private endeavor need almost identical training and skills. The nurse, the laboratory technician, the doctor in a government hospital, or the engineer or architect who designed it, perform almost identical services with those of their counterparts in business and the professions. The functions are the same, even though the incentives and feeling-tone of the public environment may be different. All of these people are engaged in public service, but are not actually administering or managing anything. When they reach the point of contributing to policy-formulation; of advocacy and negotiation; of supervising the work of others; of fostering team-work and communication upward, downward, and outward; and of evaluating the use of men, methods, money, and materials in pursuit of program objectives—then the administrative ingredient has been fused with the technical one, and usually dominates it.

Although I cannot find it in writing, Louis Brownlow used to say that the specialist appointed to a generalist job, no matter how able he proves to be, will be least effective when dealing with the subject matter of his former specialty. We have long since passed the point when we can say that these jobs need only administrative aptitude, knowledge, and insight, and that the incumbent need not be thoroughly imbued with the substantive content as well. Administrators whose careers have begun from widely different origins have achieved great eminence. A marked contrast would be that of the careers of James V. Bennett and of the late Warner W. Stockberger. Bennett began as an organization and methods man in the old Bureau of Efficiency but became the Director of the Federal Bureau of Prisons and an international authority on care and treatment of criminals. His substantive knowledge was acquired on the job, one might say. Stockberger, on the other hand, was a trained chemist, specializing in fats and oils, and became Personnel Director of the Department of Agriculture, to build one of the finest corps of scientists in the government of his day. Richard E. McArdle was the first Chief Forester to rise, not from the ranks of the rangers, but from the field of forest research and technology at a time when this was just becoming a high-priority need of the United States Forest Service. It is hazardous and premature to be too dogmatic about the best route to top administrative posts.

Much of the administrator's work will be in the field of negotiation and advocacy, and he must not only be able to expound his program and defend it but must have a certain relish in this exercise and must be able to take and reply to criticism. The rather unique system in the United States requires career administrators to defend their programs before legislative committees (an institution which many other governments do not enjoy). This is in sharp contrast to the British method in which the permanent secretary, who is equally skilled in justification of policies and in political appraisal of opposition, conducts his work vicariously through his fluent political minister, whom he briefs for the encounters on the floor of the legislature itself.

An important ingredient of the job of the public administrator is the ability to generalize. He must interpret legislation in a manner that permits delegation to his organization and enables them to apply it. In fact, his main internal job is to create an environment in which his staff can function effectively. The process of rule-making is often fraught with political pitfalls in cases in which Congress has glossed over controversial questions in order to compromise and pass a bill, and has left its intentions vague. In these cases, the administrator must, nevertheless, find a course of action, but he must be able to identify these politically "hot" instances and must know how to clear such politics upward and assure himself in advance of support by his superiors and political chiefs. The problem of school desegregation as a condition of grants-in-aid may become a classical case in this regard.

The paradoxical intervention in administration by Congress, particularly by means of appropriation riders after basic legislation has delegated so much authority to the executive, has been identified by MacMahon, Harris, and other authorities. There is also a growing area of what might be called "negotiated administration" in which the grants of authority are very wide and imprecise, and each transaction must be separately tailored, with a large amount of latitude left for judgment. Urban redevelopment and research contracts are recent examples of negotiated administration, but a long history of such cases can also be found in such fields as agriculture and conservation. The administrator is confronted with an inverse order of things, where much of the sublegislation in the form of general rules has been left to him, while he must share his authority with individual congressmen in their application to individual cases. American public administration at the federal level is watched over by 535 "Ombudsmen" in Congress, who frequently preaudit its decisions. Other levels of government have their counterparts.

Finally, much more consultation of all kinds is required today. The contemporary administrator must have a tolerance and talent for it and also the sense of timing concerning when to invoke executive cloture and come to a decision. It is evident that the clear-cut distinction between advice and authority has been overlooked in many fields and that this has confounded the tasks of public administration. But the administrator must have the patience and skill and long-term interest-span for extended dialogues inside the government, with outside groups, and now even with program beneficiaries. Trying as these conversations frequently are, if he listens carefully, he may often learn more about his agency and its operations than he would through regular channels. Furthermore, he tends to become a kind of national symbol or spokesman for the program he heads. He must instruct and inform and inspire a host of subordinates in widely varying specialties. Above all, he must encourage his staff to alert him freely on major problems arising in the field before they come to the point of impairment of a program. He should elicit conflicting opinions on major questions and be wary of the kind of completed staff work which presents him with only one alternative.

The content of the duties of top administrators in public administration, and the qualifications needed, have become almost terrifying. One of the problems of American administration and politics is how to make these jobs more bearable and more rewarding, not only in terms of emoluments and fringe benefiits but also in regard to prestige and recognition. Policy-formulation and long-term programming have become essential parts of such jobs. With the increasing complexity of programs, political executives and legislators expect initiative and creativity from the career chiefs. The day of table-pounding and of arbitrary informed decisions has passed, and the vast quantities of data now available, together with the various specialties that must be tapped before decisions are made, require the administrator to have a great analytical capacity, some comprehension of data-evaluation, and a wide tolerance and catholicity for many fields of knowledge and skill.

The administrator today must therefore have the ability and will to program the programmers, to analyze the analysts, and to evaluate the evaluators, or he will not be in a position to defend his policies and will not be in charge of his shop.

In the performance of all these difficult functions, there is still much that we do not know. The professional associations in various fields, including those of public officials, have been a strong influence in raising standards for these posts, and, in many cases, active participation in their work has characterized the careers of the men who achieved top positions.

The practitioners still need a good deal more help from the social scientists and interpretation of their findings into what John M. Pfiffner calls "operational" concepts. They need guidance from the research world on methods to identify administrative aptitudes for these difficult assignments at an early state, and to perfect the methods for developing and nurturing them. Public administration itself must learn how to make better use of its great manpower resources and must devise improved methods of executive-development and transfer of administrators between departments and levels of government, as well as between government and the professions, business and the universities. There are signs of hopeful beginnings to these ends.

Comment on Emmerich's Paper

By Herman G. Pope

I FIND Professor Emmerich's treatment of "The Scope of the Practice of Public Administration" quite satisfactory to me—sensible and sound enough to serve as a foundation for any practical purpose.

Admittedly, his paper provides less than precise boundaries, and it is possible that my commentary may blur them even more. However, if mathematics, that ultimate jewel of precision, can get along, by and large, with only an approximate value for pi, then there must also be a point of diminishing returns in striving for niceties in the field of public administration.

An appreciated dividend of Professor Emmerich's paper is his occasional indulgence in light irreverence to brighten a subject often trudged through in somewhat heavy-footed fashion. Similarly, I am glad that occasionally he risked a possible charge of indulgence in obiter dicta, for it shows that his devotion to public administration as a science is not so devout as to preclude the planting of a few value judgments along his road. I must confess, however, to a small disappointment that, in his rather amiable approach to an invitingly expansive subject, he does not include a favorite reference to "the great involuntary civil service," comprising the total citizenry of this country that is required to perform innumerable tasks on prescribed forms at prescribed times and places as a part of the governmental process.

What one sees in any subject area undoubtedly depends on the point from which he views it. The elephantine proportions of the subject that Professor Emmerich describes recall the story of the blind men who undertook to describe an elephant by feeling its various parts. In relation to Professor Emmerich's subject, it is a fascinating exercise to suggest identities for the persons involved. The blind man who feels the trunk and sees a serpent might be a scholar tempted to the sin of viewing public administration as an intellectual adornment enjoying campus parity with established disciplines. The blind man who feels the elephant's leg and sees a tree trunk might be the practitioner mentally climbing the tree that provides the fruit of his current paycheck and a lookout to even more fertile fields. The blind man who feels the elephant's tail and sees a rope might be the citizen-taxpayer visualizing a lasso that threatens to separate him from his treasure and his freedom to choose. And, judging from the generally dreary tone of most conferences that I have attended in recent years, I am quite confident that if these three principal players on the stage of public administration all felt the elephant's side and saw a wall, all would visualize it as a doghouse rather than the Taj Mahals which they picture for other fields of endeavor. Fortunately, Professor Emmerich's capacities and opportunities for studying his elephant from various vantage points over the years give him a perspective and insights superior to those of our three players, both when they research different areas separately and when they explore the same area together.

Professor Emmerich's statement that "public administration is administration that is public" is, of course, too simple and concise to please anyone. It also reveals him as probably more practitioner than academe. Without contradicting Professor Emmerich, even Webster is more wordy in defining public administration as "a branch of political science dealing primarily with the structure and workings of agencies charged with the administration of governmental functions." Also relevant are Webster's views of administration in general as "the principles, practices, and rationalized techniques employed in achieving the objectives or aims of an organization"; and in government as "the management of public affairs as distinguished from the executive or political function of policy making." As Professor Emmerich has noted, a definition of what is "public" does not come easily, and I have found none to offer here.

Professor Emmerich has arranged his paper in an orderly fashion. He provides a general philosophical and ideological introduction; sets public administration outside the private sector and the purely political acts of candidacy for office and collegial action in legislative assemblies; includes quasi-autonomous public entities within the realm of public administration; and further defines the scope of the practice of public administration by identifying the types of programs it comprises, by quantifying the money and manpower devoted to activities in the public sector, and by reviewing the job content of public administrators. Collectively, these separate elements in his approach provide both the setting for a meaningful picture and the picture itself.

As I have noted, the general sense of Professor Emmerich's views is sufficiently agreeable to me that I have no inclination to quarrel or to nit-pick. However, it may be possible to augment his paper by giving attention to several determinants of the scope of the practice of public administration that he touches on only lightly or not at all. Several of these relate both to the present and to the probable future; several reflect my wishful thinking rather than hard fact, or may be more questions than views on a particular concept or problem.

As Professor Emmerich points out, the federal establishment is so enormous as to be a significant segment of the scope under discussion. However, stripped of defense and other international activities, it pales in comparison with the size that a similarly detailed quantification of money and manpower devoted to the programs of state and local governments would show. It seems unnecessary to add this detail here, as it is readily available elsewhere, but it may be worth-while to point to several present and predictable corollaries, particularly in relation to local government.

The scope of public administration locally is changing greatly. We can expect existing services such as public works, public safety, and the rest, including regulatory functions, to continue, expand, and improve. In addition, there is growing emphasis on educational, cultural, and recreational services and on employment, housing, transportation, and other similar elements in community social and economic well-being. Developments such as these broaden the quantifiable scope of the practice of public administration, but they also amplify it in another way. They change its nature by altering the kinds of skills required of practitioners and by creating a relationship of local government to citizens quite different from that of putting out their fires or picking up their garbage. The effect of this change is all the greater by reason of the compounding influences inherent in our development of an "anthill society." Similar factors are, of course, also at work in the federal and state governments, but it is at the local level that the effect of this type of growth in scope will be most pronounced.

There are other distinctions between public administration at the federal and at the local level. Professor Emmerich's observations on the job content of the public administrator are excellent in relation to the federal level, and his remark that "public administration at the federal level is watched over by 535 'Ombudsmen' in Congress who frequently preaudit its decisions" illustrates his perceptiveness. On the other hand, the local public administrator, who lives with the people he serves, must be even more "people-oriented." The number of Ombudsmen within the scope of his work of relieving his neighbors of their money and spending it for them may, on occasion, approximate the adult population of his community. Generally, of course, an unfortunate apathy operates to keep the number of citizens involved in local affairs perhaps no larger than the number that attend big-league baseball games. And the behavior of many in these population fractions is much the same at city hall as at the ball park, evidencing a like confidence in their own technical and managerial expertise and a like license to characterize as a bum anyone who has not batted a thousand for their team that day. Also, this ingredient of direct customer exposure that distinguishes the local administrator's job from that of his federal counterpart is omnipresent whether he sits in his office, walks down the street, or runs at a riot, and it operates without the protection provided by distance and the ramparts of an impressive bureaucracy fortified by labyrinthian communications, procedures, and elusive divisions of authority. It probably should be acknowledged that, both in the environment which Professor Emmerich pictures and in the one that I have described, the door to successful performance is hinged not only on preparation but on personal traits, attitudes, and motivations.

It is probably incorrect but nevertheless tempting to include another Ombudsman, the lobbyist, within the scope of the practice of public administration. This temptation is particularly strong in relation to the state and federal levels where lobbying has developed the characteristics variously attributed to public administration as an art, a science, a process, an interdisciplinary manifestation, a profession, or whatever.

A more serious case can be made for including within the scope of the practice of public administration many of the scientific, charitable, and educational nonprofit corporations. Universities, hospitals, and a host of other institutions and entities not established for pecuniary profit have, in relation to their particular fields, characteristics and qualities more akin to those of public administration than to those of the private sector. Many of their programs augment or overlap similar activities undertaken directly by governmental agencies. Much of their manpower requires qualifications, motivations, and attitudes desirable in public administration. Much of their financial base lies in government, whether through grants, contracts, subsidies, tax exemptions, or tax-law inducements to make contributions. Many are, in practice, no less responsive to the public will than are some autonomous public agencies.

In this connection, I regret particularly that I cannot contradict the correctness of including local schools within the scope of the practice of public administration while at the same time excluding institutions of higher learning. It strikes me as an illustration of something that may be "correct" but not "right." In other words, the scope of the practice of public administration desirably should be broad enough to encompass not only the practitioner who is paid by public funds to work for the government and administer and train and do what in the environment of academia would be called research, but also his counterpart in academia, who is also paid in large part from the same source and who researches and trains and administers and does what in another environment would be called working for the government. The distinction becomes even more forced in relation to public administration as an almost academic discipline, on the one hand, and an almost practicing profession, on the other. If both or either of these two are to get anywhere, they had better get further acquainted. The illusion that they have basically different masters can be almost as discouraging to acquaintance as the notion that they are not interdependent in other ways. I can think of no instance of a field of specialized knowledge and work that has developed without full interplay between academia and practice.

Similarly, I agree with Professor Emmerich that it would be

sophistry to make contractual or regulatory ties an excuse for including the private sector within the scope of public administration. Again, however, some relaxation of criteria to define scope may be warranted. Examples may be found in relation to federal establishment in the new generation of captive nonprofit corporations popularly or unpopularly characterized as "think shops," and in relation to state and local governments in the use of building and other nonprofit corporations to evade debt or other limitations on action.

It undoubtedly is easier to circumscribe the general arena in which public administration may be found than it is to pinpoint it as the elusive "something, albeit not everything" in that arena. My regret that forerunners in our field thought of it too narrowly and neatly to satisfy the present is assuaged by my doubt about an alternative. Clearly, public administration cannot comprise the expertise of law, engineering, economics, psychology, and the like; and, as somewhat of a corollary, an exclusive and unlimited commitment to the interdisciplinary and eclectic qualities of public administration seems as likely to result in something dilettantish as in something solid. The old hope for public administration as a discipline or profession contains things that may be out of style at the moment but whose utility can be dismissed by practitioners only after something assuredly better comes along. I have, on other occasions, admitted that, in action, the fashionableness of public administration, evident in the 1930's, 1940's, and 1950's, has been dimmed by current preoccupations with political policy, with only secondary attention at home and in developing countries to management capabilities necessary to bring policies to fruition and, also, that as a fashion in academia, public administration apparently has peaked and become less than fully competitive in intramural competitions for money, teachers, researchers, and graduate students. But these developments should not obscure the predictable continuing and growing need for "the principles, practices, and rationalized techniques employed in achieving the objectives or aims of an organization"; the fact that a considerable body of these ingredients, tailored to the circumstances of the public sector of our society, are at present available and in use; and the likelihood that they can be more advantageously built upon than substituted for.

Comment on Emmerich's Paper

By Lennox L. Moak

PUBLIC administration is neither everything nor it is nothing! The major criticism that can be made of Emmerich's paper is that, although it is interesting, one still is unable to come to grips with the subject.

For many people, the term "public administration" has come to encompass the entire area of policy development, consideration, and adoption, as well as the carrying out of public policies, or executing the public business. By contrast, the term "business administration" has *not* come to have a similar reach in the field of private business enterprise. In private enterprise, "business administration" and the "practice of business administration" are almost synonymous, whereas when one considers "public administration" and the "practice of public administration," he is likely to become more expansive.

Students of public administration have come to realize that the *process* of publicly administering public policies frequently has an impact on the policies themselves, sometimes altering them, sometimes supplementing them with new ones. When that happens, the process involved is no longer merely the practice of public administration. It is a separate process which, in reality, is subpolicy determination.

To speak meaningfully within the scope of Emmerich's assignment, one must concentrate on a discussion of the "practitioners" of public administration. In that light, it becomes clear that we are not talking about everybody who is employed by government. Ordinarily, we are not talking about the street-cleaner or the epidemiologist or the teacher. Our focus is on those whom Emmerich considers under the heading of "The Content of Public Administration," but it must also include others.

Limitation of Public Administration to Upper Levels

Basically, Emmerich seeks to limit the field of public administration to the upper levels of the hierarchy. This view is an inaccurate one, arising, perhaps, out of associations too long limited to the upper levels.

The chief of the division charged with supervision of the preparation of a large and complex payroll is as much engaged in public administration as is the Secretary of Defense. In some important ways, he is perhaps more intimately engaged in public administration. The objective of the payroll unit is well understood; the time limits for processing are precise; and the absolute importance of effective public administration involved, for example, the efficiency, accuracy, and timeliness essential to organization morale, is well comprehended. Unlike the Secretary of Defense, he is not significantly engaged in policy-development, in the maneuvering for adoption of proposed policy, in elaboration of the policy statement through adjustments, or in a public defense of the policy being pursued.

Comprehensiveness of Public Administration

Emmerich asserts: "In its broadest context, the practice of public administration embraces all executive acts, subject to political control performed by public agencies, officials, or employees."

Is this not too broad a frame of reference? The process of administration should be sharply differentiated from the process of policy-formulation, even when carried on by the same persons. The scope of the practice of public administration should be restricted in concept to that of *administering* and should not include that portion of the activities concerned with policy-development.

Thus, a budget officer during the budget-development phase frequently is not engaged in *administration*. True, the executive has been given or has assumed large responsibilities of a policy character in the development of the budget. The budget officer (and the chief executive) is engaged in provision of assistance to the *legislative* branch of the government. He is not, at that moment, engaged in administration. Emmerich recognizes this distinction, yet he seeks to emphasize that "there is a large ingredient of administration in almost his [President, governor, mayor] every act." This is correct. The problem is that Emmerich seeks to embrace within the scope of the practice of public administration all those other elements which he, more or less unwittingly here, accepts as being other than administration.

SEPARATISM

Much of Emmerich's paper is concerned with the separatism within the field of public administration, for example, in education and in science. It would have been more profitable to have sought to differentiate between the elements of activity of educators and scientists which are administrative in character and those which are concerned with the performance of the acts of educating or engaging in scientific pursuit.

Thus, the teacher who is working with a class or the scientist with a test tube is not involved in "administration," but the principal of the school and many of those higher in the hierarchy are involved in public administration. True, there is a separatism. However, except at the very top, is it appreciably different from the separatism of the fire department? of the police department? of the municipal health system?

The discussion of separatism adds little to an understanding of the scope of the practice of public administration.

TYPES OF PROGRAMS

Considerable space is devoted to discussion of types of governmental programs, especially those of the United States federal government. This adds nothing which aids in the definition of the scope of the practice of public administration.

CONTENT OF PUBLIC ADMINISTRATION

This is easily the best part of the paper. It contributes to understanding of the subject. Even here, however, a preoccupation with the upper levels of the executive branch and emphasis upon policy and advocacy is noted. Important though they be in the total conduct of public business, neither policy nor advocacy is an essential part of the scope of public administration.

CONCLUSIONS

The discussion under this heading helps to underline the fact that we have no agreement upon what is public administration—

as distinguished from the other things which public officers and subofficers do.

Until the lexicon has been perfected and accepted, the job assigned to Emmerich is actually impossible of fulfillment. Confronted with it, he has moved the checkers in an interesting but not too instructive manner.

A note on acceptance of public administration

Although not germane to the subject of the paper, the interesting point is raised early in the paper concerning the *resistance to identification with public administration*. In the experience of this commentator, this is a very real problem in securing public acceptance of a profession.

Perhaps it was only my imagination, but on those few occasions when I have been a public officer, I was frequently being introduced in some of the more erudite or socially prominent circles. Did I sense or was it only in my imagination that there was a certain almost imperceptible twitch of the nostrils of those to whom I was being introduced, as if something unclean had been brought into otherwise polite company?

It is no mystery that so long as the scientist, the medical man, and the engineer are generally held in higher public esteem than is the public servant—so long will persons in the public service tend to identify more immediately with those professions than with public administration, as such. Perhaps it is not much more than the banker who identifies as such, rather than as a businessman. (There was a time within my memory—in the 1930's—in which identification as a banker was not altogether desirable, or even conducive to personal safety, for that matter.)

The manner in which the press treats public servants continuously places most of them on the defensive, whereas those who criticize or attack the public officer are frequently regarded more as guardians of the public weal.

A second consideration also prompts the narrower identification—the reality is that most of the promotions attained within government (as well as elsewhere) are *within* vocational classifications, for example, medicine, social welfare, finance, and law enforcement. It is not unreasonable, therefore, for the public servant to identify more closely with his specific field than with the general "public administration" concepts?

We have a long way to go in securing public approval for the profession of public administration, as such. Until then, the tendency to identify with specific specialties, which are more widely accepted in the community, will, I believe, continue to be the preference of most public servants as distinguished from a primary identification with "public administration."

Conference Discussion on the Scope of the Practice of Public Administration

CHARLESWORTH: The intensity of the discussion on Dwight's paper persuaded me to trespass on Herb Emmerich's time. I hope that you will understand and forgive me. Herb, our apologies to you, and will you now take over.

EMMERICH: Well, while listening to the discussion I made outlines for two additional papers, Mr. Chairman, but I am not going to deliver them. I shall try to identify the things that were left out of the paper on "the scope of the practice" which I submitted. Herman Pope was merciful in his comments and left me nothing to rebut. He wrote me, when he got your invitation to comment on my paper, asking me to write his comments for him. I declined on the grounds that I would be much harder on myself than he would be—and you must admit the truth of that statement. Nor am I inclined to debate with Len Moak. I think that his criticism of my definition of the scope of public administration is largely a semantic difference. He has said here, and he said in his paper, that public administration people have to take part in formulation and defense of policy, but that this part of their duties he does not choose to call public administration. I will not quibble with him about this as long as he concedes that it is part of their job. I regard it as the very important part of the job.

There is one point that Len mentioned to which I should respond, however, and that is his suggestion that I am not interested in the "lower classes" of public administration. My paper certainly was subject to that criticism, even if I submit that my record is not. I talked about high-level administration, and I hoped that it would include the point at which administration became managerial, regardless of the level of government. This may often be a very low point. In a little satirical article on "The Specific Gravity of Decisionism," I tried to indicate that a lot of policies are made down below and that some top administrators are the captives of their subordinates, even of those at a very low level.[1]

[1] Herbert Emmerich, "The Specific Gravity of Decisionism," *Public Administration Review*, Vol. XXIV, No. 4 (December 1964).

This is one of the continuing problems of management. I suspect it is more frequent in public management than in private management, but many examples could be found in the private sector also. There is a growing tendency for administrators to rise from the ranks—in which there has been a feeling of fraternity with their colleagues—and there is also a trend towards unionism of technical-administrative employees. These tendencies make it hard to delineate at what point in his career a man becomes a manager, when he must identify with the Establishment and is no longer representing the rank and file. This is becoming an increasingly difficult problem in our very highly organized large bureaus. Whatever may be the weaknesses, as Robert Presthus has told us, of the British administrative class, of top management by the nonspecialist, its members are definitely Establishment-identified. They know that they are going to be bosses. They are identified with the managerial element of government from the beginning of their careers, and as they are generally chosen from the educated cultural elite, they may perhaps be classified as technically incompetent amateurs. But the British administrative class has a managerial identification, whatever other weakness it may have, and its members are exposed at a young age to supervision and policy-formulation. I happen to believe that decision-making, like a muscle, must be exercised early, or it will never develop strongly. The identity with the rank and file and the desire to be a good fellow, to be liked, so accentuated now by trade unionism and seniority, makes it hard for a man at a certain point to identify himself with the management side of the table, instead of the staff side which is the rank and file. As a matter of fact, we are all mixed up today about democracy and administration, confusing advice and consultation with command and authority. We are going to get further mixed up on account of the pressures from aggressive urban groups before we learn to separate the functions of consultation and command.

On the public-versus-private-administration dichotomy, I am reminded of what an old friend of mine used to say about Russia, "I believe in coexistence but it is not necessarily cohabitation." The decisions on really major policies cannot be delegated. There are fine shadings and degrees in this area, but there is also a lot of fuzzy thinking. Everybody seems to want to buy the Communications Satellite Corporation (COMSAT) model and to incorporate the post office and other activities as well, but, in my view, if you look deep under the carpet of the COMSAT model, it is essentially a mixed corporation—a creature of the American Telephone and Telegraph Company, preponderately dominated by it. There has been quite a bit of congressional testimony which will support my view—although it is a minority view. Nor would Congress grant an incorporated post office the needed powers. We have to be very careful about extending the corporate device and about mistaking form for substance. We can persuade ourselves otherwise into all kinds of nonsense. A considerable step forward has been taken in the District of Columbia's government, and yet we find the man we call "Mayor" (a good man, who used to work for me) still reporting to the same congressional committees that hold the power of the purse, and the "Mayor" and "Council" still actually subordinate in that struggling municipality. I think McGeorge Bundy is going to have trouble with the decentralization of the management of the public schools in New York. When the time comes to find out where the money originates, where teaching qualifications are established and where teachers have an opportunity for promotion and mobility, and who has the say about curriculum and textbooks, the decentralization project may prove to be a paper dragon. Many decisions will have to be city-wide, particularly at a time when school integration and relationship of schools, city planning, and transportation are imperative.

The most glaring omission from my paper, and both Herman Pope and Len Moak mentioned it, is that I did not give sufficient attention to state and local government and its growing scope, nor did I mention the need for a new form of government, regional and, perhaps, a tier between state and local government, that many metropolitan experts think we need. Certainly, the figures which I cited from the federal budget indicate that the real growth in the need for public administration civilian manpower is not occurring at the federal level, but at the state and local levels. This is a valid criticism of my paper, for it is evident that this problem is within the scope of practical public administration, and in the training for it, we have to give much more attention to local and community and state problems than we have done. We really need crash programs in these fields to prepare people for some of the pressing, complex, and difficult problems, for this is now the front-line trend of administration. Somehow or other, we must find new ways to make that kind of vocation attractive to able people. They tend to gravitate to the glamour, the security, and the salaries of the federal service. This is a major piece of unfinished business for all of us who are interested in training people and in supplying the enormous needs that have been mentioned here for people trained and motivated to do these jobs.

I have learned more about this whole business in the last five years because I have been teaching. At the University of Virginia, they did not trust me with undergraduates, and they were quite right. I was too old to learn such tricks, but I had to deal with adult mid-career people, mostly from the federal government. I have always felt that my vocation was to be the friend of the bureaucrat, whoever he is, the men and women who cast their lot with government service. I experimented with what to do with these people sent to us by the National Institute of Public Affairs and to whom a generous government gave a year's salary.

Well, I was extremely permissive about this. For example, we had a man from naval intelligence ("weapons intelligence," it is called in the Navy), and he wanted to study Soviet history and the Russian language. His motivation was vocational, not cultural. I encouraged him and the others to range widely in their selection of courses. The only course that was required was the public affairs seminar in which Emmerich said anything he pleased. I found in this public affairs seminar that very few of them knew anything about the history of the United States, the administrative history of the United States, or the evolution of its institutions. Practically none of them had ever read a Supreme Court decision. They were unaware that things which they thought were new and different had been tried twenty, fifty, or a hundred years ago. They had no sense of continuity about our public policy problems and American institutions, and they rather enjoyed being exposed to some of the classics in the field. They were equally interested in some of the newer studies of administrative behavior. The fact that they were in a university, and not in a trade school, meant something to them, and because they rarely were degree candidates, they had the wide range of courses in a great university to select from. Their individual combination of courses was quite varied and responsive to each man's interest. These mid-career fellows had come up largely through technical and engineering schools. Almost without exception, they could neither read, write, nor talk effectively. This was absolutely shocking. They were coming to the point in their government careers where they were entering on administrative duties; communication was getting increasingly important, persuasion if you like, discussion, dialogue, communication. They had lost the habit of reading. They could not write well, and they could not talk clearly, so that some of my efforts, and some of those of my colleagues, were devoted to upgrading these basic skills. I encouraged some of them to go to the McGuffey Reading Clinic to increase their reading speed. I gave them term papers to write, and I did an editor's job on the papers and discussed them in editorial conferences. The writing, in the main, was absolutely unbelievably awful. In their essay, I encouraged them to take a position or to reach a conclusion, even if tentative and qualified, rather than merely to analyze or discuss their subject. In government, papers are expected to take a position. Well, so much for the observations of a lately arrived professor and his experiences in pedagogy.

My paper should also have stressed that, whereas we have a group here that has been discussing theory and a group here that has been discussing practice, the record should not fail to show the necessary links between theory and practice. This, I think, is also part of the unfinished business of public administration. The social sciences are still the disciplines to which we should be most closely related, although not exclusively, in training for public administration. But I hope that the social scientists will take more interest than they seem to be doing in policy-problem-solving studies and research. They are going too far in straining to emulate the physical sciences, which does not seem to me to be either a suitable objective for, or a possible solution of, the problems of the social sciences. I think that, increasingly, they will have to develop their own social science techniques and methods, and not take an imaginary construct of what they believe the methods of physics, chemistry, or biology to be. Many of them are taking a romantic view of these disciplines.

Increasingly, the social scientists are getting either into the particularism of minor studies or into total abstraction, getting more and more away from the policy-problem-solving research in which their own background, their own formulations, their own discipline, and their own knowledge would make valuable and needed contributions. By continuing to affiliate with the social scientists, public administration not only broadens its own outlook but, hopefully, can build better bridges between theory and practice.

There will be places, I think, where a professional school in public administration or in public affairs will be useful. But here I take my cue from Harvey Sherman, not so much from his comprehensive paper here, but from his paper in the current issue of *Public Administration Review*. Let us get away from Fred Taylor's "one best method"; let us have pluralism; let us have variety. I think that it is one of the things which a country of this size needs and can afford. We have had it in the past, and therefore I do not worry about the fact that this group has not reached a consensus. It would have been unfortunate, in a way, if we had, although there are certain common threads that run through all the papers. I think that this is good. This continued pluralism, the continued variety of effort, is characteristic of America, and I hope it remains so in the theory and practice of, and even in the education for, public administration.

The medical analogy has been discussed around this table a lot, and one of the papers mentioned that the practicing doctor is not the one who has added to our knowledge of medical research in the development of the science of medicine in its various branches. This is true to a great extent, but one must also add to this that in medicine there has always been an intimate reciprocal relationship between theory and practice. This is a very severe discipline. The professor in the medical school or the research institute has to prove his stuff on the operating table or in his injections or in his medications or in whatever diagnosis or therapy or preventatives he uses, and he is constantly being subjected to the pragmatic and empirical tests of whether his discoveries and hypotheses work in practice. The excessive subdivision of the specialties in medicine has been divisive, but there are now great efforts being made to overcome this and to look at the organism as a whole.

Whatever the viewpoints of public administration people are, whether we are a discipline or a profession, or a science or an eclectic smorgasbord, taking this and that and the other from various sciences and techniques, we must soon establish our own doctrine and methodology, so that when a man who has not had this kind of training suddenly finds himself catapulted from test-tube work to running a tremendous chemistry establishment and wants to go for a course or a seminar, we have something more useful to offer him. We have to do more fusing of substantive policy-analysis with techniques of implementation. Perhaps the professional school can offer this kind of opportunity, or the special institute or academy. We also need to develop a very special "Gestalt" in preparing future administrators to be interested in a more general approach than the highly compartmentalized specialist. Public administration, like political science, has within it the possibilities of becoming a co-ordinating science and of correcting the strong trend toward overspecialization in American society, which sometimes approaches almost the point of insanity. The use of the word "generalist" is undoubtedly overdone, and still the generalist point of view is the indispensable attribute of top leadership in the development of the over-all viewpoint in both the theory and the practice of public administration.

MOAK: I suggest that on this subject, until there can be a consensus on the definition of the scope of the practice of public administration, then, to use the word "sterile" which was thrown in my direction yesterday, the effort to develop a theory is sterile. I suggest that there is no agreement concerning scope. I invite you to look at the membership roster of the American Society for Public Administration (ASPA) in an effort to define public administration by attempting to define the characteristics of that membership which would entitle these people to membership in ASPA.

I honestly believe that a payroll-supervisor in a sizable payroll-processing installation is as much engaged in public administration as is the director of finance under which he serves. Let a payroll be one day late, and you will find out how important are the public administration qualities of the position of payroll-supervisor.

In my current responsibilities as head of a citizen agency seeking to cope with 250 local governments in southeastern Pennsylvania, I find that these governments run from the size of Philadelphia down to boroughs so small that you would never have heard of them. Yet, I believe that the borough manager in the smallest of these boroughs is engaged in public administration to much the same extent as is Harlan Cleveland—although not to any degree so entertainingly or provocatively as do those in executive positions in the upper levels of administration.

I want to return to the comment which I understood Waldo to make, to the effect that, if you withdraw from the field of public administration the enticing areas of policy-formulation and the securing of acceptance of policies formulated by administrators, then you decrease the attractiveness of the profession to students who might otherwise come to the field. I think that such a step, taken by itself in isolation, would create a problem in our enticement of active minds into the field. Already, I perceive that my students in the Department of City Planning are likely to be of a different caliber, and, in a number of respects, more attractive and exciting, than my students in a course in public finance administration.

But the answer lies elsewhere. The man in a small Texas college who first captured the interest and imagination of York Willbern and me, and drew us into the field of government, did so by talking to us about the art and science of government. He emphasized that we were concerned with *governing*. And what young man or woman can really resist the temptation to get in on the action? If we can get them to feel that they are in this important enterprise of being intimately, and potentially importantly, involved in the process of governing, we will attract the students—and the best ones at that.

I would suggest, finally, that in the process of trying to arrive at a definition of the practice of public administration as a "discipline"—and how I hate that word as it is so frequently used—we remember that, in its proper form, it connotes the capacity to accept restraint. I think that we are obliged to try to make this a discipline in the proper sense of the word. We must therefore be willing to draw a boundary line somewhere, within which the *practice of public administration* takes place. The other things which public employees and officers, whether elected or appointed, do in their work must be defined as lying outside the practice of public administration. Perhaps we must coin a new phrase. To use a medical analogy, psychiatry becomes something roughly related to medicine, but on frequent occasions it is necessarily distant from a carefully defined practice of medicine. Failure to recognize this necessity forecloses the possibility of our ever developing the kinds of sets of theories that will be meaningful guides to people who may be primarily involved in the *practice* of public administration. They need a clearly stated theory. Many of us need it so clearly stated that it becomes a yardstick against which we can gauge the actions which we must take, frequently almost on a reflex basis, when the opportunity may not be present for leisurely debate and selection among alternatives.

Objectives of the Theory of Public Administration

By Stephen K. Bailey

ELMER SCHATTSCHNEIDER has defined theory as "the shortest way of saying something important."

There are more elaborate definitions, but he has caught the essence. From the chaos of observation and experience, man abstracts patterns of regularity and probability and gives these patterns symbolic expression and logical connection.

Some theory-building has objectives which are basically aesthetic: the inner satisfaction of creating and discovering new order, new relationships, new logical refinements. Those, like Oppenheimer, who have referred to the "beauty" of mathematics are suggesting that certain types of theory are their own reward, and that that reward is delight.

But most theory has a broader purpose and utility. The ultimate objective of most theory is understanding for purposes of control. Even when theory begins as a simple quest for elegance, as in the case of $E = MC^2$, it may have extraordinary practical consequences.

The utility of theory as an exercise in understanding for purposes of control need not be labored. In fields like chemistry, physics, biology, and astronomy, three centuries of evolving theories—along with the arts and skills of applying them—have changed the name of the game of human existence. In key areas of environment-control, man has been transformed from a dependent to an independent variable. He has moved from being simply an evolutionary product to a new status as evolutionary partner. He has won a new entitlement to a position of centrality prematurely afforded him by an older cosmology.

Unfortunately, his new status is precarious. For his theoretical successes have not extended as yet to an understanding and control of his own nature, his social culture, and his institutional environment. In fact, his theoretical brilliance in understanding and controlling nature has unleashed forces which threaten to destroy man's tenuous grasp on civility.

In Western democratic polities, public administration may be defined as man's attempt through government to harness natural and human resources for the purpose of approximating politically legitimated goals by constitutionally mandated means. In the United States, our politically legitimated goals (diverse and contradictory as they often are) are modern interpretations of the eloquence of the Declaration of Independence and the Preamble to the Constitution. One must stress the term "modern interpretations," for the ecology of the Founding Fathers was closer to that of the Pharaohs than to that of contemporary man. The spiritual hungers have changed but little; the technological and institutional environment has been revolutionized.

If the business of public administration is as stated, the ultimate objectives of the theory of public administration in a democratic culture seem clear. The objectives of public administration theory are to draw together the insights of the humanities and the validated propositions of the social and behavioral sciences and to apply these insights and propositions to the task of improving the processes of government aimed at achieving politically legitimated goals by constitutionally mandated means. Actually, four overlapping and interlocking categories of theory are required if improvement in the processes of government are, in fact, to take place: descriptive-explanatory theories, normative theories, assumptive theories, and instrumental theories.

Unfortunately, the state of theoretical inquiry in each and all of these categories is contradictory and spotty at best. In some cases, it is virtually nonexistent. To state the need is to confess the gap.

Descriptive-Explanatory Theory

Out of the welter of laws, institutions, and behaviors that comprise the world of public administration, can propositions be abstracted which will serve as valid and explanatory models of reality?

The concept of hierarchy is one such theoretical proposition. Drawing upon assumed historical and contemporaneous evidence, early observers of public administration described relationships and explained behavior by recourse to this geometric analogue.

In recent years, as observations and insights have increased, the geometry has been elaborated. A single pyramid has turned out, in most cases, to be simplistic. Bertram Gross, for example, in his *The Managing of Organizations,* writes of multiple hierarchies and polyarchic patterns of authority. Such a new formulation, involving, as it does, multiple pyramids with centripetal points, is difficult to depict geometrically. At least an "iron cross" must replace a simple pyramid.

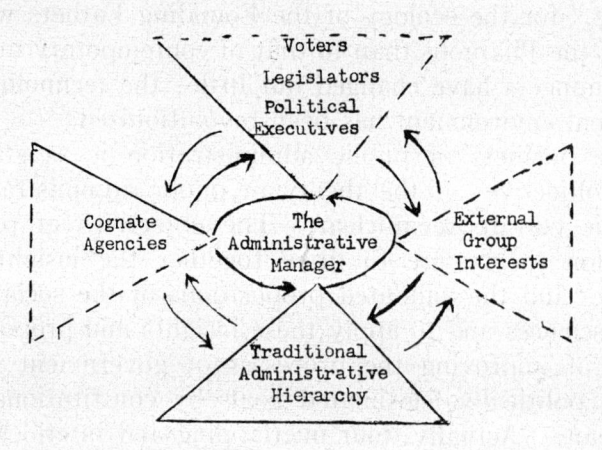

```
                    Voters
                    Legislators
                    Political
                    Executives
        Cognate        The        External
        Agencies   Administrative  Group
                     Manager      Interests
                    Traditional
                    Administrative
                    Hierarchy
```

In this newer design, administration is viewed as a pattern of interaction involving a series of formal and informal linkages. The manager is seen as a broker as well as a director. As Professor Gross has pointed out, his authority is limited by the "inverted pyramid" over him, by the lateral pyramids (to say nothing of public and private committees) which impinge upon his discretion, and by the circular winds which bypass him. Who would question that this is a more accurate description of most administrative reality in the public sector (perhaps in much of the private sector as well) than the traditional single pyramid of hierarchy?

And yet even the "iron cross" has its limitations. For any sophisticated descriptive-explanatory theory must take account of organizational typologies—that is, categorizations by identities and divergencies. New agencies behave differently from old agencies, and yet there are similarities. Agencies requiring specialized scientific and technical competence have internal problems of communication and control far removed from those of agencies dependent largely upon routines performed by lower-skilled staffs. But, again, many internal problems are shared.

One objective of public administration theory is to refine existing typologies and to invent new ones. Without further typological refinements it is difficult to imagine how progress can be made in developing descriptive-explanatory theories which have much operational relevance.

Even typological constructs, no matter how refined, have inherent limitations, however, in developing descriptive-explanatory theories of public administration. Typologies tend to be static. That is why in recent years scholars have turned with the fervor of faddism to various forms of systems analysis. Systems are designed to be descriptive-explanatory theories which account for flux. Changes in organizational behavior and performance are explained by a flow of force over time. Linear algebra replaces plain and solid geometry. Organization becomes viewed as a system of tensions—tensions which change their patterns and intensities depending upon new inputs, including feedback loops of both an indigenous and exogenous variety.

Typological analysis tends to be spatial. Systems analysis is essentially temporal. Actually, typology and system may turn out to be mutually hostile descriptive and explanatory devices, for a perverse "Heisenberg principle" may assert itself. That is, if one sees the time flow as stopped, structural definition becomes unreal. If the continuum of institutional dynamics is not stopped, structure may be incapable of being described. Any field theory of public administration must face up to this conceptual perversity.

Descriptive-explanatory models are no easier to construct in public administration than in any other field, but certainly one objective of public administration theory, drawing upon humanistic learning and upon social behavioral science, is to devise and to refine such models. We cannot improve what we cannot describe and explain.

Normative Theory

The objective of normative theory is to establish future states prescriptively. In public administration, normative theory may include such diverse utopias as "happy citizens" on the one hand,

and an idealized car-pool on the other. Norms may be set to maximize such vague and ambiguous goals as efficiency, responsiveness, accountability, economy, employee morale, decentralization, ethical probity, internal communications, innovation, participatory democracy, a manageable span of control, and a host of other articulated or assumed values.

The fact is, however, that normative theory in public administration is in substantial disarray. For one thing, it is quite impossible to separate internal agency norms from value questions at issue in the polity generally. To this we shall return. In a proximate sense, however, high tax versus low tax, local autonomy versus extensions of federal power, private versus public, privacy versus aggressive law enforcement, political control versus professional control, judicial versus legislative versus executive versus electoral accountability—these and other value controversies in the polity set the conditions within which the internal norms of government agencies are fashioned. The root values of public administration are derivative. They depend upon the peculiar mix of contending political theories and practices alive in the entire body politic.

But even those values which are largely articulated within the context of a public agency are inherently ambiguous, contextual, and contradictory. Desirables conflict. Centralization may be the friend of efficiency and the enemy of consensus. Decentralization may be the friend of participatory democracy and the enemy of economy. Accountability may be the friend of probity and the enemy of innovation. Reorganization may be the friend of innovation but the enemy of employee morale.

And the predominant values established at one point in time may produce side-effects which make opposite values appropriate at a later time. Organizational inertias often carry an agency beyond the point of optimum arrangements, and substitute new pathological rigidities for old ones.

Where are the canons of truth in normative theories of public administration? Are they comprised in "clear lines of authority"? "a limited span of control"? "subordinate and clientele participation in decision-making"? "an executive budget"? "a classified service based upon merit and free from political influence"? "a functional organizational structure"? Once widely accepted, such hortatory propositions gave the illusion of having been written on tablets of stone. Incantations are still heard, and they guide more practice than we like to admit; but the underlying conceptual God is dead.

A conditional and relative administrative ethic has emerged. "More power at the top is needed in HEW"; "less power is needed in the New York City Board of Education." "CIA needs more Congressional oversight"; "AEC needs less Congressional oversight." "AID needs more discretion to be left to the field"; "Agriculture needs to strengthen headquarters control." "The State Department needs to 'functionalize' its organizational structure"; "the Bureau of the Budget needs to 'defunctionalize' its organizational structure." "Internal Revenue needs to computerize further"; "Justice needs to computerize less."

Prescriptive future states are now created by a series of ad hoc clinical diagnoses of observed pathologies and morbidities. But a typology of administrative disease has not been developed, and therapies are insecure. "To your good health" is still a toast and a boast.

And, yet, if the supreme objective of public administration theory is the improvement of administrative practice, normative postulates are essential. How do we know that improvement has occurred unless value goals are established as a measure of approximation?

Assumptive Theory

But even if descriptive-explanatory and normative theories were clear and widely agreed upon, they could not singly or together lead to improvements in administrative practice. Public administration theory has been particularly lax in setting forth what might be called "assumptive" propositions: propositions which articulate root-assumptions about the nature of man and about the tractability of institutions. The naïvete of utopians is reflected not only in their equating of heaven with a prospective stasis; it is reflected in their uncritical assumptions about the pliability of man's nature. The glory of the utopian is his faith that he can beat history; the tragedy of the utopian is that he has not understood history. In the behavioral sciences, some steps have been made, in both motivation theory and diffusion theory, to set forth empirically based assumptive theories. Proverbial and theological wisdom abounds about the nature of man. Freudian psychology and more recent studies of man's animal imperatives are available to the theorist of public administration. A few historical and sociological studies of institutional inertias and change associated with names like Madison, Weber, Brinton, Lasswell, and Selznick have caught glimpses of useful assumptive theories. The world of literature—poetry, drama, fiction, essays, and biography—is resplendant with materials to bedeck assumptive propositions.

But, by and large, public administration theory has developed without any evidence of a careful evaluation and articulation of assumptive theories. Administrative models for metropolitan government, executive-branch reorganization, improved personnel systems, program-budgeting, and interagency co-ordination have, more often than not, come a cropper because of a failure to posit realistic assumptions about the nature of social man and the ponderousness of institutional inertias.

The inadequacy of public administration theory in this area is not to be wondered at. There are philosophical and historical precedents for almost any view of man one wishes to propose. In a world in which the Forest Lawn Cemetery is forced by bitter experience to screen personnel for necrophiliar sexual compulsions, man's depravity is empirically demonstrable. In a world in which tens of thousands march daily up the down staircase, man's heroism is palpable. Institutions are too ponderous to change; but change they do. Hate motivates; but so does love. The terror of *Mein Kampf* is eroded by the generosity of Lincoln's Second Inaugural. Rational existentialism cannot withstand irrational commitment. Bureaucracy chokes innovative energy, and then falls before it.

Too low a view of man, too "realistic" a view of institutions, make all improvements impossible and silly. Too high a view of man, too idealistic a view of institutional tractability, can only lead to frustration and bitterness. The movers in public administration tend to be those who expect more of man and of institutions than can logically be derived from most descriptive-explanatory theories; less than can be derived from utopian norms. Goethe had the precise term: "exacte fantasie."

Every public administrator has operating assumptions about human nature and about institutional tractability. But few public administration theorists have refined and articulated their own assumptive propositions. Lasting improvement in administrative practice will depend in large measure upon the ability of social and behavioral theorists to formulate a consistent and focused image of man's personal and institutional capacity. In this process, public administration theorists must help.

INSTRUMENTAL THEORY

If descriptive-explanatory theory is concerned with "what" and "why," normative theory with "should" and "good," assumptive theory with "pre-conditions" and "possibilities," instrumental theory is concerned with "how" and "when." Instrumental theory is the operating "then" of "if-then" propositions. If an administrative system operates in such-and-such a way because of this and that, if decentralization would improve its performance in realizing politically legitimated goals by constitutionally mandated means, if relevant men and institutions are deemed tractable, then what are the techniques, tools, and timing of progress?

Theory should be useful here, but useful theory is sparse. H. G. Wells once wrote a book called *The New Machiavelli*, but the content is short of the title. ICP cases and a welter of administrative biographies and autobiographies describe—often with eloquence and elegance—how administrative changes have, in fact, been accomplished in the past. The Public Administration Service (PAS) and others have produced "How-to-do-it" manuals. The better management consultants are instrumentally sophisticated. Charismatic politicians often ply the channels of change with virtuosity. Bethel sensitizes the task-oriented to the dynamics of the group.

But little systematic theory has emerged. Perhaps it never can. Perhaps administrative change is so contextual, so dependent upon accidents of leadership and mortality, so related to ineffable realities of "climate" and "organizational style" as to defy the creation of useful, general propositions. But human curiosity will not let go, and certain kinds of instrumental theory lie all around us. The Book of Proverbs ("A soft answer turneth away wrath"); Aristotles *Rhetoric* ("Appeal to feelings of friendship, gratification, and pity in exhortation, of envy and hatred in dissuasion"); the gentle fables of Aesop; Dale Carnegie's *How to Win Friends and Influence People*; and scores of works exposing the sullen trades of Madison Avenue—all of these contain instrumental theories of possible value to the public administrator.

Perhaps what is needed is simply a more careful articulation of existing theory in the institutional and ethical context of public administration.

In any case, instrumental theories are essential. They are the "pay-off" theories. All else is pedantry. A man may be knowledgeable about reality, inspired in his sense of what is needed, and profound in his understanding of human nature and institutional tractabilities. But if he lacks instrumental wisdom —operational theories of tools, techniques, and timing—he might just as well have stood in bed. The British physicist Milliken once defined "power" as "the art of using machinery." There would seem to be no inherent reasons for believing that man is incapable of producing useful, middle-level theories (perhaps what the psychologists call "theorettes") which could help in the practice of this art. In truth, modern game theory and diffusion theory are attempts to develop propositions of precisely this kind. The fact that such theories run into difficulties when applied to specifics does not erase their utility; it simply suggests what is possibly a hopeful conclusion: that instrumental theory in public administration is haunted with a sufficient number of variables and perversities to preclude the easy and predictable manipulation of others. Imperfections in instrumental theory possibly constitute mankind's ultimate margin of freedom and dignity in a highly technical and interdependent world.

To this point, we have argued that the ultimate objectives of public administration theory are to draw together the insights of the humanities and the validated propositions of the social and behavioral sciences and to apply these insights and propositions to the task of improving the processes of government aimed at achieving politically legitimated goals by constitutionally mandated means. We have argued further that four types of interdependent theoretical systems are needed if this objective is to be reached: descriptive-explanatory, normative, assumptive, and instrumental. Improvements in practice depend upon the artistic interrelating of these theoretical systems in terms of specific objectives in time and place.

But this leaves a central and somewhat hoary issue left hanging. Are "politically legitimate goals" and "constitutionally mandated" means simply the "givens" of the public administrator's universe? Or does his universe presume his partnership in shaping political and constitutional ends and means? Is the administrator's role simply to discover and obey, or is it to participate and create as well? This latter-day statement of the policy-administration dichotomy of a generation ago is not meant to reopen an old discussion. The post-Appleby world cannot return to its former innocence. But the question remains of the extent to which public administrators should consciously attempt to shape the political and constitutional environment which ultimately governs them. Have we now reached the point, prophesied a generation ago by James Burnham, where a "managerial revolution" has, in fact, occurred? where the agenda of public policy is so complex, so specialized, so technical, and so interdependent that only an oligarchy of managers using computers and the soft-sell can keep the system going efficiently and benevolently? Is their expertise now the major determinant of politically legitimated goals for the society? Is the public administrator's discretion, in a *de facto* sense, the final arbiter of constitutionally mandated means? Do administrators, in fact, manipulate the "iron-cross" of influences depicted on an earlier page? What is really left to the legislators, the elected executives, the courts, the press, the electorate itself, in terms of ultimate value-definition? Is the public manager (often in league with self-serving private groups), in fact, setting the value priorities and goals which were once believed to be the prerogative of the general citizenry and its panoply of elected representatives and high judicial officers? Is democracy nothing but the inner-directed manager's skill in adapting Aristotle's *Rhetoric* to the manipulation of committees, caucuses, and communities? Has it ever been more than this? Is the clash of adversaries in our society in reality limited to interfraternity squabbles in a controlling college of social engineers? If, in fact, the managers and their technical satraps are being interfered with by untutored politicians and publics, are not the society's collective interests thereby imperiled? Is politics the enemy of administrative rationality?

Warning flags flutter in every breeze, but the winds are variable and the flags fly in different directions. Dangers of managerial manipulation most certainly exist. So do dangers of political interferences in the managerial process. Computerized central information systems including reasonably complete personal records of every private citizen are now being discussed. Without such information can a large and interdependent society be effectively governed? With such a system, how long can individual privacy and dignity be preserved? Can the crime rate be slowed without foregoing the Bill of Rights? Can country health services be wisely and efficiently provided as long as private hospitals are around? On the other hand, can man sustain his humanity unless his compassion can take the form of voluntary gifts for local and categorical ends? Can city hall be trusted without an Ombudsman around? On the other hand, can administrative equity persist if an Ombudsman can intervene in specific cases? Can we afford to let politicians decide life-and-death questions about the appropriate mix of military hardware and deployments? But if not politicians, then who should decide —the military? the foreign service? economists? the Rand Corporation? Should a Planning-Programming Budgeting System (PPBS) decide educational goals and optimum resource allocations for achieving them? Should such goals be determined by a blind political market?

These are questions so fundamental to the future of mankind as to warrant the attention of the most thoughtful, sensitive, and civilized people on the face of the globe. For the answers to these questions will come close to defining what is meant by the "politically legitimated goals" and "constitutionally mandated means" which public administrators are supposed to pursue with improved competence. Here is where public administration theory blends inexorably with social, political, and constitutional theory. Our existing faith is that the tensions in our polity—between centripetal and centrifugal forces, between public and private interests, among competing professional and economic interest groups, between generalists and specialists, between and among politicians and administrators, between and among levels of government—will continue to produce a reasonably benign mix of competence, compromise, and consensus.

For if history teaches anything, it is that neither Plato's philosopher-kings nor Jackson's untutored citizenry can safely manage a free society. Something besides natural or divine law must contain the propensities of the powerful; something beyond the transient prejudices and groupings of the demos must determine the end and means of society.

Within this framework, public administration theory must attempt to fashion descriptions of reality, postulates of betterment, sophisticated assumptions about the capacities of men and institutions, and workable tenets of instrumentation which can improve both the ends and means of democratic government.

Comment on Bailey's Paper

By Albert Lepawsky

WE can readily accept Stephen Bailey's four basic categories of administrative theory. From the most fundamental to the most implemental, these may be relisted as: (1) the assumptive, (2) the normative, (3) the instrumental, (4) the descriptive-explanatory.

In searching for a meaningful body of theory applicable to any discipline concerned with human behavior and societal conduct, nothing would seem to be more basic—to use Bailey's own well-chosen words—than "the root assumptions about the nature of man and the tractability of his institutions." Bailey's principal complaint here is that we students of administration are remiss in having failed to articulate an "assumptive" theory about human behavior.

It is true that we have been relatively quiescent on this matter, but our discipline is rife with basic assumptions and conceptualizations about sociopolitical institutions and human organization. Moreover, more so than any other group of disciplinarians, we devotees of public administration take it as axiomatic that men under all conditions, however primitive they may be, tend to administer their affairs and institutions with at least a modicum of systemization and rationalization. Our comparative studies of developing and dictatorial governments during the last generation certainly reinforce this assumption of ours concerning the administrative inclination of mankind. From this body of evidence alone, it seems clear that the arena of politics may sometimes be partially disbanded, but the structures and functions of public administration, including the essential processes of policy-formation, thrive and proliferate.

True, public administrationists are twitted today for treating man as a conforming victim of the rule-making, rule-enforcing Establishment. No doubt, we shall have to concede that there are some men, such as hermits and hippies, who flee society and try to live outside the pale of administration; although I have yet to discover a hippie community which does not administer itself in part or else has to be administered by others. In fact, I venture to assert, in the ultimatumated style of the day, that if any one refuses to accept this notion that man is an administrative animal, he had better move over, or power-minded people who presume a differing role for public administration will move over him.

I would like to see us exploit more effectively some of these inexplicit theories of ours concerning administrative behavior. We should argue, not merely that man must be better understood in order to be properly administered, but we should insist also that man has to be administered in order to be fully understood. What a rich harvest awaits the alert researcher who is willing to capture and record the substitutive administrative processes now being concocted by militant leaders and activist citizens on college campuses, in public squares, at city halls, and before higher halls of hierarchical authority!

One elementary explanation for the universality of administration is the very ambivalence of human nature which seemingly confounds our assumptive speculations. Man administers precisely because he is a creature of the conflicting impulses of rationality and irrationality and of the diametric instincts of love and hate referred to by Bailey, and exactly because, as Bailey further indicates, man's complex motivations confirm the existence of "philosophic or historic precedents for almost any view of man one wishes to propose."

I would conclude from all this that public administration, the root values of which Bailey rightly regards as being derivative from the primary social science disciplines, borrows from these sciences its basic doctrines about mankind, yet adds to this some of its own lore about human nature. Public administration probably deserves credit for thus marshaling its intellectual resources wisely and for proceeding to unfold largely as an "assumptive" field of study.

In moving from the assumptive to the normative realm, we encounter more indigenous theories of public administration. Despite his disappointment at the disarray in which he finds our normative theories, Bailey reveals how promising is our theoretical potential even here. But the most immediate opportunities for fruitful normative theory lie in the policy-making realm for a society overwhelmed, as ours now is, with unanswered problems of public policy and public administration. As to whether public administration should continue to go beyond its traditional concerns with technical rationality and to exploit further these matters of policy content, it seems to me we are beating a dead horse. A substantial number, in fact, the majority, of our specialists in public administration have long been simultaneously scholars of some subject matter in one or more substantive fields, selected areas of comparative government, certain levels of American government, or the policy process generally.

While I do not want to get into this question of scope, which is next on our conference agenda, I would like to make the relevant point here that if we are intent upon cultivating a relevant body of theory, we should not be deterred from freely roaming, as we habitually do, the policy disciplines and sociopolitical sciences. Certainly, Bailey's analysis leads us in this direction, thus reminding us also that, under the open-ended rubric of "public affairs," he and his colleagues at Syracuse have foraged well among all the relevant disciplines, not only in political science but in the social sciences generally. Should not our whole discipline now assume the initiative of codifying these cross-sectional and cross-disciplinary subjects of inquiry? Public administration theory should embrace the organization of our knowledge as well as the organization of society.

As to our underlying constitutional questions of choice—the relationships of executives and legislatures, national and subnational authorities, private and public bureaucracies—where can you find a more involved and, in many ways, a more "disciplined" expertise than among our organizational and administrative theorists? The danger is not that the administrative experts armed with inhuman computers will become, as Bailey puts it, "the major determinant of politically legitimated goals for the society." Perceptive politicians and irate citizens are beginning to put supererogatory administrators and planners in their proper place under our particular brand of pluralistic democracy. The main danger is that these counterpressures may sterilize a public service which, when all is said and done, is probably in the best position to provide the neutrality needed to harness such a seething system of power politics.

This brings us to one of the most crucial of the normative issues that our discipline has to face. How can we preserve the viability of public administration in the face of a threatened displacement or our prevailing patterns of political consensus by those of political conflict? Specifically, for example, are the pressureful and rising forms of clientele or constituency administration tenable? Are they consistent with our basic assumptions about human relationships and societal roles and with our norms for viable administration? I speak now not of administration *for* special groups and interests in our society—to this demand we have long yielded—but of administration *by* such groups and interests.

With this type of self-help administration we have had a longer experience than we realize. The network of farmer committees employed in our agricultural production and soil conservation programs in the United States, has involved, at its height, 100,000 participants. This popular form of action-administration raised few eyebrows at the time. Yet, we are now seriously questioning the urban expression of a similar self-help movement.

Are we doing this only out of concern for the efficiency of public functions, or also because we are disturbed by this threat to traditional norms of public service and existing concepts of public administration? Despite a growing tolerance toward "citizen service," many of us are worried (and I admit I am harassed myself) lest our cherished "civil service" be converted from a minor priesthood to a major proletariat. Our past experience offers some evidence, however, that in an upgrading society, we can popularize the processes and yet protect the purposes of public administration—providing we remain prudent and plucky in projecting into the scene our own already available body of interrelated socio-politico-administrative theory.

Moving along from Bailey's normative category to his instrumental theories, I very much like his stress upon the fruitfulness of innovative models and of middle-level theories. These lucrative "theorettes," as Bailey colorfully calls them, might compensate for our over-all lack of systematic theories concerning administrative instrumentalism. Although there is always the danger here of going off on analogies and metaphors rather than discovering the intrinsic verities, I recognize as one of the most attractive of the theorettes suggested by Bailey's paper his treatment of social tensions and their related medical and clinical implications.

It is quite possible that, in response to the social pathologies of the times, the administrative and related sociopolitical sciences will strengthen their future ameliorative or adjusting role and, like the omnibus science of medicine, will now concentrate more on the basic remedies or public policies needed for an unstable (or is it merely a rapidly changing) society and for an ailing (but it is also a mending) body politic. In any case, when societal problems call for the application of strict diagnoses and drastic therapies and when the diverse disciplines converge in seriously pursuing these problems, the scientific and theoretical possibilities are greatly enhanced.

For this reason alone, I feel especially congenial toward Bailey's instrumentalist view that the most basic objective for the theory of administration is primarily to respond to human needs while also pursuing scientific values. This is not a popular stance to assume among our more devout codisciplinarians, with their primary commitments to the behavioral and social sciences. But it represents, I am convinced, a valid theory of human behavior in the realm of the intellect, even in the case of some of our most puristic and physical sciences.

Although Bailey extolls our rapidly mounting pile of descriptive-explanatory theories, he is not beguiled by their current sophistication. Throughout, Bailey leans toward the kind of theorizing which serves lasting values rather than those tuned to transient styles of inquiry and thought. He is particularly concerned with what he describes as the "Heisenberg" perversity in our theorizing habits. By this he means our theoretical shortcomings in handling the time element.

With this characterization of what is probably our leading theoretical failure, I heartily agree. For explanations which are continually revised, current constructs which black out former experience, and models which are always being remodelled are theories built on existential quicksands. They may do much to recalibrate our instrumentation and to help elaborate our explications, but they contribute modestly to normative theory and meagerly to the distillation and cumulation of usable knowledge and meaningful understanding about human behavior and societal conduct in the realm of public administration and public affairs.

Comment on Bailey's Paper

By Emmette S. Redford

I FIND Bailey's four categories of theory acceptable as distinguishable but interlocking approaches and as together yielding a comprehensive perspective for study of public administration. My commentary only elaborates and rearranges these categories.

The Normative Category

Normative administrative theory relates ideals to administration. Inevitably, it will be of interest to some students of administration because they understand the profound significance of administration on men's lives and are concerned with the kind of lives which men will have in society. With respect to administration, normative theory is both general and particularized. In its general aspect, it is part of political or social philosophy and may include three kinds of questions: What are the ideals that men strive for in a culture? What are the highest ideals man can envisage? What ideals might be attainable, men and institutions being what they are? Particularized with respect to administration, the question may be what ideals *are* served by administration, in which case the inquiry is another aspect of descriptive-analytical theory. It is an inquiry into what is, rather than into what men aspire to or should aspire to. Or it can deal with the conversion of ideal into administrative practice. It looks for the ideals men do or might set for administration—for goals *for* administration. In this case, it is strictly normative and becomes administrative theory, not merely general philosophy. Bailey by defining normative theory as prescriptive restricts it to goals for administration, and thus places it in a different category from descriptive-analytical theory.

The function of the normative theorist is to define the ideals for administrative practice and search for the ways in which these might be implemented within it. He may take the concept of the dignity of man, or of democratic government, or of political supremacy over administration, and expand it into a theory or concept of the way administration should operate.

The potential span of normative theory is not generally understood. It may deal with ultimate values, as in Golembiewski's discussion, in *Men, Management and Morality,* of the dignity of man. It may deal with the social purposes that have been politically legitimized—good education, stabilization and growth in the economy, security against hazards of life—and the ways of implementing these in practice. Or it may be concerned with instrumental values—such as decentralization, hierarchy, or clientele participation.

Bailey is correct that normative theory is in disarray. This is, I think, due to the fact that both basic ideals, such as democracy, and instrumental administrative ideals, such as hierarchy, are being re-examined. There is, therefore, a challenge to normative theorists to reanalyze both ultimate and instrumental values, particularly in their relationship to each other.

Pure Science

Insofar as we can aspire to pure science, we must use two other of Bailey's categories: the descriptive-analytic and the assumptive. These are the two parts of our vineyard in which we, as students of administration, will spend most of our time. Without knowledge of reality, normative theory will be superficial, utopian, and futile, and instrumental theory will miss its mark entirely.

I think descriptive-analytic theory has also been in disarray. Old concepts based on monistic and legalistic assumptions have been shown to be lacking in reality, but there is still need for theory that incorporates new concepts and retains what is valid in the old. The old assumption that politics and administration were separate has been routed, but, as yet, we have only fragments of theory about political administration. With some exceptions, notably Fred Riggs, we have not, since John Gaus, related the function of administration to ecological factors which lie back of the immediate political influences on administration. While behavioralists and institutionalists quarrel or look askance at each other, we await theories which will explain why men act as they do because they occupy positions in institutions.

My own opinion is that for the purpose of comprehensive description and analysis the language of system and subsystem offers us the largest hope. It enables us to encompass all the factors—ecological, structural, physiological, historical, and contemporary—that produce politically oriented administrative operations. It allows, however, for search for typologies which explain variations within and among systems. In short, the systems concept permits broad objectives in theory-building without inhibiting narrower approaches.

Although in descriptive-analytical theory we may have rounded second base, in assumptive theory we have probably not touched first base. Assumptive theory may differ from descriptive-analytic theory only in form—substituting hypotheses for propositions, conclusions, or models. And it can, of course, be meaningless, because it deals with matters that have little relevance to the concerns of men. There are thousands of hypotheses that can be tested and many of them of concern only to the man who tests them or to a few people talking to each other. Bailey, however, sets a wide range for the inquiry: the nature of man and the tractability of institutions. He is thinking, I believe, primarily about the operation of administration. I would add another dimension: the effects of administration on things beyond it. What, for example, are the correct assumptions about what can be accomplished through regulatory administration? What can be achieved through welfare-administration that provides payments on the basis of individual need? Can rehabilitation be achieved? And what are the by-products in terms of human dignity, administrative costs, and other relevant factors? What assumptions can be made about the results of public-private federalism, now becoming prevalent in so many areas of public policy? or about the results of participative democracy? What I am suggesting is that part of our search for assumptive theory should be program-related. What, in brief, are the limits and capabilities of instrumentalization of program objectives?

Applied Science

In his category of instrumental theory, Bailey moves into applied science. If we have perception of "politically legitimized goals," and of "preconditions" and "possibilities" of administrative achievement, then we can aspire toward theory about manipulation of administration to achieve purpose. It may be questioned whether if the other forms of theory are well-developed, there will be much place left for instrumental theory as a distinct category. If, for example, presumptive theory has taught us what to expect from the operation of flat organizations and tall organizations, then what is left may be pure application. But this probably assumes more than will ever be taught from pure science, and hence there is left some room for theory in what we call administrative wisdom and art.

I think that the most significant thing about Bailey's discussion is that it assumes the interrelation of these four categories. The instrumental objective establishes the relevance of the search for theory, for administration is, after all, an instrument made by man for his own purposes. And the instrumental objective fuses normative with descriptive-analytical and assumptive theory. The ultimate objective of administrative theory is, as Bailey explains, to draw together the insights into values and into practice so that they may guide the policy-maker. We need theory that explains to the policy-maker whether, to what extent, and in what ways the purposes of men—ultimate, policy, or instrumental—can be achieved in the practice of administration.

Conference Discussion on the Objectives of the Theory of Public Administration

CHARLESWORTH: Al, are you ready?

LEPAWSKY: I am not ready, Mr. Chairman, but I shall jump in. As I indicated in my comments, I was grateful to Steve for bringing some order into this opening subject on our agenda. Moreover, I see eye to eye with him generally, except, perhaps, with regard to his criticism concerning our lack of "assumptive theory" in public administration. True, we do not have much of our own, but, as I indicated, I feel that we may be wise in having accepted the sediment of assumption in the primary social or behavioral sciences as a basis for our own speculations about human behavior.

I find little wrong in accepting the body of behavioral doctrine and social concept as it develops and is refined, and, in fact, as we help to refine and develop it in our studies and applications to political man and to administrative man. I believe that we are learning to sift out the useful and demonstrable theory and doctrine here fairly well. Of all disciplines, as I have indicated, our own accepts the fact that man is a creature of both love and hate, and it is for this reason that we implicitly hold to the assumptive theory, if we may dignify such a truism by this term, that man has to be governed and administered or learn to govern and administer himself. I realize this may be regarded as an oversimplification among the more sophisticated body of assumptive sociopolitical theory, but it is something basic to begin with in public administration and political science.

But I would like to pass on to other significant issues which Steve's paper raises but to which, understandably, it does not arrive at full answers—issues which will be raised in the remainder of our discussions. I refer to questions dealing with the definition and context of our discipline which will, I am sure, recur when Dwight Waldo presents his paper for discussion.

Nevertheless, it is relevant at this point to indicate some of my leanings on these issues.

First, I lean toward the public rather than toward the sheer administrative side of our subject matter. In this respect, I suppose, I do differ somewhat from the predominant emphasis in the discipline. I do not think that the bucket can be carried on both shoulders. If it is administration that is our main concern as a behavioral science, then we have to face up to the fact, revealed by the actual history of our discipline, that we have not provided the basic ideas or the seminal theorists, with due respect to the accomplished thinkers among us. We have furnished excellent illustrative case materials and have done some supplementary model-building, but, for the most part, we have been revivalists—very good ones, however—for the social theorists, political sociologists, and social psychologists. I stand to be corrected on this point, and I hope that it will come up for further discussion. But we have been flying other peoples' kites, and, perhaps, that is all to the good.

If, on the positive side, we should seek to make our original contribution on the public side, rather than the administrative, I do not think that we should be beguiled by the question of whether economics or business, as well as government, is "public." We now know that economics or business of certain kinds, or at certain dimensions, is an extremely public affair, just as the administration of some nongovernmental, and even industrial, institutions is public in nature. I would like to see us put more emphasis on the definition of the public interest.

Whether we should go so far as to define public administration as administration in the public interest, thus denying the imprimatur of the public interest to the administration and conduct of nongovernmental institutions, is a more delicate question. The possibility of proceeding with this kind of analysis may be enhanced by the proposition that while the subject matter of our field might deal with administrative behavior, the core and context might stress the public and policy aspects, taking into account sociopolitical behavior more broadly.

In any case, we will get less mileage out of our discipline, both scientifically and professionally, if we adopt the broader view, because this also permits us to exploit its interdisciplinary aspects more fully. This, it seems to me, is one of the main lessons which we can learn from the physical and biological sciences. Moreover, they are also less worried than we are, or than we think they are, about the line between basic and applied science. They are interested in operational generalizations which push forward the frontiers of both prediction and control, and are not interested merely in playing around with pure concepts and constructs.

With respect to our sister social sciences, some are becoming so methodologically puristic but substantively irrelevant that I think it is safe to predict that they will soon be subject to serious review and reconsideration. They will probably be reaching back into both the empirical and the normative realms of public administration and public policy. Otherwise, more scholars may leave the fold of political science, for example, as it is now structured and conceived.

Finally, with respect to the comparative approach referred to, our own internal experience with our comparative method deserves consideration. Although I think that we have unduly neglected the study of American government, any move to abandon the comparative field at this stage will be scientifically and professionally unrewarding. Nevertheless, as part of the comparative approach, I would add the historical dimension, which has been almost wholly neglected by us in our studies of politics and administration. What is the scientific difference between a comparison of two contemporary societies and of two systems separated in historical time but richly comparable in character and significance? I would apply this to the American scene itself. Case studies of administrative syndromes and policy systems as between, let us say, the New Deal period and the present, or between our earliest developmental periods and the present, would be richly rewarding.

SHERMAN: I would like to ask you, Steve, a question about your definition. There is one aspect of it that I do not think is explicit. You define public administration as man's attempt, through government, to harness natural human resources for the purpose of approximating politically legitimated goals by constitutionally mandated means. This definition is not explicit as to what role the public administrator plays in defining these politically legitimated goals or in influencing them. I raise the question in terms of Harlan Cleveland's paper, in which he takes the position, as I understand it, that the public administrator frequently decides for himself what the goals are, or at least that they are not given to him by the same group that used to give them to him.

BAILEY: Harvey, I would only refer you to the last three pages of my paper, where I try to suggest that public administration really blends inexorably with social, political, and constitutional theory. And I go on to say that our existing faith is that the tensions in our polity between centrifugal and the centripetal forces, between public and private, among competing interest groups and professions, among generalists and specialists, between and among politicians and administrators, will continue to produce a reasonably benign admixture of competence, compromise, and consensus. This refers back, in turn, to my point that, inevitably, public administrators are part of the group that defines constitutionally mandated means and politically sanctioned goals. Administrators do not wait around for somebody else to do this. They are part of a creative partnership that continues to be at work in defining the ends and means of government.

SHERMAN: I completely agree with what you have said. But I think that this is one point on which the papers are in disagreement. Some of them would make public administration that broad, and some of them would not.

NAFTALIN: It seems to me that we have before us three questions that are interrelated. We are dealing, first, with the role of higher education in training for the public service—and this, I believe, is the most urgent of the three, at least to most of us attending this conference. This is the question of what higher education should do to meet the the manpower needs of government, and subsumed as part of this question is the further issue of defining the relationship between the teaching of public administration and the teaching of political science.

The matter of training for the public service is much different from the second issue (the issue, incidentally, that I thought was the main purpose of this symposium), namely, the search for an improved formulation of the methodology, the scope, and the objectives of public administration so that this field of study and training will have greater relevance to present-day needs. This question, I believe, should be studied in its own right and ought not to be confused with the first question.

The third issue raises a host of questions concerning current and critical substantive problems in administration and government, the kinds of questions advanced in Harvey Sherman's paper.

All three questions are critical and deserve our attention, but we should keep them separated. If we do not, this will be a disjointed discussion which gets nowhere.

I was strongly attracted to Steve Bailey's paper because I thought we were to discuss a new formulation of theory and to explore our experience in relation to that effort. It seems to me that Bailey's categories break new ground. He appears to me to be talking not only about public administration but about action-related activity generally. For example, his category of the *descriptive* and *analytic* is what has historically defined the work of the social sciences. We abhor the category of the *normative*, regarding it as antiscientific, and we have never paid much attention to the *assumptive*, because we have not regarded the question of defining the ideal society in relationship to man's potential as our responsibility, nor have we concerned ourselves with *instrumental* questions.

Bailey appears to me to be saying that, if we are to train for the public service, we must be more than explanatory or descriptive or analytical. We must also worry about the normative, about values, about goals; we must raise questions concerning how man relates to society and to himself; we must even ask about man's potentiality; and, finally, we must deal with the instrumental questions that tell us about the strategies for realizing our goals.

So I think that Bailey's framework is helpful for exploring central questions of administrative theory, but I do not see the necessity of limiting the theory to public administration. Would it not apply to social workers? and to teachers?

BAILEY: I was commissioned to write a paper on the objectives of the theory of public administration, and if what I propose is applicable to other fields beyond that of public administration, you know, I am flattered and delighted, but I have not consciously raised issues of broader theoretical relevance.

SAYRE: Steve, let me put Art's question this way. If you substituted the word, "government," for "public administration" every time it occurred in your paper, what violence could you do to your argument? I think that this is a way of paraphrasing Art's question.

BAILEY: Wally, in most areas of my paper, it would do very little violence.

SAYRE: You are claiming for public administration the scope which is usually claimed for, or associated with, government?

BAILEY: Yes. I would take exception only in terms of elections and congressional procedures. My emphasis relates to bureaucracy. I am not referring to the external party system at election time, or to the legislature.

SAYRE: Let us leave out the electoral aspect. Your conception involves political parties, interest groups, bureaucrats, and the legislative body. So in the way that you have organized your argument, one could substitute the word "government" for "public administration."

BAILEY: Maybe you are right about this fuzziness. I think that I would make this distinction, though: legislatures tend to function across a very substantial range of policies, and have a very important function of legitimizing the work of the administrator. The administrator tends to operate within a fairly narrow range of policies, and he functions only within the framework of authority established by others.

SAYRE: Like governors and mayors and presidents.

BAILEY: This is true, of course, when you get up to the level of top executives. If you are trying to get a poverty program developed and carried out, a Sargent Shriver, who is in the business of getting the President on your side, trying to get group interest organized, trying to get key people in the legislature in a supportive mood, trying to formulate a yearly budget—a Sargent Shriver is inevitably involved in the totality of the process.

SAYRE: Yet, this might not be a typical sequence.

BAILEY: If your argument is that the generic process of policymaking is simply the blind interaction of group interests, then I must disagree. The major function of the public administrator, including the political executive, is to homogenize and moralize the struggle of groups. The administrative (or legislative) function is not simply a derivative of group interaction.

SAYRE: I do not think that you are quarreling with anybody.

BAILEY: I think that I am.

SAYRE: What you are saying is that he is an aggregator.

BAILEY: This is right. He is—an aggregator and a moralizer.

SAYRE: So that is the essence of leadership?

UNIDENTIFIED VOICE: Steve, would it be fair to say that if you broadened the term, "public administration" to include public policy, your position would be even more tenable and that possibly Wally might then accept the point? One of our troubles may be that the term "public administration," whether we meant it to do so or not, has tended to exclude this important normative phase of the subject which is so inherently a part of political science and public administration.

BAILEY: Well, let me rephrase my answer this way. First, I would not be disturbed about substituting "government" for "administration." I would only say that if you want to understand either, you have got to talk about a lot more than traditional political science.

WILLBERN: I want to shift the ground a little bit because I would like to take exception to Steve's four-part classification of theory. Partly, I want to do this for the record because both of the commentators appeared to accept it without question, and I think that, because it is so well worded, it is likely to be picked up and used by a lot of people in a lot of places. It gives me a little trouble because I would say that two of the four are just aspects of one of the four—that what he calls assumptive theory and what he calls instrumental theory are, to me, just types of descriptive-explanatory or descriptive-analytical theory. Theory about the nature of people and the nature of institutions, that is, what they are and what they are capable of doing, is, it seems to me, just theory which describes people and institutions. The evidence about such theories is not significantly different from the kind of evidence that is required about any social fact or relationship. And pretty much the same thing is true in regard to instrumental theory. If you want to achieve such and such a goal, then such and such a method is appropriate; this is just a statement of a social or a physical relationship, which, again, is a descriptive statement. This kind of phenomenon tends to produce this kind of result; or, if such a result is desired, then such and such steps seem to be appropriate. To set these types of theory apart may have some utility for some purposes, but I think that we are actually making a mistake if we put them completely on a par with the other two. That leads to the conclusion that I do want to make very strongly, which is that the real value of this analysis is that we cannot settle for either the descriptive explanatory or the normative theories, that the two are inextricably tied together, although they are fundamentally different. For example, the points that you were raising in the last pages of the paper which Harvey asked about—these are both descriptive and normative, that is, the role of the administrator or executive is capable of being described and analyzed, and important data can be found about it. But you can never escape, it seems to me, even after you have described and analyzed it, the normative matter about what it ought to be or what you would prefer it to be. Those two kinds of theory are fundamentally distinguishable, whereas I do not think that the other two are on quite the same plane.

BAILEY: York, I accept your criticism. I guess I put these into separate categories because of my feeling that in my own learning process I was taught precious little about what I have called assumptive and instrumental propositions. I guess it was my own sense of this lack, and a sense that these were terribly important aspects of any total descriptive-explanatory theory of public administration, that induced me to factor out these categories for special consideration. But, intellectually, I am sure that you are right. We are talking, really, about descriptions and explanations of observable phenomena, and these would surely encompass human nature and instrumental processes.

RIGGS: May I respond to what York has said by agreeing with his basic classification of administrative theory under two major headings: empirical and normative. Under empirical theory I would prefer to speak of the descriptive-analytical type as *system theory*. This involves looking at the public administrative system as a subsystem of government, trying to explain what it is and how it works. Much of our literature is concerned with this system. What I hear you saying is: Let us expand the range of empirical theory to include instrumental analyses of cause-effect relationships or *theories of change* in administrative systems. Such knowledge, which can be empirically tested, is of great value to practitioners of government. I also hear you saying: Let us look at some of the assumptions regarding—what I would call the *ecological*—relationships between administrative systems and nonadministrative variables which clearly affect public administration, providing an environment which both conditions and may be modified by administrative behavior. Thus, empirical theory includes three main types: administrative systems, change theories, and ecological theory.

Just as empirical theory contains several varieties, so I think we also need to recognize several kinds of normative theory. We have not emphasized them as much as we should.

One type is concerned with the goals of action. We are talking about the objectives of public administration, and these lead into the objectives of public policy, the objectives of politics and, indeed, of human society and existence. I cannot say much about this type of normative theory here, but I recognize its profound philosophical and practical importance.

Rather, I would like to stress *another type* of normative theory, a type which may be even more important for the everyday practice of public administration. This involves analysis of ethical and normative constraints on administrative action, involving not ultimate goals but matters of day-to-day operations. Such constraints set limits on the range of choice of administrators. For example, in civil administration we do not consider killing people without due process of law—even when we think them guilty of serious crimes. The police department might like to line up accused criminals and have them shot. It would simplify life for them. In some countries they do just this, but in American public administration, this is forbidden.

By contrast, our military services consider that if you classify someone as an enemy and you are engaged in war, it is perfectly permissible to shoot not only known enemies, but civilian women and children who get in the way. We have been doing a good deal of this in Vietnam, I might add.

The taking of life is an extreme example, but there are others of a more subtle nature. For example, we are now engaged in a debate about police eavesdropping, about the use of wire-tapping. This is a moral and constitutional constraint. To what extent does our interest in catching violators of the law justify us to use means which violate inhibitions designed to protect the privacy and human rights of individuals?

I believe that if you examine the whole field of administration, you will find it crammed with such moral and ethical questions. What limitations do we impose on ourselves, even though they reduce the effectiveness of administrators, because failure to respect these limitations would violate the consciences or cultural norms of our citizens and of the administrators themselves?

This question brings us back to the subject which I raised earlier, whether we should be talking in this conference about American public administration only, or public administration in general. We tend to take for granted the legal and moral constraints under which administrative action occurs. But in different countries such constraints vary widely, with important consequences for what can and cannot be done administratively. The weight of family obligations, for example, makes nepotism not only unavoidable but even praiseworthy in some countries. This clearly has implications for efforts to introduce a merit system in such governments.

Can we not extend this aspect of normative theory to a consideration of Dean Bailey's definition of public administration as an effort to use government to approximate politically legitimated goals by "constitutionally mandated means." You have expanded the scope of your definition, Steve, to include not only the United States but also other Western democratic polities. But if we are to have a theory of public administration (not just of American administration) we need to go beyond this. Are the principles of public administration relevant only in democratic polities, where the rule of law also prevails, that is, where constitutionalism exists?

Since many of us have worked abroad and have therefore had to test the relevance of our administrative theories there, I think it germane to raise this issue. If our theories are irrelevant overseas, we ought not to use them as a basis for technical assistance in countries which lack democratic, constitutional regimes. But if they are relevant, then we ought to be able to talk about them in a world-wide, not just an American, context.

Let me illustrate my meaning by referring to a conversation I had last summer in Greece with some civil servants under the control of a military regime which had seized power by unconstitutional means. Certainly, the Greek case is not exceptional. What we see in Vietnam today is far more extreme. Now, by Bailey's definition, what these Greek civil servants were engaged in was not public administration. They were carrying out laws, but the laws were not politically legitimated by constitutionally mandated means.

These civil servants faced an agonizing moral choice, which brings me back to the question of moral constraints. If you had been a civil servant in Greece when the government was ruled by a parliamentary constitutional regime, what would you have done when a military group seized power by violence? Would you try to resign, even though the price might well be imprisonment, loss of your property, and persecution of your family? Would you, perhaps, say that the interests of the public override those of constitutionalism, and that you would, therefore, try to serve the public despite the regime?

Such are the perplexities facing officials today, not just in Greece but in many countries around the world. It seems to me that we cannot refuse to face such problems if our theories of public administration are to be relevant to the problems of a changing world. Alternatively, if we admit that public administration has nothing to say about problems of government under unconstitutional authoritarian regimes, then we ought to be frank enough to say so, and admit that we have a body of knowledge and doctrine of limited relevance, limited, that is, to our own conditions in America and to those countries which share our form of government.

BAILEY: I recognize the limitations of my paper's terms, as they are self-imposed. I told you the idea when I started writing this, in trying to extend this beyond my own culture. Precisely the kinds of questions that you are now raising came into my mind, and apart from the pretty general statements like, "public administration is carrying out of public's business," I found it next to impossible to develop any kind of definition that would take account of constitutionally mandated means, which I looked at, as well as procedures and processes, in the terms which we mentioned above; and all of this is what I mean by politically legitimated goals, in terms of our own culture. I do not have the knowledge, even the experience or ability, to try to formulate the kind of definition for the carrying out of government's business, which would mean that public administration is something that carries around the world.

WILLBERN: May I make a comment on that point? For instance, I was puzzled, too, by what you meant by constitutionally mandated means, but I tended, perhaps, to misinterpret you by assuming, for instance, that the kind of structure and procedures that prevail in the Soviet Union are constitutionally mandated means for that society. Or am I wrong? By constitutionally mandated means, do you define this to be the processes of the democratic societies of the West, or would you say that your definition would fit the Soviet model within that context or society?

BAILEY: I have not had enough instruction on the Soviet Union to know whether the constitution of 1936 is ever referred to by the ———

WILLBERN: Would you agree that the British constitution can be used as a model here? Not necessarily a specific body of legal procedure but that which is socially acceptable, what has been going on in practice in the society?

BAILEY: Yes. But, you see, I would then say that in order to have constitutionally mandated means you have got to have some sort of precise instrumentality for defining what is constitutioned. In Britain, they have it in the parliament. In our country, we have it in the courts. When I used this phrase, I did not have the Soviet Union in mind. Even in the case of the United States, of course, definitions change. The Supreme Court cannot be oblivious to what is acceptable to society. I do not suggest that the Supreme Court of the United States conducts a Gallup Poll before making its decisions, and on many occasions the Court runs counter to accepted beliefs. But the Court is a dynamic not a static interpreter of "constitutionally mandated" means.

CHARLESWORTH: Steve, do you mean by "constitutionally mandated," mandated by the recognized heads of state? Do you have to have a constitution in the Western democratic sense? Now, let us take the Roman Empire, not the Republic, but the Empire. They did not have any constitution; they had rescripts and so on. The statement can be made and defended that public administration had more to do with the continued ongoing of the Roman Empire than did the army or the law. Now, the administration of the Roman Empire, was that constitutionally mandated?

BAILEY: I do not know. I started off within the context of democratic politics created during the last 150 to 200 years. You now push me back to the days of the Roman Empire. That there are analogies and parallels I do not doubt. The power of proconsuls in the imperial administration of Rome was in many ways similar to the power of the British colonial servant in Africa in, say, 1920.

CHARLESWORTH: Now, you would not be offended if I say that the Latin word "constituere" merely means to arrange or determine. But our constitution has semiroyal, semimystical, semimoral connotations. Which kind of "constitution" do you mean?

BAILEY: Let me put it this way. I mean by the term "constitution" something quite precise. I mean the attitude of mind that developed in the Western world over centuries of time that suggested that the law applies to the state as well as to subjects.

GLADIEUX: Steve, I wanted to revert to the question which was originally raised by Harvey concerning pages 137–139 of your paper. I believe that you have raised a profound question there concerning both the definition of public administration and the role of the administrator, and I want to be sure that I catch your message. As I understand it, what you are saying is that the concept of the value-neutral public manager, who has pretty much the role of a generalist, is really an anachronism. You are advocating a very positive role with regard to program-development as an integral part of leadership on the part of the political administrator. In other words, you are suggesting that the art of public administration and the role of the new-style public administrator does consciously involve the shaping of the environment which ultimately governs him. Yet, I got the impression— on pages 138–139, where you say that our existing faith is that the tensions in our polity will continue to produce a reasonably good government—that you seem to be relying more on external forces and circumstances. I was not quite sure then that you were coming down on the positive side here: that the role of the political administrator was consciously to lead and to help shape the environment. I just want to be sure that that is what you are saying.

BAILEY: What I am saying is that public administrators are not the only movers in our society, the only policy-makers. But they do have an important role to play, and they should not be embarrassed about it. I am saying that they are one force among many forces which have policy-initiation interests. I happen to think that a lot of the agenda of modern public policy, particularly where it gets extraordinarily complex, is set by the public administrator as an aggregating and moralizing agent. He is a key element in the whole process. However, he is not the only element, and he is, and should be, bound by contextual forces.

GLADIEUX: I understand. Incidentally, in my 1935 Maxwell days it was the economy and efficiency values which were predominant. That was the ideal concept of public management. Policy and program were secondary. It seems to me that we have come a long, long way since then.

MOAK: I think that we have come a long, long way from it, but in the wrong direction. We talked about Jim's country-boy derivation of the name Charlesworth. I am a kind of simple-minded guy who has worked in the field of local government all my life, and most of the people with whom I worked would upchuck at some of this conversation. I think administration is, and should be, much more Appleby, even pre-Appleby, rather than what it is reported that Syracuse is talking about. This does not foreclose our casting the administrator in dual, triple, quadruple, or whatever number of roles we want to cast him. But I think that we do the whole field a disservice by becoming impatient with the constrictions of the definitions of administration. This process leads to our gradually embracing the universe. Shortly, everything includes everything.

It does not add to the understanding of anything when we get into that position. This is not to reject the proposition that there are interrelationships; certainly is not to reject the proposition that a man involved in public administration at the appointed level is not frequently involved in policy-development. Otherwise, I think that he is an awfully sterile character.

In the few times that I have been in public office, I spent more than half my time trying to influence public policies. During that use of time, I do not think that I was engaged in public administration. I think that I was engaged in another process—that of policy-development; of trying to secure the political legitimization to which you make reference. I would very strongly urge that we should seek to make the scope more discreet; that we return to a concept that administration is the process of putting into effect public policies, and is not the process of making public policies. This would be superior to the process generally tried by these papers, that is, the attempt to broaden the scope of the definition of public administration.

BAILEY: Well, Len, all I can say is that the world as you understand it and the world as I understand it are not the same worlds. This does not mean that you are right or that I am right. It just means that yours is a different world from mine. I know of no experience in administration which I have had personally where it was possible for me to distinguish between public administration and public policy making.

MOAK: Are you talking of public administration as the carrying out of policies made?

BAILEY: Take an example. I have recently studied the implementation of the Elementary and Secondary Education Act of 1965. In the first place, every step of the administration of the Elementary and Secondary Education Act involved a whole series of discretionary judgments by administrators. These judgments are absolutely necessary in the implementation of a general law. Legislative intentions are necessarily general. This means that administrative regulations and guidelines have to be developed in order to give the law specificity. Somebody puts down notions as to what he thinks Congress might want. He tests these notions against what is deemed reasonable by various clientele groups: chief state school officers, local school superintendents, the conferences of mayors. These give him feedback. He rearranges his regulations and guidelines on the basis of who is going to get hurt, how badly he is going to get hurt, and how important it is if he gets hurt. He carries out this discretionary process on a day-to-day basis. In actual fact, the administrator has an enormous amount of discretion. As soon as you have discretion, you cannot ignore political consequences. Making judgments in terms of political consequences is my definition of policy-making. There is just no way of separating the policy-making function from the administrative function.

MOAK: Well, I have indicated that my experiences were primarily in local government and in the field of public finance. I understand clearly the difference between the development of the budget and the execution of the budget. In the first one, I am engaged in policy-formulation, and if I gain a reasonable comprehension of the decisions that were made in the course of the development and the approval of that budget, it is then that I can engage in a fairly adequate job of administering the budget to carry out the policies which were validated thereby.

BAILEY: Len, did you have any transfer power?

MOAK: Yes, I had some, and I repeat that, in the exercise of it, I was fundamentally engaged in pursuit of the policy-decisions that were made in the course of the development of the budget. Alternatively, if it represented a formal adjustment of policy, it was usually done through the involvement of people in the policy level—mayor and city council in this case. I concur with you that, at the very apex of hierarchy, we have great difficulty in making this distinction, these separations, but I do not believe that public administration *per se* is primarily concerned with policy-execution, not policy-formulation.

BAILEY: Len, I had a peculiar kind of finance officer when I was mayor, and I had also a very peculiar kind of corporation council. I was very fortunate in both. I came in and said that I wanted to do something, and they looked at their job in terms of finding ways of helping me to do what I wanted to do. My finance man had been around a lot longer than I had. He was terribly helpful in making suggestions, not only concerning what we ought to do but also concerning from which pocket money ought to come in order to achieve our goals most expeditiously. I see nothing preordained about a finance man's being a helpless neuter.

The American Public Executive: New Functions, New Style, New Purpose

By Harlan Cleveland

THE business of the public executive has always been to bring people together in organizations to make something happen in the public interest. What that something was to be, and where the public interest lay, was traditionally a "given" in his life and work. The ultimate aims were set by the whims of kings or bishops, the compromised wisdom of citizen legislators, or the calculations of political generals and generalist politicians.

But in our own time, in the United States of America, something odd has happened to the role of the public executive. It is still his business to bring people together in organizations to make something happen in the public interest. But what that something is, and where the public interest lies, is ultimately for himself to judge.

The public administrator's new ethical burden is only part of the fallout of invention, innovation, development, modernization, or whatever you want to call the accelerating complications around us. New functions for the executive, and a new executive style, are also children of complexity.

I am presuming in this article to describe the changes that the American public executive is bound to feel in his functions, his workdays, and his purposes. But, first, we had better update our analysis of the environment of executive complexity in which he lives and works. The American public executive should be in a good position to see what is happening, for he tackles more unprecedented problems and manages more large systems than anyone else.

THE MULTIPLICATION OF DECISIONS

From the public administrator's angle of vision, the striking thing about the process called "development" is the rapid expansion in the number and variety of public-interest decisions requiring to be made from day to day. I do not know how to count them, and neither does anybody else, so I will assert with confidence that since the beginning of this century, topics to which governmental authority and administration are applied have increased by a factor of several hundred. Each year that goes by, the pell-mell pursuit of scientific truth further multiplies the subjects about which governments have to make decisions.

Before the atom was split, public authorities did not have to decide about the testing and control of nuclear weapons, or think about insurance against nuclear accidents. Before we knew that we could get to the moon, nobody was seriously working on the politics and law of outer space.

Until the first earth satellite was launched, no parastatal agency was budgeting for a global communication system and the Weather Bureau was not planning a World Weather Watch.

Only when powerful drugs were invented that could change the balance of nature and affect human personality did governments think hard about rationing their use and controlling their effects. Until most people had to live in or near cities, the problems of urban transport and congestion and pollution that worry us now worried us not. Before the scientific revolution in farming and medicine, there was not, effectively, a "world food problem" or a "world health problem"; there was merely a regrettable prevalence of starvation and incurable disease. Now that something can be done about these ancient afflictions, decisions have to be made by somebody to do or not to do that something.

These new kinds of decisions do not seem to displace the older kinds of decisions; they are, by and large, additions to the quantum of public responsibility. To get the expanding volume of decisions made, new social forms had to be invented. They are strikingly different from the public organizations of even fifty years ago—and from our inherited image of what big organizations are like.

Decision-Making in Modern Organizations

Modern organizations must, of course, be big enough to encompass the enormous issues arising in a continental industrial society. And growing size seems to be directly correlated with (a) the wider dispersion of real power inside each organization and (b) more sharing of responsibility with outsiders.

The large pyramid of authority with all control at the top, which is still celebrated in song and story, does not survive in the developed industrial state. What develops instead is a congeries of large organizations in which control is loose, power diffused, and centers of decision plural. And the more each organization is conceived by its managers to be affected with the public interest, the wider is the range of *other* organizations which are deeply involved in "its" decisions.

Decisions are thus typically a committee process, as much in totalitarian as in free societies: "collective leadership" is not an index of democratic feelings but a technical imperative of bigness.

What is involved here is not just devolution of the decision-making authority. In our largest organizations, the executive almost never writes a letter he signs, or signs a letter he writes; but that is only an index of vertical size. The point is that size also multiplies the horizontal span of specialties and interests which need to be brought into each decision. New appointees to top positions in government are often appalled at the way their options are narrowed by lateral brokerage among their professional subordinates before important matters are pushed up for "decision." The "technostructure" which Galbraith has discovered in American industry, and which he says makes all the decisions, is old stuff to students of governmental process.

Even when a "decision" seems clearly within the jurisdiction of a single organization, the person in whose name it is announced is expected to consult, and to be seen to consult, with all the relevant kinds of expertise and all the concerned interests. It is not enough for the President to announce a tax program; he must produce in its public support his financial and economic advisors. If he proposes a measure of national defense, the Joint Chiefs of Staff, the Secretaries of State and Defense, and the leading congressional specialists on foreign affairs and armed services must have been visibly brought into the decision process.

At every level of government, the complexity of the subject matter widens the circle of executives whose special knowledge is essential or whose oxen are gored. In every community, and notably in the metropolitan areas, a new pattern of leadership now spreads the power to affect the community's destiny, breaking the leadership monopolies traditionally held by businessmen, business lawyers, and early-arriving ethnic groups. In the new competition for influence, any group can play; the ticket of admission for its leaders or hired professionals is now skill in organization and a working knowledge of intergovernmental complexity. For every decision is shared with other groups, and every major improvement—a new hospital, a downtown plaza, a poverty program, a community college, a metropolitan water plan, or whatever—involves the creative manipulation of multiple public authorities.

It is true that the degree to which leadership is collective varies according to the activity that is administered. The spectrum of public administration still ranges from organizations where at least some formal orders go down the hierarchical line, to organizations where nearly everything is done by lateral bargaining; a Marine platoon, a family business, or an established local trade union are still to be found at one end of this spectrum, and the administration of hospitals, research laboratories, and academic faculties is still somewhere near the other end. But in the process of modernization the whole spectrum shifts—away from the more formal, hierarchical, order-giving way of doing business and toward the more informal, fluid workways of bargaining, brokerage, advice, and consent.

Aptitudes and Attitudes

The modern public executive thus has to learn to move in a fluid environment. To the beginning student of administration, or the detached observer if any, the large-scale organizations of our big democracy may still look like square and static diagrams on a two-dimensional chart. But to the practitioner they feel like chemical reaction in a liquified solution. It must have been a perceptive analyst of modern administration who first said that a task of public management was as difficult as nailing Jello to the trunk of a tree.

If you look around at the American public executives who are managing our destinies these days, you do not find that they share any coherent set of ideas. But you do find that they have in common a set of aptitudes and attitudes which are clearly necessary to the administration of complexity. It goes almost without saying that they enjoy complexity, relish change, and have a talent for self-induced optimism. Less obvious, perhaps, are the other priceless ingredients of fluid executive drive:

They have brains, and like using them.

They are "low-key" people, with high boiling points and soft voices.

They feel responsible for their own sense of direction.

And because they have learned to swim around in their environment, they feel free.

The Obligation to Think

In times past, it was sometimes said that a good executive could always hire brains, the implication being that other executive qualities were really more relevant. Thirty years ago, Chester Barnard listed intelligence last, and it seemed reluctantly, among the talents the executive required. There are still executive-training programs which teach that the executive's main task is to get good men and delegate them full responsibility for clearly defined pieces of the work to be done.

Modern complexity has rendered this conventional wisdom both unconventional and unwise. Nowadays, the best executives are the men and women who know that it is a mistake to ask for "completed staff work" on important matters, and who immerse their own minds most deeply in the decisions they make.

The executive's work, after all, consists in meeting a series of unforeseeable crises on the road to an undefinable objective. It helps to plan, that is, to try to foresee the unforeseen; but the planned-for contingency never happens—something else happens instead. So the planning produces, not a usable plan, but a better-trained group of people who can continuously adjust their analyses to changes in the real world, and winnow for the responsible decision-makers (usually plural, as already noted) the choices that simply cannot be fudged or postponed.

This process requires all the specialists and staff assistants to have some understanding of what it is like to be an executive and what it takes to frame a decision that will "stick." But it also means that the ultimate decision-makers must themselves participate in the planning, measure the options, and filter the imagined consequences of each through their own personal computers, which are their own brains.

The objection is sometimes made that the problems of a modern organization are too complicated for any one executive's mind to absorb and master. The objection is without merit.

The human mind is an unimaginably intricate, phenomenally rapid, and extraordinarily sensitive computer, able to take in millions of observations, weigh them according to their multiple relevance, store them in a memory of fantastic dimensions, retrieve them with enormous speed and accuracy, organize them into options, come up with a line of action, and transmit the necessary implementing instructions to other parts of the body, all in a fraction of a second.

A recent incident in a crowded airport can serve as a pale illustration of the mind's indescribable capacity to cope. On the "down" escalator during a rush hour, a family of small children stumbled and fell over each other at the bottom. In the circumstances they were destined to be crushed by the rest of the crowd on the escalator, falling on them in a heap. But one man in that crowd, who happened to be a military officer with a mind trained to the analysis of complex situations, calculated the choices and came up with a relevant answer in a second or two. He turned around on the descending stairway and shouted to its passengers to walk rapidly upstairs, as the escalator kept moving down. In a moment, the children had unscrambled themselves and were safe. An alert free mind had triumphed over "destiny" again.

If the executive is not himself plowing through the analysis, there is no sense in which he is "making" a "decision"; he is merely presiding while others decide. The obligation to think hard is the one executive task that cannot be delegated. And this means that the modern executive has to be reflective, curious about ideas—something of an intellectual, not only by education and training but by instinct and temperament as well.

The Modern Style of Leadership

The more the modern executive has to wrap his own brain around the corner of complexity that he is hired to manage, the more he finds that a certain style of leadership works best. The trademarks of this modern style are the soft voice and the low key.

I have recently had occasion to visit a number of military commands related to the North Atlantic Treaty Organization (NATO) defense system—armored divisions, fighter squadrons, and warships at sea. It is noticeable that the men who are running things in our Armed Forces find little need for a loud voice or a parade-ground manner. They seldom shout; if they want to reach large numbers of troops, they speak quietly and let electronics do the amplifying. Even with subordinates, an officer seldom raises his voice; some even frame vertical orders as "suggestions," much as a dean would deal with an academic faculty.

A growing proportion of each officer's time is spent in dealing laterally with people not subject to his orders anyway. A captain who calls in air support for his beleaguered company is not dealing up and down a chain of command, but negotiating across several chains of command. The colonel "in command" of an air base may find representatives of fifteen or twenty different United States military organizations camping on the two square miles of "his" base. None of the officers in charge of these operating tasks is responsible to the base commander; they deal with him laterally, as a tenant deals with a landlord.

The proposition can be generalized: the more complicated things get, the more every person working in a large organization is clearing horizontally with people he cannot order around and who cannot order him around. In short, military administration is more akin to hospital management or the academic administration of scientific research than it used to be.

The more critical the function and the more split-second the timing, the more likely you are to find in charge executives with quiet voices who manage by indirection and understand the importance of loading onto each staff member the maximum personal responsibility for the successful operation of the whole system. If you sit above the flight deck of a modern aircraft carrier, watching the "air boss" at work, you find him depending heavily on the extemporaneous originality, the ability to adapt known procedures to unknown emergencies, of every member of his staff. He is responsible for the whole process of catapulting planes from the deck and landing them safely on the deck; it is an intricate and dangerous function. Yet, the air boss infrequently gives an order; most of the time, he is monitoring a complex but familiar procedure, and intervening only when, with his wider knowledge of the system as a whole, he sees trouble developing which the men running around on the deck cannot yet see. Since the flight deck in use is a noisy place, the key participants in its complicated choreography are wired for sound. The air boss can hear what they say to each other, and that is how most of the work gets done; the boss can pre-empt a decision, wave off an incoming plane, or call up reinforcements to handle a momentary crisis, if, with his wider knowledge, he judges it necessary to intervene. But the system would not work at all if it depended on cumbersome vertical recommendations and approvals. Most of the time, the air boss is watching, calculating, thinking ahead—and letting the training and sense of responsibility of each man carry to completion a drama in which the actors are too busy to feel dramatic and too professional to feel anxious about how complex it all is.

A "low-key" style works best for the modern public executive because the administration of complexity is conducted at such high tension; the more complex the system, the higher the tension. Organization is not people, but their activity in concert, as Barnard put it. But if diffusion of power and collective leadership are the secret of success in large-scale administration, the public executive's primary problem is not to get people to cooperate. Most people do that all too readily. His problem instead is to construct a web of relevant tensions, and then maintain within it a fruitful friction between staff members "representing" all the specialties and interests that have to be stirred together to accomplish the executive's purpose.

The tensions he encourages must, of course, be drained as far as possible of their emotional content. The complex technical processes of modern industry require close attention and instant intercommunication, and people who get too easily excited are likely to get in the way.

What sets the "developed" off from the "underdeveloped" societies is precisely the presence in societies at later stages of development of large numbers of people capable of depersonalizing their relationships in order to play an executive role. A "developed" society, crammed as it is with complex systems of organizations, requires of each executive that he act in each office he holds in the way in which it is functional for a person in that position to act. He must be able to deal with other executives in the system not merely as himself, but as surrogate for a specialized function or a special interest. He must be able to argue forcefully with colleagues without "taking it personally" when his view does not prevail.

In the more personalized cultures of the less developed lands, the executive's family or his tribe or his regional affiliation still tends to override his loyalty to the function he represents in society, and this clogs the complex system with too many considerations that are extraneous to it. In the developed industrial cultures, an official may come to his task from Texas politics or from a trade-union background or from a Proper Bostonian tribe, but for purposes of his official task, these elements of personal background are supposed to be subordinated to the fact that he is the deputy assistant director of this or that. That is why a main purpose of education in the developing nations is, or at least ought to be, to imbue people with attitudes that enable them to function as specialized parts of large complex systems.

The Definition of Goals

In the new environment of executive complexity, the reflective men with the soft voices find that there is plenty of responsibility to go around. Packaged with their new functions and their new style, they are discovering new ethical burdens. For the first time in the story of man, the public administrator is more responsible for defining the purpose of his work than anyone else is.

From prehistoric times until the day before yesterday, leadership in public affairs was exercised by a comparatively small number of strong men. Their aim in contending for political power was, then as now, a polity with themselves in charge. Once in power, the changing objectives of organized society were established and announced from the top, which is to say by the strong men.

The more successful strong men collected as advisers the most intelligent men they could find, to suggest where to go and how to get the followers to follow. The professional managers—sorcerers and warriors and public administrators—hired out to the most congenial bidder, or were pressed into service by force. They probably originated most of the "policy" that emanated from the top, but did not themselves presume to be *responsible* for the goals of statecraft.

If these public executives wrote about their work, it was "how to" stuff; the earliest book of record on personnel-administration was written by a man who served local princes in China 1,700 years ago. It is a valuable literature; of the codified insights which serve us today as general theory in public administration, the most durable seem to be the legacy of reflective practitioners from Lao-tse through Machiavelli and Clausewitz to Barnard and Nicholson and Appleby. But the angle of their vision was that of a senior servant, civil or military. The purpose to be served was the Prince—the growth of his sway, the perpetuation of his power, the conception and prosecution of his program. The first concern of the political leader is necessarily the enhancement of his own power, as Richard Neustadt says of the American presidency; and most philosophers of civil and military service have not allowed themselves, or been allowed, to forget it.

Thus, down through history, the environment of hierarchy, with its sharp distinction between policy and administration, enabled the professional administrators to finesse the question, "Where are we supposed to be going, anyway?" Theirs was an ethic of effective manipulation, leaving to others the choice of a general sense of direction.

"Whate'er is best administer'd, is best"; in half a couplet Pope captured a philosophy for the administrators of all time—until our own time.

But nowadays, for the public executive in a modern complex system, it is different. "Policy," for him, turns out to be largely the decisions which he himself negotiates with other public executives. The broader guidelines that he needs are not available from oracle or priest or political boss, and often not even from the "higher" levels of an increasingly nonhierarchical hierarchy. If he asks where he, or his organization, or America, or the world, is and ought to be heading, he finds that his best authority on the subject is himself. If he cannot figure out in what direction to push his fraction of the public business, the frustration of running hard toward indefinable goals will sooner or later drive him into some less demanding line of work.

For those executives of middle age who step into government from other pursuits, the first experience with fuzzy goals can be traumatic. If the new public executive came from a private company not deeply involved with government, he will not have spent much time and energy on defining goals and projecting purposes; the self-justifying purposes expressed in the balance sheet, the competitive position, and the reaction of those who use the company's products serve him well enough as distant targets for day-to-day executive work. Moreover, he can, without undue philosophizing, relate other more "public" purposes to his company's aims—either because the company is deemed to serve them automatically (full employment, prosperity, a better America, a favorable balance of payments, a stronger defense), or because the public purpose is deemed to override the company's admittedly narrower goals (as when he pays his corporate tax and subjects his product to the government's standard-setting authority).

But take the same business executive and elect him mayor or ask him to run his state housing program or appoint him Secretary of Defense, and he perceives an enormous change in the environment. Instead of spending most of his time and effort in working toward objectives about which nobody is arguing, he finds himself presiding at meeting after meeting in which the real agenda, hidden or overt, is a question: "Where are we supposed to be going, anyway?" For some executives, this state of affairs carries its own exhilaration; the confusion of purposes adds to their own discretion and enhances their sense of freedom. But for others, who persist in regarding ill-defined aims as an abnormal condition to be instantly corrected, the frustration builds up and the desire to serve wider purposes drains away. They may then echo the sardonic comment of a former Army Controller. The art of public management, said General William Reeder shortly after his retirement,

consists of issuing orders based on inaccurate, incomplete and archaic data, to meet a situation which is dimly understood, and which will not be what the issuer visualizes, orders which will frequently be misinterpreted and often ignored, to accomplish a purpose about which many of the personnel are not enthusiastic.

"Principles" Are Too General

There is, of course, no lack of general principles to which the public executive can relate his work. He can readily find some general formulation of a sense of direction in a book of scripture, of philosophy, or of law; he can find whatever such formulation best rationalizes what he has decided to do next. New principles of universal application do not need to be written, by him or by his ghost writer—they have been uttered already by the Old Testament prophets, the teachers and saviors of the world's great religions, the ancient Greeks, and the eighteenth-century philosophers.

When, in the last year of his administration, President Eisenhower appointed a Commission on National Goals, that wise and sophisticated group commissioned a hundred studies, held several long meetings, and concluded that it was hard to improve on the Declaration of Independence. When they came right down to it, the commissioners held these truths to be self-evident: that all men are created equal, that they are endowed by their creator with certain unalienable rights, that among these are life, liberty and the pursuit of happiness; that to secure these rights, governments are instituted among men, deriving their just powers from the consent of the governed.

Jefferson and his colleagues were clear that they were writing for "all Men." And, indeed, the modern piece of paper on which these ideas about freedom are most persuasively and authoritatively expressed is not a private manuscript penned in the dead of night by some monastic scholar, but a very public document called the Charter of the United Nations, a tract pasted together by politicians and public executives in a dozen international committees, which in time became a state paper ratified by a hundred nations through a hundred constitutional and unconstitutional processes.

These liberal doctrines have proved out well, we Americans naturally feel. They provided both the motive power and the governor for our efforts to tame a continent and build a great nation. They somehow justified the science and technology that created the complexity in which the American public executive pursues his *metier*. But they do not, of course, provide the answers to the tactical questions of the day—whether to deploy an antiballistic missile system, how to cope with riots and poverty and discrimination, what to do and who should do it in Berkeley and Newark and the Congo and Vietnam. They are even less helpful in deciding how to chair a committee meeting or whether to hire Miss Zilch.

The Public Executive's "Ethical Hunch"

"Next steps" have always been the executive's stock in trade; what sets the modern public executive off from all of his predecessors is the seemingly limitless opportunities inherent in his very next steps in the years just ahead of him, to affect whole societies for good or ill—if he can only tell the difference.

Increasing knowledge is breaking down the distinction between human conduct and natural events, an Indian philosopher-scientist has recently said. He meant that more and more human behavior can now be explained in mechanical terms. But the converse also applies: as man learns more about the mastery of his environment, he is privileged to apply his free will to its increasing mastery.

For we do live at a very specialized moment in mankind's long ascent toward civilized behavior. It is clear enough now that a kindly God has placed in our brains the technical genius to meet before long all the basic physical wants of mankind—in North America and Europe in our lifetime, in the rest of the world in the lifetime of our children. Without a single new scientific discovery or insight—and what a conservative assumption *that* is!—we know how to limit most of the hunger and disease which has been the chief preoccupation of society's political leaders and administrators through the millennia of unremembered time.

At the same time, a God who seems to believe in self-help has placed in our brains the intellectual equipment and social skills necessary to organize people on a scale large enough and complex enough to put our full technical know-how to work in solving the "whether" and choosing the "what." We are not yet doing this at all well, either in urban affairs or in international relations. This is the sense in which the American public executive is exploring the new frontier of a great society where the puzzle is not whether we can manage enough progress for everybody, but what kind of progress we want to manage.

And at this moment in history, with that taste for irony that has always characterized the story of man, we have used our technical and administrative skills to invent and perfect the power to end it all—or, in the alternative, to make the experiment endless.

So during the years immediately ahead, public executives in the more developed societies, and especially in the United States of America, will have less priestly guidance and more obligation to take far-reaching decisions than ever before. No one will have to carry the ethical burden all by himself—the collective processes that are natural to complex systems will take care of that. But if nobody is fully in charge, everybody is partly in charge; for making the choices and taking the chances just ahead, every public executive will be more dependent on his personal moral gyroscope—his own ethical hunch—than ever before.

We have been prepared for these choices and chances by an uncounted infinity of mutations, by half a million years of human evolution, by a dozen millennia of history known and surmised, by a brief but brilliant period of systematic thought—through Chinese human relations, Greek logic, Indian philosophy, Christian ethics, Western science, and the rest. From all this teaching, we know that the choices are ours, that there is no shelter from the social fallout of science, that we cannot duck the questions it raises, nor turn them away, nor refer them to higher authority, nor leave them unanswered.

And of all the men and women who face this frontier, it is the public executives who will carry the greatest responsibility, and will be rewarded by the liveliest sense of freedom. For it is they who make the crucial choice: which people to bring together in organizations, to make what happen, in whose interpretation of the public interest.

Comment on Cleveland's Paper

By Arthur Naftalin

HARLAN CLEVELAND has articulated a thesis of major significance in the study and practice of public administration. His view of the changing role of the public executive challenges many conventional notions concerning organization and procedure, and suggests that a re-examination of some time-honored assumptions may be in order.

In reacting to Cleveland's description of the "*new* functions, *new* style and *new* purpose" of the public executive, it may be helpful to view the decision-making authority as existing on a continuum that moves from an *administrative* pole at one end to a *political* pole at the other.

At the *administrative* end, decision-making is automatic, mechanical, and impersonal; authority flows downward from the individual in command at the top. Here we see the administrator in his classic role, Cleveland's Marine captain exercising leadership by command and sharing the decision-making authority with no one.

At the other end of the spectrum, decision-making is *political*. Here authority is shared and decisions are arrived at after consultation and negotiation and are based on consensus and agreement. They reflect the blending of diverse capabilities and the moderating of competing interests. In its purest form, the *political* process reflects total equality of power among all members of the organization. The decision is the collective expression of those who share a diffused authority.

Of course, decisions seldom occur in their pure form. At any time or place, the purely administrative act is affected by the executive's impulse to share responsibility, and the purely political act is modified in some measure by the natural authoritarian assertiveness of the political leader. Every decision is, to some degree, compounded of shared responsibility and the leader's resoluteness.

Cleveland's thesis is that our growing cultural complexity is having a fundamental effect on the decision-making process, that it is creating the necessity for a wider sharing of responsibility in the typical administrative situation, and that the process is shifting from the administrative pole to the political pole. He is saying, in effect, that the administrative process is becoming *politicalized*. He shows clearly that command from the top as an administrative practice is progressively disappearing and that increasingly in administrative situations there is the horizontal merging of specialized insights and capabilities. As a result, the effective administrator is becoming something of a political broker, one who relates and organizes the needed specialties in a horizontal sharing of power, in contrast to the public executive who, in a less complex time, administered by sending his orders vertically down the organizational pyramid.

One might contend that two different types of public decision-making are involved in this analysis, those at the political end of the spectrum being *policy* in nature, embodying public preferences and programmatic choices and concerned with the ends and objectives of governmental effort, while those at the administrative end are *instrumental* in character, representing decisions that relate to implementing predetermined policies and concerned with the means and strategies of governmental effort.

Cleveland has shown so clearly how the *instrumental* decisions increasingly require the meshing of talents and knowledge possessed by many and the skillful threading through a maze of coequal agencies and institutions. Thus, "a new role, a new function, a new style" is becoming evident among public executives. It is a role of co-ordinating, directing, organizing, and leading in the midst of increasing complexity; it is a function of fashioning appropriately new and adaptable instruments for executing policy; and its style, of necessity, is one that is democratic in spirit, low-key in manner, and respectful of knowledge and capability. Because knowledge is specialized and therefore diffused, power is diffused, and the public executive must know how to organize the diffusion. Can it, perhaps, be argued that there is a corresponding shift from the other end of the political-administrative spectrum? Is there, conceivably, a tendency for the political (policy) decision-making process to become more administrative in character?

As a converse to the Cleveland thesis, is it perhaps possible that the political executive, too, is taking on a new style and that his is less *political* and more *administrative*. Where once the political public executive counted votes and low-keyed the exercise of his authority, is he perhaps today more prone to *administer* policy?

I do not quarrel with Cleveland's thesis that the role of the executive is changing in the direction of a wider sharing of power. I think that he has persuasively demonstrated the point. I think that it is important, however, that we identify the different types of governmental decision-making and that we differentiate between the administrators whose responsibilities tend to be policy-oriented and those whose responsibilities tend to be instrumental.

Cleveland's main point, in my view, is valid, namely, that the effective public executive as viewed traditionally in the study of public administration, finds himself increasingly involved in the horizontal exercise of authority. Granting the validity of this thesis, many questions occur concerning its implication for administrative theory. For example, if diffusion of authority is an inevitable product of social complexity, should the administrative management of such diffusion be institutionalized? Should, for example, we deliberately plan structural forms as alternatives to the classic pyramid?

I happen to operate as mayor in a structurally diffused system, with administrative and legislative authority widely shared among the mayor, the city council, and numerous boards and commissions. I have long complained about the lack of the mayor's executive authority, but I recognize that it has been possible, historically, for individuals, often hidden in the structural maze, to provide creative leadership in particular situations. It would be helpful to know whether the diffusion in the system produces some positive value or whether the external pressures are of a nature to make some measure of constructive policy-formation inevitable, and that with a less diffused structure the constructive results would be much greater.

Does awareness of the Cleveland doctrine argue for less vertical structuring of the power relationship, a partial abandonment, perhaps, of the classic pyramid in favor of some more horizontal arrangement? Is it, perhaps, desirable to recognize formally the new character of the authority of the typical public executive so that public understanding is enhanced?

With respect to procedures, Cleveland's theory explains why decision-making has become so cumbersome, why delays and endless reviewals are inevitable. It certainly explains why it takes so long to accomplish even relatively simply tasks. When power is shared, more persons must be consulted. The question arises, having been made aware of the theoretical relationship, whether we can now devise more expeditious methods of obtaining the required agreements and necessary clearances without increasing the time-lag. In other words, can we invent new forms that will enable the new public executive to perform his functions more rapidly and at the same time retain his effectiveness?

Another question arising from Cleveland's statement is the proper emphasis on decentralization in administration, the moving of the ultimate decision-making responsibility from a central point to a series of regional points. Do we, in fact, aid in the decision-making process, if we do not fully relate such decisions to the availability of the requisite specialties?

Also, the Cleveland thesis should lead us to re-examine some age-old questions that most of us have come to take for granted. For example, are we justified in insisting that a new political administration should have the authority to change all *top* policy-making officials or should we recognize that future decision-making might benefit from carrying over some executives from the previous administration?

Harlan Cleveland's analysis is, as always, provocative and challenging. It relates public administration to the profound changes occurring in society. It is certainly an important contribution to enriching administrative theory.

Comment on Cleveland's Paper

By Eugene H. Nickerson

HARLAN CLEVELAND has perceptively identified the new environment of the American public executive. It is more organizationally fluid and more technically demanding. But, for the American *political* executive, these new functions are best understood and appreciated within the total complex of political and administrative milieu.

To achieve the ideal that Cleveland has set up is difficult. The burden of decision still remains with the political public executive. He must be able to weigh policy matters. He must deal with professional and citizen pressures for new programs and new actions. No change in organization, no modification of procedure, can be instituted without affecting some political participant. And he must be re-elected. Thus, each political participant, be it the bureaucracy, the party, or the industrialist, has certain access and information routes which are available and focus on the public executive. They bar him from making a decision or keeping an operation on keel as easily as Cleveland would suggest.

In short, our job is not easy. We must administer a government, *and* we must be re-elected. We must provide services, *and* we must reconcile interests. Unless our entire political system is changed, these forces and limits will remain very real and important factors in any executive's functions, style, and purpose.

On the other hand, the quality of a chief executive can make a very great difference in the workings of government within those limitations. I refer specifically to a spirit of personal leadership that far surpasses the "traffic cop" functions which Cleveland cites in the case of the air boss on the flight deck or the hero in the escalator incident.

A good chief executive must force the pace of government; and at this stage of history, he is still able to do so at all levels of government.

This ability can still play a forceful role in setting programs and people in motion even within the changing role of the

American public executive vis-a-vis his changed executive environment, which Cleveland has analyzed so well.

The continuing extension of scientific developments into the arena of public responsibility has ranged from production of interplanetary spacecraft to the design of devices to eliminate water pollution and to medical equipment. How does a public executive decide which program is most feasible or monitor its operation? How does he select the program which is most in the public interest? Clearly, these decisions and roles are not easy, and he cannot make every decision. He must immerse himself in modern program complexities. He must seek the advice and counsel of all supporting specialists and technicians. He must continually encourage interaction and cross-communication. He must delegate a certain amount of staff decision-making. But he himself must set the tone, pace, and goals which guide all decisions.

Cleveland has clearly posited a new style and purpose of the American public executive. I would suggest two qualifications to his description.

First, when we speak of public executive, we must clearly differentiate between the *political* public executive and the *administrative* public executive. The political chief executive's office is the apex where government and politics must coalesce. My role as county executive of 1,500,000 people and a budget of $250 million is quite different from the roles of any of my three deputies or any of my departmental commissioners. Obviously, this distinction prevails in any federal, state, or local public environment. Cleveland's article is more consistent with the administrative executive role.

Second, the functions, style, and purposes described by Cleveland are applicable to only a relatively small number of American political executives, namely, the President, some state governors, some mayors, and some county executives. For the great majority of the more than 30,000 public executives, workdays remain substantially unaffected in any direct way by the "technostructure." The programs of public works, welfare administration, police protection, health and mental health administration, for example, may utilize computers to speed up mechanical operations. However, most of their operations remain untouched by advanced management techniques.

Cleveland has set up an ideal model of how an American public executive is likely to operate. However, there are a number of powerful forces constantly seeking to constrain and divert the *political* public executive in the decision-making processes with respect both to daily operations and daily policy-making. They must not be minimized or neglected since they mitigate against the political executive both in making decisions and in overseeing operations. They obstruct the public executive in the formulation of his new "ethical burden."

I group these forces in the following three major categories.

INSTITUTIONAL FORCES

Cleveland has isolated the public executive within the administrative structure. However, the judiciary, the legislature, and his own bureaucracy constantly seek to influence the public executive's decisions. Additionally, a significant portion of American public executives have limited executive power. Most state constitutions diffuse power among many elected and other officials and boards. Municipal charters are subject to state regulation. Local public officials are severely restrained by local legislatures. Each of these factors serves to retard change.

The resources at the command of the bureaucracy in particular are enormous. Bureaucracies have their own staffs specialized in each particular field of interest. They can reveal information as they see fit and retain some information which a "traffic cop" executive, rather than a "leader" executive, may never ferret out for his own use. In their enthusiasm for specific programs or out of fear that their power positions will be attenuated, department heads and their subordinates may, at times, seek to "slant" information, deliberately and discriminately. How, then, is the political executive to gain information and make a decision as described in the Cleveland frame of reference?

Max Weber clearly recognized this in the early 1900's:

Under normal conditions, the power position of a fully developed bureaucracy is always overtowering. The "political master" finds himself in the position of the "dilettante" who stands opposite the "expert" facing the trained official who stands with the management of administration . . . . Every bureaucracy seeks to increase the superiority of the professionally informed by keeping their knowledge and intentions secret.

The increasing specialization described by Cleveland heightens the difficulty faced by a political executive in understanding the range of problems presented to him. He is thus faced with the decision of attempting to immerse himself in detail in every problem, which he cannot generally do, or relying upon his staff of department heads and advisors. This latter alternative presents a further, most serious problem of finding talented people who also are trustworthy. The result is that many chief executives select those who are either trustworthy (generally of the same political party) or those who are highly specialized in their field, generally unknown, and sometimes of questionable rapport and loyalty.

The political public executive must evaluate decisions in terms of his personal perspective, which lies outside merely technical, efficiency objectives. He must bear the greatest burden of this responsibility. Richard Neustadt described this principle in *Presidential Power*:

A president needs all the guarding he can get . . . . And he, himself, the layman in most areas of policy, has no better protector than concern for his own power.

Operational Limits

In Cleveland's ideal, the executive is pictured as being able to watch over his operation and make decisions when trouble arises. There are a number of practical, operating limits on this process. The institutional constraints outlined above sometimes serve to obscure the quantity and quality of information reaching the public executive. If he tries to avoid an active role, relies on his staff, and permits them to make all decisions, he jeopardizes his position.

Assuming that he is confronted with a problem, as Cleveland suggests, what are some of the other limits in the decision-making process? There are limits of time allocated to administering (and to campaigning). There are limits of money, manpower, and over-all cost and benefit. There are limits to the amount of particular time he can devote to analysis and discussion of issues; always, there is the need for additional argument and consideration. There are the limits of previous commitments, perhaps of his own party, perhaps of his own previous decisions with which he must live.

These are real limits that tarnish the Cleveland ideal.

Community Forces

Perhaps the most influential forces pressuring the public executive are those generated by groups within his constituency. These include political parties, including his own; other local and state and federal governmental jurisdictions; commercial enterprises; labor interests; leisure and social societies; manufacturing and heavy-industry groups; various professional organizations; church and civic associations; and the press.

Most analyses by students of community power structure indicate that the real power in a community often resides in a relatively few men, who may or may not include a government man, possessing substantial financial resources in relation to the community.

To effectuate programs vis-a-vis Cleveland's "new ethical burden," a political executive must convince this amorphous power structure of the efficacy of his programs. Here again, what I consider to be the key to a successful chief executive—active leadership—will determine whether this substantial political pressure is used to mobilize a program. The passive executive will be led by the pressure.

In either case, decisions must be based upon consideration of these voices. Furthermore, and most importantly, the voices significantly affect the decisions of legislative bodies upon whom the chief executive is dependent for resources.

This problem is particularly acute at the state and local level. Here, governments are local and by definition accessible. Each program, therefore, has immediate, definable, and vocal adherents and antagonists. The public executive characterized by Cleveland would have a difficult time indeed sustaining his low key and soft touch within this environment.

I would suggest that the American political executive should be far from low key. A strong executive with strong convictions can still succeed in today's changed environment. There is an urgent need for more energetic and committed leaders to enter and transform individual governments. It has been done before, and it can be done now.

Conference Discussion on the Objectives of the Practice of Public Administration

CLEVELAND: It seems to me that Steve's definition produced discussion because it says that there ought to be politically legitimated goals, that there ought to be constitutionally mandated means. I would argue that there always are. The trouble is that some of the political forms of legitimation are more attractive than others.

That so many kinds of legitimations and constitution-making are so unattractive to us here partly reflects the nature of the society in which we have grown up and in which we have learned about public administration. In this sense, we are at the frontier of the development of the subject, not only because our society is more scientific, more technological, and more complex, but most of all because we have set out to do something really quite extraordinary in the United States—to run a society in which nobody is in charge. Consequently, we are in the process of developing theory to explain what seems to be a new state of mind in the world. Today, we actually believe that it is possible—indeed, that it is probably technologically imperative—to have a society where nobody is in charge, where there is no ultimate decision-maker, where everything is checked and balanced, and where the kinds of tensions to which Steve Bailey refers do, in fact, countervail each other enough to make sure that nobody runs very far with the ball on any one play.

In that type of society, certain kinds of people make the most effective leaders, and we need disproportionately more of them as complexity gets more compounded. I have tried in my paper to describe several of the characteristics which they must have. The most interesting of these, for purposes of view of this colloquy, is that today's leaders should be increasingly responsible for deciding where they are going, where their organization is going, and where it ought to be going.

I rather expected those who criticized my paper to object that public administrators should not really write all their own legislation, draft all their own presidential speeches which they will use later themselves as their "politically legitimated" mandate. Maybe my doctrine did not seem so shocking to the two critics of my paper because they are both political executives. In any case, the critics tended to concentrate on the normative questions: Where *should* we be going? Why is there not another section of the paper telling us where we *ought* to go? What *are* the proper goals? In short, the criticisms reveal a felt need to investigate more thoroughly the area of normative theory—and that is comparatively new business in the field of public administration. We have touched the corners of the "why" and "where" questions, but have reached only the unsurprising conclusion that everything is related to everything else—and that, therefore, the public administrator has to be an expert on everything. But if we are going to train people, especially adults in mid-career, as the administrators of the future, we really have to persuade them that nobody is going to tell them where to go if they do not know themselves. They have to work it out for themselves. The provision of a certain degree of inner-directness, focused around the values of Western society, is going to be an increasingly important part of the process of training the public administrator. It had better be. Over to you, Art.

NAFTALIN: I am very much taken with Cleveland's thesis, as you know from my written commentary. My experience confirms his view of the *horizontal* exercise of authority: the importance, for example, of the administrator with the high boiling point, one who can put together all the complex components of a problem. He has the view of what should be done and the capacity to stay with it, through confusion and frustration, negotiating and compromising to a final resolution of conflict. These administrative types emerge with a special personal force in response to the failure in our system to provide mechanisms through which power can be accumulated. They emerge in response to the fragmented character and the inefficiency and the inadequacy of our governmental framework. These types provide the integrating force for the administrative process. They make it work.

I wondered, as I read Cleveland's paper, whether what he is describing is simply an expedient adjustment to a system that has become completely inadequate. I worry also about administrators becoming politicians. There is something alarming in the notion that the administrator is the one who holds the luncheon, works over the contending parties, and fashions the compromise deal. This is certainly at the opposite pole of what we have regarded as the role of the city manager or chief administrator who, presumably, never is involved in determining goals or objectives but just automatically and objectively administers the law without introducing his own preferences. Meanwhile, at the other end of the spectrum, as I constructed it in my paper, is the politician. My spectrum is meant to suggest that at one end there is *administrative* behavior and at the other end *political* behavior. I wonder if the role of the politician is undergoing a complementary change, if he is becoming less the politician and more the administrator, and perhaps in response to the same forces that are making the administrator more the politician. I am suggesting that the political leader now administers the policies produced for him by his staff and by the line administrators.

CLEVELAND: He has to do that, does he not, in order to arrogate, in our kind of society, enough political power? If he is going to be in politics, it is necessary for him to become more and more an administrator.

NAFTALIN: Probably so. I was going to offer an illustration in my paper, but I did not know quite how to handle it. I was thinking of President Johnson and Vietnam and was wondering if the policy that the President finds himself administering is not really the product of the specialists, Rusk, MacNamara, and Westmoreland, who, in their turn, accept and administer policies determined by their subordinates who are even more specialized. I get the sense that here is the chief executive behaving not quite like the politician but rather like an administrator. In the same way, I find that, as mayor, my program is often the product of the administrative and technical specialists and that, more and more, our City Co-ordinator (very much like a chief administrative officer) is called upon to advance and support publicly programs that are highly political, such as urban renewal and public housing. We do not expect him to be neutral as we once did. Thus, Cleveland's thesis, I think, is very suggestive.

I mentioned in my paper that I operate in a highly diffused system with many boards and commissions and with the City Council serving as an administrative body. I have been a fierce advocate of reorganization that would place the mayor at the top of a conventional administration pyramid. I still strongly favor this reform, but I have, from time to time, speculated as to whether there may be some mysterious wisdom in the diffusion. I recall Harlan's piece in the *Public Administration Review* some years ago, in which he described the horizontal character of administration in colleges and universities, and such diffusion has been, because of my experience, a constant preoccupation with me. There may be some real strength in it. It takes forever to accomplish very much, but it has a certain kind of stability and continuity. I sometimes wonder, if this form of diffused structure were to be deliberately institutionalized, whether we might not evolve a mechanism of value. There is no doubt that the system about which I have long complained has certain advantages and certain elements of strength. It is precisely this kind of exploration that I have in mind when I say that I think new theoretical approaches may be helpful in public administration.

At another level, the question of diffusion is further relevant. I am thinking about the fragmentation of authority that exists in every metropolitan area. In my area—the Twin Cities of Minneapolis and St. Paul—we have some four hundred governmental units, and it appears most unlikely that we will ever have reorganization that will give us an integrated governmental approach. How can we get meaningful action from governments that share the authority for public policy. Are there, perhaps, elements of strength in this particular form of horizontal diffusion? Is there, perhaps, a form of specialization among the units that has value? If so, what are the approaches to realizing a larger degree of effectiveness?

Finally, Cleveland's central thesis underscores the growing importance of knowledge and information in public administration. He appears to me to be saying that, in a complex organization, knowledge is power and that is why the specialist comes to share the policy-making or political role. And the administrator who can relate and integrate the knowledge of the individual specialists is the one who will most fully discharge his leadership responsibility. If we are executing an urban renewal program, our administrator must know what bankers and developers and neighborhood leaders have to offer by way of specialized information, and the better he understands their role, the greater his power. I think the development of this central thesis holds many insights for the further development of the theory of public administration.

CLEVELAND: Power is in rank, in other words?

NAFTALIN: That is right.

CLEVELAND: Though, certainly, not necessarily and often not, anyway, in a method of operation.

SHERMAN: I would like to ask a question to help understand Harlan's position. Harlan, the last sentence of your second paragraph, which I take to be a key one, states: "But what that something is, and where the public interest lies, is ultimately for himself [the public executive] to judge." Now, I do not think that the rest of your paper really supports that. Perhaps, in some metaphysical sense, it is always true that each man must judge for himself. Even if he decides to follow somebody else's opinion, this is a judgment he makes himself. But it seems to me that when you get to pages 166–167, what you are really saying is that no longer do the legislature and the chief executive have as much influence over the individual executive's decisions as do the technical people, the groups, and the committees that he must work with. On page 166, you say that growing size is directly correlated with a wide dispersion of real power and more sharing of responsibility; that more decisions are a committee product. So I think that what you are really saying is that the powers that influence the public executive's decisions are different from what they used to be, and not that the public executive himself is making any more decisions than before.

CLEVELAND: The point is that he now has so many options available in his situation of things to be for, so many philosophies to say that he is implementing, and so many potential sponsors for any line of conduct that he decides to follow. He has an enormous and probably growing degree of freedom. But it is freedom defined in a peculiar, interesting, modern sense, a freedom vouchsafed only to those who take the trouble to figure out how their environment works, and who know that it is essentially a bureaucratic environment.

SHERMAN: But, because of the experts, he may have limited freedom. For example, if his engineer tells him that a building will fall down if built in a certain way, that way is virtually precluded.

CLEVELAND: But then there are lots of other engineers. Every administrator constantly has the experience of being told by experts that it cannot work, that it will not happen, that he cannot get the money for it. He overrides much of this with unwarranted optimism, unwarranted by the advice he is given. That is, indeed, his function in life. He does that in our type of complex society by multiplying the expertise, by using committees of experts instead of single experts, by getting competitive expertise, from which he is then able to pick a direction that is technically sound but also compatible with his own administrative and political judgment.

SAYRE: Harlan, if we are to be normative, I am puzzled as to what we are to be normative about. Public administration in the interwar years was highly normative. The report of the President's Committee on Administrative Management is a highly normative document. It is a prescription for the proper organization of the executive branch. The literature through these interwar years is full of these prescriptions—for example, the executive budget, position classification, and optimum span of control. In other words, we have been, in our time, highly normative. Now, in the 1960's and 1970's, what are we to be normative about? about democracy or about constitutionalism, or what?

CLEVELAND: About *order*, or about *ourselves*.

SAYRE: Are we to be political philosophers or what?

CLEVELAND: What I am saying is that because nobody is in charge and because so many of the levers of power are in the hands of the executives in public organizations, it is increasingly hard for the administrator to find anybody to tell him where to go. He increasingly has to work it out for himself. By a social process, not off in a monastic cell, he ultimately is himself in charge of where he goes.

SAYRE: He is to be normative then about policy output.

CLEVELAND: About policy with which he is concerned as an administrator.

SAYRE: He should be partisan about his programs. Is that what you mean by normative?

CLEVELAND: Yes, but even before he has a program, he has to be partisan about the development of that program; about making sure that the phrases that he wants get into that presidential speech or into that law; about the process of political legitimacy, or, if you will, about the substance of what is administered, not merely about the way any substance ought to be administered.

EMMERICH: I am trying to find a way to state this question. The question is: "Is there really an essential difference in administrative behavior and the outlook and operation of an elected and of an appointed executive?" This question is suggested by both the Nickerson and Naftalin papers. At the risk of my question becoming a speech, I would reply (on the basis of observation and conventional wisdom rather than on research) that as the appointed official becomes more and more prevalent in our society, as opposed to our early days when we elected everybody, he tends to identify with his program, with the specialists. He administers in terms of the substantive content of his program, and by God he will fight for it. And if he has career tenure, he has to achieve a balance concerning whether a policy that he advocates will be acceptable to the present administration and to what extent it may last through another. His loyalty is, first of all, to the long-term program. The elected official will tend to give a higher priority of loyalty to the party or to the administration or to the electoral process or to his own electoral succession. Now, this is an entirely different kind of approach. There is a substantial difference between the behavioral outlook and actions of an elected official and those of an appointed one, whose loyalty is to the party, and only incidentally to the program for which he is fighting—although these are not absolute differences, and both the elected and appointed officials may end at the same point, the elected one by becoming identified with a program policy and the appointed one by bowing to some of the electoral pressures. But they start with different assumptions.

WALDO: I wish, Harlan, that you would say something on

the subject of leadership in relation to the other matters in your paper. Now, what you have said impresses me, as far as it goes. As a sometime teacher, you will appreciate the compliment of my saying that your paper is full of good examination questions —splendid, arresting statements that one can quote and use. There is in most of us a receptivity to the idea that power ought to be shared. I understand your argument from the technological imperative, and it ties in with power-sharing on a purely "moral" basis. But then I find myself coming to the line of thought and argument which I have been impressed with, too: that at some point somebody has to be "in charge," has to be a leader. I remember Barnard on *The Functions of the Executive,* and I think of John Gardner's famous speech on the antileadership vaccine, and I really wonder whether society can run without this vital ingredient, whatever it is. I am influenced also, I suppose, by the events at the University of California three years ago when there was a crisis that brought the University, in the words of the day, to a grinding halt. My own interpretation of the events was that some leadership would have prevented that painful result and that, for all of the intelligence and all the skill in manipulation and negotiation, this vital ingredient was absent.

CLEVELAND: Nobody was fully in charge—perhaps, under the circumstances, no one could have been.

WALDO: Nobody was in charge. Certainly not the Chancellor, nor the President. I suspect most of us have the ambivalence that I expressed. Most of us would buy your argument in general terms. But with reference to the Eisenhower administration, we would say: "This was a bad administration." Why was it bad? It was bad because he did not *lead.* This tension between wide participation and leadership is not an insoluble problem, perhaps. I would like to have your thoughts on it.

CLEVELAND: I would argue that the proportion of the population that has to become leaders is going up very rapidly, partly because the leadership on any given subject is so widely shared. Thus, the leadership which most people exercise is not what one might expect; it is the kind of thing where effectiveness at a round table is much more important than effectiveness on a platform. No matter how good-looking he is, if a person is fundamentally stupid, he simply cannot absorb the substance of the problems on which he has to exert some leadership because the issues are too complicated and they require too much homework. Consequently, you do not find fundamentally stupid people running for major elective offices or, if they do, they do not get very far. The kinds of characteristics that I tried to list—which are the consequence of our society's increasing horizontalness—are affecting the kind of people who succeed, not only in administration but even in elective office. And, of course, most of the public leadership jobs are not elective.

UNIDENTIFIED VOICE: I am sure that there is a divergence—or I am not sure that there is—between Herb's interrogatory statement and Harvey's response just now. I would like to lean toward Harlan's latest comment, namely, that there seems to be a convergence between the functions and roles and characteristics of leading people elected to office, not only chief executives but executives at various levels. I do not know whether Harlan meant to say this, but if York can ask a question to make a point, I can make a statement to make a point. I would just call your attention to the fact that many of us have tried to make this kind of description on the administrative side, and I think that one of the best of the attempts has been that of Wally Sayre, when he presented his famous wheel (I do not know whether to call it that) of administration. He put the administrator at the center and then, by segments, defined the various quadrants of influences that seem to come into play. One of them, of course, if I remember correctly, Wally, was the legislative or elected official, chief executive as well as the legislative official, the party pressures, the pressure-group pressures, special-interest pressures, and the professional pressures, not only in professional groups that the administrator himself has to deal with, but among his own professional peers. He has to respond to them because, as a matter of fact, in my judgment, administrators are always worried about their colleagues, particularly those at the universities. And last, but not at all least—and it is of growing importance—is the re-emphasis that I would like to give to York's comment. The public itself, not only a pressure-group public, but a congeries of publics, including the general public now, in one form or another, is getting very articulate. I am going to raise the question whether the really biggest new influence in administration is not about to be—or is not already—the public pressures. And I do not mean only concrete pressure groups represented by each of the bureaus, historically, but public pressures generally, the generality of public pressures, directed upon the administration and the administrators and special pressure groups.

Whether this description of Harlan's is not accurate only insofar as, traditionally, we have made this distinction between our legislative leadership and our administrative leadership, as well as how long this new type of pressure will last, is hard to judge. Whether it is viable in a representative, let alone a democratic, system is something that not all of us are sure about. It may be unworkable to expect the real pressures upon administration to come, not from the appointed chief or the legislative committee to which he reports, or even his own profession or some concrete pressure group, but from this newer direction, which expresses itself by methods of demonstration, as well as by more radical methods of opinion-bearing. I mention this because I think that there is some evidence, though this has to be checked very closely by our fellow social scientists, that there is an upgrade, regardless of whether we are talking about democracies or not, of the understanding or assumed understanding of members of the public, large numbers of the public, about what policies should be and how those policies should be enforced at almost every stage of thinking, making every step of the administrative process, for a change, a controversial question. Now, it may be that this is quite the contrary, but I do not believe it. I believe that in our society generally we are upgrading the articulateness at least of our public. I think that it is something for us to take very seriously, not only as we come to our administrative teaching or learning or research or operations, but also as we define the realm and the role of administration. In fact, if you are going to limit yourself to American administration, in terms of your interests for the next decade, I would say that this is the one single factor: what I would call clientele-customer-constituency administration or participation in the administrative process—participatory administration. I do not think that we are ready for this at all. I am not saying that we should defer to it entirely, and we have to keep ourselves subject-matter pure, technologically pure, and organizationally correct as much as possible, perhaps. But I think that we may be missing one of the main points for discussion at this conference.

MOAK: Well, you are almost suggesting that, as this applies to public education, we are returning to the little red school house in which the parents always told the teacher what to do. Strangely, we have almost reached this point in the Philadelphia school system. All of the segments of the community tell the superintendent what to do, in different ways, every day.

I would like to come back to a point that Cleveland raised earlier about this man in middle passage whom you bring back for additional training. What relative emphasis in this training is going to be placed upon the securing of acceptance of the policies in which he may have an interest versus the carrying out of the programs which are authorized? What kind of emphasis are we going to place on those two facets of development of the man who has become a specialist and now comes back for the postgraduate courses that you mentioned earlier?

CLEVELAND: I think that the central thing at each stage of his career is to immerse himself in his function, to think hard about the process in which he is engaged, including its politics, its norms, and the like. I think that we should place more emphasis in training programs on putting people who are going to be leaders to work in situations where they have to figure out their own sense of direction. They should not wait around for the people-in-general or the newspapers to tell them where they ought to be going, because that is more their business than anybody else's. The tendency in the past has been, rather, to assume a program environment with a sense of direction, where the purpose of the exercise is to try to get to the agreed-upon goal in the best way that one can. That assumption does not seem to be the typical environment anymore.

NAFTALIN: I would like now just to try to tie this exchange which we have just had back to the general consideration of theory of public administration and its spoken objectives. I think that I did some of this when I was in government, probably not unconsciously. I do think that there is a very special function of the public administrator—even though that term has just been written off a bit—or whatever individual we are talking about. I think that he has to have a particular sophistication on the relationship between policy and desirable objectives and implementation. I think that he has to have real skill in that, so that my answer to Len Moak's question would be "both." The administrative man has to have interest both in formulating plans that can be implemented and in implementing plans that have been adopted. He has the particular "know-how" in his field of how to reach a desired goal and of what kind of goal can be reached.

WILLBERN: I would like to comment a little on about two or three of these things that relate to Harvey Sherman's point awhile ago and, much farther back, to Wally Sayre's query to Harlan Cleveland about what is prescriptive, what is normative, what is descriptive, and the like. I would suggest that there are two kinds of normative theory, one of which is only pseudo-normative. If you say, "I would like to go from here to New York," then you can say, "the better way to go is such and such," or "you ought to go by such and such a way." In a sense that is an "ought" statement, a prescription, a normative statement; but I would say that it is pseudo-normative. That is really a descriptive statement—saying, given that certain factors in a relationship are such———

CALDWELL: Steve calls it instrumental.

WILLBERN: Instrumental, yes, that is an instrumental kind of statement. Much of the prescription that we do is pseudo-normative. A goal is assumed, and the choice is made concerning the most effective means. Between the wars, public administration people would prescribe with great force and conviction. These prescriptions rested on two theory assumptions, one of which I would say is really normative and the other descriptive. The really normative theory assumption was the ethical value of democratic government—that the people *ought* to control their government; the descriptive theory was that the most effective way, given the social relationships and so on that we know about, to achieve that goal was through a hierarchical-responsibility relationship—lower levels to the executive, executive to the legislative, and so on. What they were prescribing was really more of the second, or instrumental, level than of the first, or truly normative, level. They were not really questioning the first. This was taken for granted. I have a notion that most (I think that it is correct to say most) of our worry about the wisdom and desirability of a policy can rest upon these descriptive matters. To reduce the traffic in the city, the choice between whether you do it by traffic engineering or by subsidizing transit is a priority choice, but it is not really a normative choice except in this pseudo-normative sense. It can be subjected to careful scientific analysis as to which of those is likely to be more effective.

CHARLESWORTH: Is busing school children pseudo-normative?

WILLBERN: It could well be. Let us put it this way: someone said a while ago that increased participation in administration is a good, a desirable thing, with sharing of power and responsibility. That can rest on either of two bases, and usually rests on a mixture of both. One is that it is just *ipso facto* ethically and aesthetically desirable; it is satisfying to many people. Or the other can be that this is a more effective way of securing certain policy goals which are also held to be desirable. This is capable of being researched, whether or not that last statement is true. And I think that these two things are often combined with each other. I would argue that the ultimates in terms of values—these aesthetic, ethical axioms—are relatively few, and that most of the questions which we have to worry about can at least be analyzed to a far greater degree than we have analyzed them.

WALDO: The conversation came back to a point that Len Moak raised. Briefly, one pro and one con, so to speak. I was arrested by your remarks, Len, because, as you know, they broke a train of thought, took us back to something which we were not thinking of. Your remark that the trend of the conversation would make some of your colleagues ill was an arresting statement, and I think that you have a point there. I would admit that our grand generalizations tend to ignore or gloss over times, places, and circumstances in which they do not seem to be particularly relevant, in which, in fact, they may seem not only irrelevant but pernicious. Paul Appleby used to say that that which is to be decentralized must first be centralized, and that if there is no centralization and order first, then one cannot talk about decentralization. All one has is chaos and confusion. Similarly, with regard to the talk which one hears about doing away with the "merit system" and having a *real* merit system: this move becomes appropriate or relevant only when there has been an intermediate period of a civil service system which introduces a new era and a new set of expectations.

The other point: I understand your reservations on both semantic grounds and strategic grounds against expanding public administration until it seems to include everything. But what I want to call attention to is that the "narrower" or more technical you make it, the less power it has to attract students and to motivate them. I think everyone here who has tried to teach public administration will agree with me on that. Put it this way: I think that the historic textbooks may have had a negative recruitment effect, may have attracted the least imaginative, the more stolid students from a group. Now, in the Depression days it did not make any difference: a job was a job, and government jobs were *good* jobs. Too, an inspiring teacher, a Sam May or a Paul Appleby, could overcome the seeming mechanical quality that was in the textbook and make the subject matter seem important. But certainly, with today's crop of students, if you tell them that public administration is about how you implement government policy efficiently, that it is tools and rules, the better ones are going to leave in droves and you will have the less imaginative ones remaining for the second course.

BAILEY: I would like to comment on York Willbern's statement. I am bothered by his concept of pseudo-normative problems. I may have misunderstood you, York, but if I have understood you, I really do disagree. The question of a new state highway would seem to involve—and there are many engineers who look at it this way—simply a kind of cost-benefit analysis: if one wants a road to go from here to there, what is the straightest line that will cost the least. I would submit that the decisions in the real world of administration are laden, not with pseudo value questions, but with the most fundamental value questions that one can ask. Is it worth the destruction of the scenic beauty of the Grand Canyon to put a road through the Grand Canyon? Is it worth the destruction of an important historical landmark, say, a piece of Georgian classic architecture, to satisfy the engineer's definition of road-building economy? I do not think that these are pseudo value questions at all. I think that they are absolutely fundamental questions, and I think that there are an awful lot of Planning-Programming-Budgeting System (PPBS) types who are way off the track in this. They assume somehow that accomplishing certain kinds of goals can be handled with a slide-rule, that the most efficient way of accomplishing something is in terms of an engineer's cost-benefit analysis. In actual fact, the most efficient way of doing something in slide-rule terms may be the most inefficient way in terms of maximizing values other than dollar economies. The nature of government is that one is constantly confronted with value trade-offs in the implementation of policies, and I do not think that these involve pseudo values. They are of the heart of the day-to-day value problems of government.

EMMERICH: Steve, did you happen to see the beautiful case study in an article on the problems that they have encountered in routing the new London–South Wales motorway through England? It was odd that you should just happen to choose that topic as an example, but you might be amused by the two excellent essays by Roy Gregory, in *Public Administration*, entitled "The Minister's Line, or the M-4 Comes to Berkshire."[1]

LEPAWSKY: Rowland Egger, some twenty years ago, described in our *Public Administration Review*, I believe, a similar issue which arose in his home, Charlottesville, Virginia. But if you concern yourself primarily with descriptive science in a technological society, you will be driven into a corner and will have to confine yourself to pseudo norms, minor decisions, and matters of mechanics. Besides, we have made considerable progress in public administration with the ends-and-means chain and can now treat the meandering borderline between the two more assuredly than previously. Still, one can easily get involved in a series of questions of shrinking significance. Before you know it, your ultimate question could become, "If I make this or that decision can I be elected to this-or-that post, or will I be fired from this or that job?" And then you may really be receding into the lower levels of decision-making.

CHARLESWORTH: That is why I asked the question about busing the school children.

LEPAWSKY: Yes, and the ultimate decision in your life is,

[1] Roy Gregory, "The Minister's Line, or the M–4 Comes to Berkshire," *Public Administration* (London), Vols. 44 and 45 (Summer 1967 and Autumn 1967).

"Do I go to heaven or do I go to hell if I make this kind of emphasis or the other kind of emphasis?" But I think that we, as practical academicians and academic practitioners both, should try and make some tentative decisions here concerning which way we lean with respect to this basic issue that is again presented to us in Bailey's latest remark—and, I think, in Cleveland's paper, in a different form. I do not want to drive us into an attempt at consensus, but I certainly hope that we attempt to do some rethinking toward a consensus, without in any way uttering any conclusions at this conference.

CHARLESWORTH: I know that we have to adhere to our timetable, but I want to put a question to the group. I would like you to think about this question this evening and give our committee here an answer tomorrow morning. It is quite evident that the greater part of the conversation here has subsumed a high position for the administrator. We have been talking about department heads and mayors and ambassadors. We have not been talking about modest bureau heads and the like. Now, I would like you to give your editors some instruction on that. Are we to have a little Foreword in this volume saying that we are talking about policy-making administrators, and not mere implementers? Would you think about that one, please?

SHERMAN: The question has a wrong premise.

CHARLESWORTH: What is wrong about it, Harvey?

SHERMAN: There are no such things as *mere* implementers according to Harlan's paper and my own view. Certainly, every supervisor at every level makes policy of certain kinds.

CHARLESWORTH: There is only a slight difference between 59 degrees and 60 degrees, but there is a lot of difference between freezing and boiling. When the degree of difference becomes sufficiently great, it becomes a difference in kind. That is what I am talking about.

BAILEY: Well, Jim, I was listening to what Harvey was saying, and I agree with him. The difference is between 59 and 60 degrees, and not between freezing and boiling. You take these so-called specialists operating at the low levels, say, GS-9's. As I observed GS-9's around Washington, if they are bright and concerned with specific aspects of public policy, they are often extraordinarily influential.

UNIDENTIFIED VOICE: Nevertheless, as Jim put the problem, our records should reveal, not the answer to the problem as he puts it, but the proposition that is now being restated around the table. If Jim is wrong, that the difference is not between freezing and boiling but between 59 and 60 degrees, or to put it more accurately, between freezing and the next degree above, if I can move you along the scale, that, too, is an important issue to which we will have to address ourselves: to say something about the differential in questions raised concerning policy-making.

CHARLESWORTH: I see that I might have made a mistake by recruiting only important people for this conference. I should also have brought in a couple of letter-carriers, to see what they had to say about whether everybody is a policy-maker. The letter-carrier might go down this side of the street first or go down that side of the street first. Nobody cares about that, and that is not public policy. I submit that there is a difference.

Methodology in the Theory of Public Administration

By Lynton K. Caldwell

1. IT would be easy to demonstrate in a few brief sentences that the title "Methodology in the Theory of Public Administration" is not susceptible of intelligible discussion. The conceptual and operational referents of the title are not self-evident, nor do they represent commonly understood and agreed-upon definitions. In a word, the title is ambiguous, and it is the author's task to make of it what he can.

2. The conceptual and semantic difficulties associated with the term "public administration" suggest the expedient of abandoning the expression in favor of an alternative more clearly congruent with the phenomenon to which the term allegedly refers. But it is difficult to jettison a term that enjoys conventional currency in favor of some new expression that would be unfamiliar, would probably imply a restructuring of knowledge regarding government and administration, and, in consequence, would require a reorganization of that knowledge as expressed in the structure of universities. Yet, even if the term is retained, its conventional content will have to be changed, and the resulting intellectual and institutional inconvenience will have to be endured, if the concept "public administration" is to remain fully viable. In time, an approximating term, perhaps "macroadministration," may replace "public administration" in scholarly usage. This replacement would occur most probably in a society in which *all* large-scale administration, however organized, had come to be perceived as "public," thus rendering the term "public" redundant. This latter circumstance would appear to prevail in the Soviet Union and the People's Republic of China. In a *functional* sense the activities of all large-scale organizations in the United States and other advanced technological societies have become public, although their political economies may continue to distinguish the public and governmental from the private and personal, particularly as regards the ownership and management of property.

3. If, as this essay is premised, the term "public administration" refers generally to an aspect of social behavior of highest importance, if the term as commonly understood is increasingly incongruent with the set of operations to which it ostensibly refers, and if the existing term cannot be easily replaced by one more generally satisfactory, the primary task of theory would appear to be one of redefinition. The term "public administration" must be reinterpreted so as to have continuing operational validity. The main body of this paper will, therefore, be concerned with the alternatives available for a realistic theory of public administration and with the methods by which such theory may most effectively be validated. But before this is attempted, it will be useful to consider briefly why we have not heretofore developed a satisfactory body of theory concerning public administration and why it has become necessary for us to do so now.

Why a Theory of Public Administration?

4. If the expression "public administration" made no sense whatever, its survival during the past half-century would be hard to explain. The difficulty with the term is that it has had a contemporary and conventional utility, but its meaning has failed to adapt to the changing phenomena that it purports to describe. It once described, with apparent satisfaction, an aspect of government to which Woodrow Wilson directed the attention of scholars in his essay on "The Study of Administration" (1887). Public administration, as an American academic concept, took shape in the years between the initial efforts of the American Political Science Association (1911-1914) to promote university training for the public service, and the publication of Leonard D. White's *Introduction to the Study of Public Administration* (1926). White's book, and the first academic courses in public administration, appeared during the presidency of Calvin Coolidge, when the distinctions implied by the terms "public," "personal," "governmental," and "private" enjoyed a transitory appearance of clarity. The clarity was specious, and the actualities of American public life became progressively inconsistent with conventional concepts. But academic public administration was cast in a mold which corresponded to this contemporaneous set of assumptions,

and was not easily reshaped to be consistent with the social and technological changes that transformed the nation and the world in the ensuing decades.

5. The increasing incongruity between the form and content of academic public administration and the world of public events has been noted with dissatisfaction by numerous critics both within and without the field of study. There has been growing recognition that we have no satisfactory generalizing theories of public administration that are operationally reliable. And there has also been a growing body of belief that, in the absence of a more adequate understanding of administration as a generic social process, no operationally valid theories of public administration are likely to be developed.

6. It would be easy to blame the leaders of academic public administration for not taking more seriously the growing conceptual and semantic problems of the field of study. In their defense, however, several extenuating circumstances should be pointed out. Most importantly, perhaps, the American people and their political leaders have not been notably enthusiastic about the study of public administration, in any sense. At best, their sympathies have been bounded by conventional assumptions regarding the role of government in society and the nature of organizational behavior. Academic public administration tended to become what it was widely assumed to be: training for the contemporary civil service. The rapid growth of government, particularly at the federal level during the 1930's, not only stimulated training efforts, but drew the attention of scholars to the analysis and description of new governmental agencies and programs. Administrative case-writing refined and enlarged the body of descriptive literature and simultaneously revealed ramifications and complexities in the actual process of public administration that lay beyond its conventional academic interpretations.

7. To the limitations of public sympathy, and to the preoccupation with contemporaneous tasks of training and description, there needs also to be added the handicap of an inadequate basic behavioral science. The leaders of academic public administration might have more readily supported a better way of organizing its study *if* that better way had been readily apparent. In the absence of a demonstrably superior way of conceptualizing the

study of public administration, conventional assumptions prevailed. But we have now reached a point of development at which new and more realistic concepts of public administration not only are possible, but are necessary. Behavioral science and organization theory are now able to contribute significantly to the informational base which students of administration, public or otherwise, have been constructing. Moreover, emerging social and political developments are adding urgency to the formulation of operationally valid theories of public administration. The public efforts of our times cannot be sustained by assumptions as widely discrepant from reality as those which may have served academic public administration well enough in the past, but can no longer do so today.

8. We need an operationally valid theory of public administration in order to exercise wise and effective control over those far-reaching social developments of our times for which history offers little guidance by way of precedent. Administration in *any* context is a business of coping with uncertainty, but the rapid, far-reaching, and frequently irreversible nature of the changes induced by present-day man, make ad-hoc experiment a costly and dangerous way to proceed over unfamiliar terrain. The task of theory is, therefore, to provide, so far as feasible, a systematic organization of all knowledge relevant to understanding administrative behavior; to reveal, so far as possible at any given time, the gaps and inadequacies in that knowledge; and to provide validated bases for projecting alternative courses of action and their probable costs and consequences. Most importantly, it is in the larger aspects of organized human behavior in which complex organizations and multiorganizations interact to constitute national and international affairs that operationally valid theories of public administration are needed to enable men to foresee and, if possible, to control, the consequences of their collective action.

9. To reject the attempt to marshal all knowledge pertinent to administrative behavior on the ground that the goal is unattainable is to misconstrue the purpose of the effort. Human knowledge is always an imperfect understanding of reality; the significance of knowledge changes with time; and the absolute totality of existing knowledge can probably never be organized systematically. Nevertheless, the pursuit of complete understanding is

the ultimate objective of science. If we cannot know the limits of our own capacity to learn and to understand, is it not more prudent to pursue this unattainable goal than to constrain the reach of our knowledge by self-imposed limitations? It is the *effort* toward comprehensive understanding that I urge. The goal lies in the effort, not in the attainment of the unattainable. Comprehensiveness, and freedom from constraints not imposed by the phenomena of administration itself, are thus characteristics of a methodology of theory that holds promise for advancing our understanding of public administration, however defined.

Alternative Approaches to Theory

10. The first step toward theory is identification of the phenomenon to which it relates. If the purpose sought through theory is a firmer basis for understanding and for the advancement of practical knowledge, then the validity of theory depends upon its consistency with objective reality. To be adequate, a theory must have taken into account the essential elements of the phenomena that it purports to describe. To pull out from the total functional phenomena some part, which is then treated as if it were the whole, will not provide a reliable basis for a theory of the whole. As with conventional definitions of public administration that have been bound by parochial, cultural, or academic perceptions, the convenience of a manageable body of subject matter is obtained at the price of ultimate futility. This approach can only lead to a dead end of self-imposed limitation.
11. The total functional system is the field of relevance, and nothing less is the proper scope of theory. Parts of the total field may, of course, be studied separately if their relationship to the whole is taken into account. But a theory of public administration must identify its total field of relevance, not because it will attempt explanation of everything that is relevant, but in order to obtain as far as possible an accurate estimate of the form, scope, and internal-external relationships of the phenomenon. One should not infer that the tasks of theory cannot be successfully undertaken until all parameters of the relevant phenomenon have been identified. This identification of parameters and the mapping of the field of relevance *is* the primary task of

theory. It is, moreover, most realistically perceived as a continuing task of extending, modifying, refining, and reorganizing our understanding of the phenomena of public administration. The task is not likely to be finished short of the advent of Roderick Seidenberg's Posthistoric age.

12. To begin to identify the phenomenon of public administration, it is necessary to clarify the semantic confusion surrounding the term and its associated concepts. The term cannot faithfully represent the phenomenon as long as its referents are confused. At least three alternative concepts of "public administration" are available as avenues toward theory. Each has had its advocates and has influenced the study of public administration in the United States and abroad. But these three distinguishable concepts of public administration, whatever other merits or advantages they may have, are not equally productive of the advancement of knowledge or the development of theory. This categorization of viewpoints should be understood as a convenient method of analyzing the conceptual basis for theories of public administration. They are not "water tight" intellectual compartments, nor can most students of public administration be assigned a fixed place in any of them. Nevertheless, at particular times and places, these concepts have been held by particular scholars and have been evidenced in the curricula of universities. With the hope that the reader will not take these categories more seriously than the writer has intended, they may be summarized as follows:

(1) The phenomena of public administration are unique; the variables associated with each administrative act make comparative study or generalizing theory impractical.

(2) Public administration is a complex but coherent class of phenomena, different in its more important aspects from any other aspect of behavior to which the term "administration" has been applied. This concept affords a limited basis for comparative study, generalization, and theory-construction, but it encounters difficulties that may be insuperable in defining its parameters.

(3) Public administration is an aspect of the more comprehensive social phenomenon called "administration." Based

upon an understanding of administration as a generic social process, the principal semantic problem in this concept involves the meanings attributable to the word "public." Unless the term "public" can be applied to a universally valid referent, this concept of public administration may find itself backed into the same culturebound cul-de-sac that frustrates the preceding concept.

13. Regarding the first of these concepts, little need be said. If all administrative actions are unique, the scope of theory can be hardly more than an attempt to explain the singularity of the phenomena. This concept obviates public administration as a field of analytic research or of preservice training. The administrative activities of public officials are perceived to be derivative mixtures of personality-endowment, subjective experience, and circumstance. This atomistic concept of public administration provides no rationale for theory in any significant sense, as it assumes that the phenomena are not amenable to generalization. Thus, it follows that the academic study of public administration would be largely restricted to description.

14. The second concept—public administration as a distinctive and independent class of phenomena—is not easily defined. This is primarily because it represents a range of interpretation extending from the atomistic concept of uniqueness to the concept of administration as a generic social process. Within this range fall the interpretations of public administration that have been predominant in the American academic community.

15. Within this general concept, there are differences of interpretation involving semantics of the term "public administration" itself. The meanings attributed to the term appear to influence the perceptions of the phenomenon to which it refers. Opinion within this concept of public administration has been divided over whether the phenomenon is monistic (a discrete class of phenomena fundamentally unlike any other) or is syzygyous (public and administration correlatively yoked together to form, in the Linnean sense, a distinctive order in the class of phenomena called administration).

16. Public administration from the first viewpoint would more accurately be spelled "publicadministration." In the lexicon of

American academia, "publicadministration" has referred to the activities of the executive and independent civil agencies of conventional political government. The phenomenon has been perceived as fundamentally distinct from administration in other contexts, for example, in business; and even governmental administration within judicial courts or military establishments has usually been held to be beyond its purview.[1] Similarities between "publicadministration" and other aspects of organizational behavior have been considered to be superficial. For example, "publicadministration" and business administration have been said to resemble one another only in their relatively unimportant aspects, and neither field of study could be expected to yield knowledge or insight useful in the other. This interpretation of public administration is now seldom articulated, but was assumed in Leonard D. White's *Introduction to the Study of Public Administration* (1926). It may still have a kind of tacit acceptance among those persons who see the study of public administration as belonging almost exclusively to the discipline of political science.

17. From the second viewpoint, public administration appears as one of a number of species of the class of behavior called administrative. This interpretation approaches, but does not quite reach, the point of viewing public administration as essentially an aspect of the general phenomenon of administration.[2] Public administration, business administration, education administration, police administration, and hospital administration are different kinds of

[1] The evidence appears in the earlier textbooks on public administration, for example, Leonard D. White, *An Introduction to the Study of Public Administration* (New York: The Macmillan Company, 1926).

[2] I would associate the earlier work of John Pfiffner as illustrative of this viewpoint, for example, see *Research Methods in Public Administration* (New York: Ronald Press, 1940); and Luther Gulick and L. Urwick (eds.), *Papers on the Science of Administration* (New York: Institute of Public Administration, 1937) as marking the crossover to a generic theory of administration. But it would be unfair to type any individual with a particular concept, first, because a scholar's viewpoint may change in the course of his lifetime, and second, because his written work may reflect the prevailing academic orientation, and not his more advanced thinking. This possibility is especially pertinent in the case of textbook writers. At the close of his career, Leonard White's concept of public administration was much broader than his published work, and John Pfiffner has continued over the years to be an innovative thinker.

administration whose differences are as significant as their similarities. This conceptualization permits comparisons among the several kinds of administration. It does not, however, require the postulation of a generic process of administration of which these various types of administration are aspects.

18. This conceptualization of public administration as a distinctive aspect of behavior, independent of all other phenomena, suffers a major semantic difficulty in the meaning of the word "public." Failure to find a universally valid referent for this word has been a major cause of parochialism in the study of public administration in the United States, and has been a major handicap to the development of theory. From its very beginning in the exhortation of Woodrow Wilson to American scholars, academic public administration in the United States has been artificially bounded by particular circumstances of time, place, and culture. Public administration was not, and could not be, studied with the methods of science. It was instead a normative, pragmatic response to the demands made upon government by a society in transition from a decentralized, agrarian state to an interdependent, urbanized, technological society. This context, however, tended to deprive the study of public administration of historical depth.[3] There was little interest in placing contemporary developments in public administration or government on a time trajectory in which their possible futures might be conjectured. Thus, poverty in the historical dimension of public administration, as studied in the United States, meant also impoverishment in the substance of public administration theory.

19. Public administration, as understood throughout most of its academic history in the United States, has been a concept of very limited transferability. This is largely attributable to the fact that the term "public," in the lexicon of American public administration, has customarily been used in a restrictive legal sense. In this sense "public" has usually been equated with "governmental." The consequences of this usage become evident if one attempts to compare the scope and substance of public administration in the United States, France, and the Soviet Union.

[3] Leonard D. White's notable volumes, and occasional articles in scholarly reviews and papers presented at meetings of the American Society for Public Administration do not refute the generally nonhistorical bias of American academic public administration.

20. There is a functional-descriptive sense in which all large-scale organized activities in these and other countries can be compared, regardless of legal status. But culturebound assumptions regarding the meaning of "public" do not permit this comprehensive approach to be fully exploited. Not only is culturebound interpretation of the term "public" nontransferable, but it is also vulnerable to the changing perceptions of publicness that occur within particular cultures over periods of time. A major handicap to theory and practice in public administration in the United States today is the slowness of their adaptation to space-age realities. New concepts of administrative organization and action have been widely publicized: for example, project-management, matrix organization, and structural innovation in uniting the respective skills of government, industry, and universities for attack upon large social problems. But there has yet been only minor evidence of change in the perceptions that are reflected in public administration as taught in the universities or as verbalized in public life. The heretofore generally accepted academic concept has been comfortable to live with, but has not proved helpful in guiding us toward more effective ways of dealing with the complex social problems of our times. In brief, the semantic difficulties inherent in the concept of "public administration," as a phenomenon different and apart from all other aspects of administration, outweigh, so far as theory-construction is concerned, whatever advantages the concept may otherwise possess.

21. If persistence of the term "public administration" is not to be obstructive of a realistic approach toward understanding organizational behavior, the meaning of the term itself must be made consistent with what actually happens in society, and not merely with a culturebound interpretation of what happens. This is not the place to argue the epistemological question of how much we can know about what actually happens. It is sufficient for our purposes to obtain a definition of public administration for which a valid set of corresponding operations may be identified and to which the term is therefore applicable regardless of how particular societies or individuals elect to perceive it. Comparative studies of politics, government, and business will continue to explore the nature and significance of cultural differences in administrative behavior. But comparative study of public adminis-

tration will have practical utility only to the extent that it is possible to distinguish generic from variable elements. A generic sociology of the administration of public affairs is a necessary concomitant to a valid comparative study of public administration.

22. The approach to a theory of public administration that seems most likely to possess operational validity is the previously suggested third alternative. Public administration under this concept is neither a unique nor an independent class of phenomena. It is instead an aspect of a form of organized social behavior called administration. The connotation of "public" is not legal status, but involvement in the collective or communal affairs. Public administration loses its syzygial character; "public" becomes an adjective, modifier of the noun "administration." In this context, "public" must have a meaning of universal applicability. Webster's definition—"of, relating to, or affecting the people as an organized community"—if functionally interpreted, would seem sufficiently general. The test of the relevance of any institution or event for the student of public administration would, therefore, be the extent of its involvement in or impact upon public affairs. To illustrate: in the pluralistic technological society of mid-twentieth century America, the Boeing Corporation or the United Automobile Workers *may be* as significantly involved in public administration as the Post Office Department or the Office of Indian Affairs.

23. Although the degree of publicness is not necessarily commensurate with the magnitude of an operation or event, the very large undertakings in society inevitably assume a public character. The public aspect of these efforts, whether of national defense, telecommunication, or the manufacture of automobiles, is public or macroadministration. The internal management of individual firms and government agencies is essentially microadministration and is relevant to public administration only in so far as policies, procedures, or technical operations impinge directly upon community interests. There is no impervious barrier between the macro and micro aspects of administration, and the student of public administration will inevitably be concerned at both levels. But the major concern of public administration is not with the management of organizations, for as James D. Thompson has written: "Social purposes in modern societies increasingly exceed

the capacities of complex organizations, and call instead for action by multi-organization complexes."[4] The largest of these complexes are the larger national governments, but the largest national and international industrial technostructures exceed, by most measures, the magnitude of lesser national governments.

24. The public administration of the future, whatever its *form*, will in *function* be the co-ordination, nurture, protection, and direction of *res publica*, the public affairs of society. The methodological approach to a theory of public administration, so conceived, would be concerned with government in the sociological sense, and not merely as defined by law or custom. It would include, but not be bound by, presumptions of law or culture. It would be concerned with generic phenomena, not with transitory classifications of governmental, nongovernmental, personal, and private. It would not ignore the realities of cultural variables in the phylogeny of societies and the ontogeny of organizations, but would treat them *as* variations in the generic process of administration conceived as a universal human experience.

Costs—Methods—Opportunities

25. In a world of unprecedented change, requiring new forms of public effort—where the time-span for action is frequently compressed—usable, reliable knowledge is of highest value. For the administration of *res publica*, where the outcomes affect the welfare and survival of the whole society, a large fund of usable knowledge is needed as a frame of reference against which to estimate the effects of policies and actions. A general theory of administration with emphasis upon its public or large-scale aspects affords the most adequate basis for organizing and extending this fund of knowledge. But the advantage cannot be realized without payment of intellectual and institutional costs.

26. The intellectual costs of a viable theory of public administration are twofold. The first and more difficult of these is a reorientation of thinking about the emerging structure of late-twentieth-century society and of the institutional relationships through which it operates. The inadequacies of conventional

[4] James D. Thompson, *Organizations in Action: Social Science Bases of Administrative Theory* (New York: McGraw-Hill, 1967), p. 157.

narrow-based concepts of public administration became evident when they were unsuccessfully applied in international technical assistance programs. An improved though less than satisfactory effort was made to compensate for the parochialism of American public administration concepts by infusing their overseas application with heavy doses of cultural anthropology. But the conventional concepts were fast becoming no less inadequate at home, where they were not proving adaptable to the realities of the new technological era of electronics, bioengineering and aerospace systems. Perceptions lagged behind events.

27. It is easier to see the need for a more realistic perspective on the meaning of "public administration" than it is to determine what changes in academic organization are necessary to facilitate and implement this development. There are several points of clarity however. *First*, it seems clear that the actual scope of public administration is too great to place its study exclusively in any one discipline. If public administration is termed a "discipline," then it is a discipline of an order different from political science or sociology. Its substance would be derivative from more basic disciplines, and its methodology would be largely one of synthesis. *Second*, the construction of valid theories of public administration requires especially the continuing assistance of behavioral science and the study of complex megasystems. It is difficult to see how a valid theory of public administration can be constructed in the absence of a validated general theory of administrative behavior.

28. The shaping of academic organization for the study of administration is beyond the purview of this paper, but the establishment of centers, institutes, or schools to facilitate multi-disciplinary focus upon administrative phenomena would appear to be moves in the most promising direction. No dramatic revelations, however, should be expected from the first of such institutions to be established. Time will be required—hardly less for scholars than for the general public—to see clearly that the society emerging in America today is not the one that we have known; not the one that the textbooks still describe. It is a new thing— this society of the scientific superculture—and few of those now aware of its advent are prepared intellectually or emotionally to think seriously about its meaning.

29. The foregoing observations do not, however, imply that study of administration as a generic social process obviates need for a separate focus upon public administration. Even when conceived in the broad context that has been advocated in this paper, public administration is a distinguishable aspect of the general process. Focus upon the administration of public affairs may be as sharp as our data and our insight permit. The study of public administration, although largely an examination of macroadministration, may be as specific within this context as inquiry proves fruitful. The practical substance of knowledge concerning the organization and management of public institutions and affairs need not be dissolved in a sea of generic abstraction. The fuzziness and inconsistency of concepts that have diminished the practical and theoretical value of the old academic public administration should not and need not be perpetuated in the new orientation. This newer and broader concept is not intellectually unmanageable. It seems difficult because it is unfamiliar, and admittedly it is also more complex and more varied than its academic predecessor—but so also is the reality that academic theory attempts to describe and interpret.

30. Because of its broad scope, and complex and varied subject matter, there is room for almost every method of inquiry in the development of theories of public administration. But not all methods are equally useful. The traditional methods have been: (1) recollected experience, (2) deductive reasoning, and (3) empirical observation. These familiar approaches to theory-construction still have value—albeit diminishing. They do not easily allow for independent confirmation of evidence, and their predictive utility has been low. The search for operational validity and predictability moves the investigator to greater reliance on two other methods of inquiry: (4) heuristic analogy and (5) inductive inference. A brief explanation of the reasons for their special utility is in order.

31. Heuristic analogy, which in this context implies recourse to models and to simulation of administrative behavior, is a substitute for the rarely feasible controlled experiment in actual administrative situations. The development of the computer as a research tool has facilitated this method of inquiry, particularly through its capacity for handling vast amounts of data and for

foreshortening the sequence of events in time. Heuristic analogy thus contributes directly to the realistic study of the dynamic processes of administration, and indirectly through its use in the study of complex systems of all kinds.

32. Inductive inference as a method of research and theory-construction draws upon all other methods insofar as their data are amenable to objective testing. It is the common method employed in the natural sciences, and is sometimes acclaimed as *the* scientific method. The claim is exaggerated, but the value of the method for the advancement of reliable knowledge is beyond question. Its reliance upon controlled experiment has been its principal drawback when applied to human behavior. The method involves: (1) devising alternative hypotheses; (2) devising appropriate experiments (or the simulation of an actual experiment) with alternative outcomes, each of which will, as nearly as possible, exclude one or more of the other outcomes; and (3) repeating the procedure to obtain the elimination or refinement of sequential hypotheses.[5] Through the progressive elimination or correction of invalid hypotheses, reliable theories are ultimately obtained.

33. The objection invariably raised to this method of inquiry is the difficulty of applying controlled experiment to human individuals and institutions. But it is the misuse of the method that should be impugned, not the method as a system of reasoning. The current inadequacy of applied technique is a problem to be solved—not an answer to conclude debate on the feasibility of the method. Moreover, the method is not equally appropriate for all inquiries. Tightly quantified data and statistically controlled manipulation are not necessarily evidence of scientific method—they may be no more than exercises in mathematical ingenuity. And, as John Rader Platt has pointed out, quantification, although necessary to scientific inquiry, is not identical with it, nor does it substitute for the type of logical analysis, which he calls "strong inference" and which may not require the assistance of mathematics at all.[6]

34. Method is not solely, or even most importantly, a matter of

[5] Cf. John Rader Platt, *The Step to Man* (New York: John Wiley & Sons, 1966), p. 20.
[6] *Ibid.*, 48 ff.

technique. It is first and foremost a way of thinking. Inadequacy of technique may, of course, constrict or foreclose methods of thought. But techniques have been devised in response to the needs of method, and the choice of methods among rational men will turn ultimately upon their objectives.

35. What do we want to know about human behavior within the context indicated by the term "public administration"? The published evidence suggests that we have been concerned primarily with descriptive contemporaneous information regarding administrative operations and events. The pressures of public life and our curiosity about human behavior in government have not yet pushed us to a serious effort to get at fundamental knowledge. Twenty years ago, Robert A. Dahl observed that "we are a long way from a science of public administration." [7] We are still a long way, not merely from a science of public administration, but from the refinement of a methodology and the establishment of an academic environment in which operationally valid theories of administration, public or generic, can be devised and tested. Our society has not demanded—and the academic community has not volunteered—an effort that would give us more reliable control over administrative behavior in the ascertainable future.

36. It would be as presumptuous to argue that reliable prediction and control with respect to administrative behavior will never be possible as to assert that they will be achieved. More pertinent is the question: Do we wish to develop a capacity for administrative control and for controls over administration that may be dangerous as well as beneficial? Our choice may be between whether we attempt to hasten the growth of administrative knowledge, or whether we (so to speak) let nature take its course. Knowledge appears to exert a pressure for its own expansion, and this force, augmenting the human tendency to seek relief from uncertainty, seems likely to impel the advancement of knowledge available for administrative purposes. Science and technology are making administration an ever more powerful instrument of social policy in a world in which there is ever growing occasion for its use. Persons who hope that the "ad-

[7] Robert A. Dahl, "The Science of Public Administration: Three Problems," *Public Administration Review, III* (Winter 1947), p. 11.

ministrative state" may be socially responsible and democratically controlled should logically advocate an expanded and refined study of public administration. It is possible to control institutions and processes that are themselves not understood, but the risks of failure or inadequacy are high. And if knowledge can reduce risk and increase the prospects for success, why incur unnecessary hazards through self-imposed philosophical limitations?

37. Administration of the scientific superculture and of its complex and dynamic technological infrastructure might well be the Toynbee-esque challenge upon which the survival of our form of civilization will depend. The preservation of international peace may seem to be a more urgent matter; yet it could be that the persistence of war is, to a large extent, a consequence of our failure to cope effectively through government with the social problems brought about by the growth and misuse of knowledge. The inadequacy of public administration in the management of the human ecosystem may be a major factor in the survival of war as a social practice. Control of the vast and complex organizations and multiorganizations through which modern societies operate can no longer safely be left to crude empiricism or conventional wisdom. Among those aspects of knowledge that must be advanced before the reliable prediction and wise control of administrative behavior becomes possible are: (1) the influence of human personality in organizational interrelationships, especially in leadership; (2) the costs and effects of size or scale in organizational structure; (3) the tolerable limits of organizational or procedural complexity; and (4) the relative effects of organizational instability and homeostasis, and the conditions required for organizational self-renewal.

38. Knowledge concerning these aspects of human organization is necessary to any support of a valid theory of administration—public or otherwise. The sequence of events daily widens the gap between what we know regarding the organization and management of societies, and what we need to know to avoid social disaster. The human race has worked itself into a position of responsibility for the management of its present and the direction of its future. In the past, societies have often (but not always) been able to survive the irresponsible discharge of this task. But modern man through his ingenuity and optimism has, in effect,

raised the stakes in the game of survival. In the difficult task of using the unprecedented powers of technoscience for self-improvement rather than self-destruction, "public administration," as we have defined it, is a crucial element.

39. The most practical methodology for a theory of public administration is therefore one that permits theory to become prophetic. One of the tacit theses of American public administration has been the proposition that man does, in fact, consciously shape his future, and that his history is not merely the unfolding of predetermined events. The proposition was stated implicitly at the outset of our national experience by Alexander Hamilton, first Secretary of the Treasury in the government of the United States and a principle architect of American public administration, when he wrote:

It seems to have been reserved to the people of this country, by their conduct and example, to decide the important question, whether societies of men are really capable or not of establishing good government from reflection or choice, or whether they are forever destined to depend for their political constitutions on accident and force.[8]

40. Translated into the context of our times, this challenge goes far beyond maintenance of the viability of a political constitution as Hamilton understood it. It now becomes maintenance of the viability of the greater society itself, in which government and citizen, science and technology, enterprise and philanthropy are interrelated in a new form of political order as different from that of eighteenth-century America as Newton's physics differs from Planck's quantum mechanics. The complexity and dynamism of this new age cannot be mastered by simplistic concepts that fail to accommodate its realities. An ultimate task of public administration, to which contemporary man is necessarily committed if he seeks survival, is maintaining the viability of spaceship Earth and giving its evolution a direction beneficial to humanity. This is less than the total task of government, but is of formidable proportions measured by any historical precedent. This is the dimension of the challenge to which any useful methodology of theory in public administration must respond.

[8] *The Federalist*, ed. by Edward Mead Earle (Washington, D. C.: National Home Library Association, 1937), p. 3.

Comment on Caldwell's Paper

By G. Homer Durham

PROFESSOR Caldwell has rendered a significant service. He urges more meaningful foundations and content for what he introduces as having an "ambiguous title," (1) with the further assertion that it is the "author's task to make of it what he can." The very name and past formulations in the field are thus challenged, if not swept away, at the outset. Public administration, he tells us, must become "more clearly congruent with the phenomenon," both for reasons of satisfactory generalization (1–4) and of operational reliability (5).

His essay is more than a critique. The quest for new directions is clearly urged in forty enumerated sections. Each "verse" of this scripture invites textual criticism. Such discussion should be encouraged. Textual criticism, especially in the universities, can be relevant to the current tasks of methodology and the effort to formulate general statements. Positive suggestions beyond this stimulation, however, are outlined by Professor Caldwell. New hypotheses, computer-simulated models, and "heuristic endeavor" (31) are encouraged. But I wonder if the directions he points, from what he makes of his "task," do not efface "public administration" and cause it to disappear in "generic" seas. Albert Lepawsky inquired in 1949 if the overwhelming importance of "administration" did not require its own school, like medicine and engineering, "for the survival of modern civilization."[1] I believe that a case can be made for "syzygous" public administration to find a place in the university, for the same reason. The considerations raised by Professor Caldwell are provocative. Is public administration worth saving? Can whatever passes or could pass for administration, in the generic sense, in the future, include a significant "public administration"?

The paper is innovative, takes a bold stance, stimulates and provokes a variety of reactions, as the editors hoped. But I

---

[1] Albert Lepawsky (ed.), *Administration* (New York, Alfred A. Knopf, 1949), p. 668.

feel that Caldwell's new wine can and should be added to the old bottles.

Should the theory of public administration, as it has emerged and developed in the United States, be abandoned? Should the connotations, legal and governmental, of the word "public" be discarded? Is it true that the activities of the United Auto Workers (UAW) as a large entity have as much significance for public administrative theory as do those of the Tennessee Valley Authority (TVA)? Have such entities as the UAW become, in the functional sense, as much "public" as the National Labor Relations Board (NLRB) or other governmental service? Is the state of society and the nature of today's world, is the quest for theory (including operational reliability), such that there is no real distinction between governmental administration and Boeing Aircraft? between public administration in the United States and any enterprise (all "public") of the Soviet Union? Should, in time, the "theory of public administration" be replaced by Henri Fayol's "General Administration" (1916), or Caldwell's possible "macroadministration"? Should (I say "should" rather than "can") public administration be a variation "in the generic process of administration conceived as a universal human experience" (24)?

Is the expectation of "uncertainty," the reliance on psychological, behavioral, social science—indeed on "all knowledge" (8, 9)—such that education for public administration must be completely revamped and restyled? Or do we still include a view towards the background of public law?

Professor Caldwell's broad vistas are challenging. But I have grave doubts (8) that "a systematic organization of all knowledge relevant to understanding administrative behavior" is possible. Some theologies deny this possibility even to the gods, who, though omniscient, are yet circumscribed by Prometheus and the doctrine of free agency. If law and government as disciplines are viewed sociologically, rather than in terms derived from law and political theory, does not *public* administration disappear? Methodology in theory may so aspire, but its fruitful focus must surely include the legal and governmental as special considerations. I would therefore rewrite Professor Caldwell (24) by asserting that public administration is, in fact, bound, and will continue to be bound, by presumptions of law and culture, and that these are the data which *do* permit a comprehensive approach —rather than *contra* (19). Theory is a meeting place for philosophical generalization and specific scientific description. Methodology must account for both the specific and the general. The tests of theory are experiential and pragmatic. Many universities in this country, as a practical matter, are willing to expend limited resources on a school or program in public administration —due to the impressions held concerning the nature and significance of the problems of government. But establish the idea that the job can be done as well or better in "macroadministration," or in a new sociology, and the same programs could soon disappear. Medical schools might theoretically be consigned to a grand academic division of psychobiological sciences, in a generic system. But would it serve the pragmatic interests involved in surgery, diagnosis, and mental health?

Despite the "publicness" of certain large contemporary states, the challenging phenomena of international and global life, some disappointing overseas experience of American public administrationists,[2] and the deep involvement of large and small organizations in public affairs, I argue the case for public administration: for public administration apart from business administration, with room for distinctions, based on law and government, from the administration of Gum's in Moscow or transportation in China. Public administration must stand on firm foundations as a peculiarly significant branch of political theory because of the nexus which public administration provides for study of the classic problems of man and his claims regarding government, and the nature of the state.

Public administration presents a point of departure in the necessary study of how legal processes and official acts affecting humanity vary from culture to culture. Based on this foundation, all possible methodologies and approaches should be poured into the quest for sturdier, more "operationally reliable" theory. Professor Caldwell's appeal—quoting Hamilton (39)—to substitute intelligent determination for accident or force in the quest for "good government" involves such selection and such a foundation.

[2] Due to language difficulties, in my observation and experience, rather than the failure of our "theory."

Public administration is inescapably related to political theory. Public administration in Hamilton's and Madison's state has a different character than in a state of another nature and theory. So runs the argument for "syzygous public administration."

A developing theory and schools of macroadministration can necessarily assist and serve public administration. But a firm place remains for public administration. The varied character of public administration from state to state, especially as it relates to such concerns as life and health, liberty, property, transportation and mobility, marriage, the family, religion, preferred goals established by law, and different groundings in political systems expressing selective political theories, presents challenges for both methodological and theoretical endeavor.

Concern for the broad and complex values involved in execution of the relevant public law, and the subsequent rights affected, is an important key to the truly scientific ordering of public administration. The matter need not there remain.

Professor Caldwell's third and "syzygous" concept (Section 12) is, I feel, the hopeful one. But I do not feel any "major semantic embarrassment" in the word "public." Public administration *is* governmental administration. The shades of difference in mixed or quasi-public enterprise are distinguishable by legal considerations, as with National Aeronautics and Space Agency (NASA) contracts, and by the degree of relation to and responsibility of government. I applaud the sentence (Section 19): "Public has usually been equated with governmental." This is where methodology in the theory of public administration has to begin. If public administration loses its "syzygial character," its connection with law and government, its past most useful and durable concept is forsaken. The Boeing Aircraft Corporation is not as significantly involved in public administration as the Department of the Interior, and certainly not in the same ways. Boeing's goals and methods, although influenced by law and government, have not been so limited and prescribed, nor its public responsibility so controlled, fixed, and subjected to legal change and political clienteles. The methods of maintaining Harvard University and Indiana University differ. Sociologically, the differences may be slight. But politically and legally, the differences are real, even in securing and administering federal grants. The basic difference is *public* administration, as discriminated and related to the government, and the legal processes of the state of Indiana.

The difference in theorizing about "macroadministration" and public administration is like the difference in Robert Frost's poem:

> I shall be telling this with a sigh
> Somewhere ages and ages hence:
> Two roads diverged in a wood, and I—
> I took the one less traveled by,
> And that has made all the difference.[3]

The challenge of theory in public administration, as Caldwell says, is to become prophetic (39). This involves maintaining the viability and values of a political constitution, as German theorists learned to their sorrow after 1933. Unless political constitutions remain prescriptive and prospective, open and viable, the controls (36–37) in a "greater society," or any new form of political order, may, indeed, permit constraint and force to interfere with deliberate and discriminating efforts for "good government." Some theorists and practitioners in public administration must help "prophecy" to provide ample room to sustain certain values. The operation of future "modern societies . . . cannot safely be left to crude empiricism or conventional wisdom" (37). New knowledge to surmount "the scientific superculture" and the complex "technological infrastructure" must indeed be won. Its use, by government, under law, will continue to challenge and call for all accumulated wisdom, both in our politics and in our past "syzygous" public administration.[4]

[3] "The Road Not Taken," *The Collected Poems of Robert Frost* (New York: Henry Holt, 1930), p. 131.

[4] See my "Guards for the Future," in Don L. Bowen and Lynton K. Caldwell (eds.), *Program Formulation and Development* (Bloomington: Indiana University Press, 1960), pp. 83–87. Reprinted in 1961 by Bureau of Publications, Arizona State University, Tempe, Arizona.

Comment on Caldwell's Paper

By York Willbern

AS a major first step in the consideration of the theory of public administration, Professor Caldwell proposes a new organizing definition of the term and of the field itself. He recognizes that his approach is not completely new, but he rightly asserts that what he suggests differs substantially from the organizing approach now most commonly used. His argument is well stated and provocative, but not completely persuasive.

In any specialized field of study, a set or class of phenomena are selected for examination and attempted explanation through theory. The selected phenomena, or behaviors, have certain characteristics which associate them with some neighbors, other characteristics which associate with other neighbors. The question in selecting criteria, for the choice of data and relationships to be examined, is whether the similarities chosen as those governing the choice of this particular set seem to be more powerful in understanding and in explaining the phenomena than some alternative set of criteria, some other way of subdividing the happenings, on another axis.

The choice of names or of terms to apply to the events being studied may be very important in the building of theory, since the words convey to hearers and readers, directly or by analogy, a class of things with certain characteristics in common. It is entirely appropriate to argue, as Professor Caldwell does, that both the naming and the definition of the universe to be studied, and its contextual relationships, are fundamental first steps in the formation of theories about it.

Consider the following two statements. Statement 1: Administration is a generic social process, which may be subdivided into governmental and private sectors (each of which may, of course, be further subdivided). Statement 2: Government is a generic social process, which may be subdivided into politics, legislation, administration, international relations, and so forth. I think that both of these statements are true and that both are useful. But the study of public administration will be substantially different if Statement 1 be accepted as the primary or basic assumption than it will be if Statement 2 is thus accepted. Either scheme of primary and secondary classification of phenomena will lead to theoretical generalizations. I think that both have been profitably used—and that both will continue to be used. But, in a conference on the "Theory and Practice of Public Administration," attention to which of the two may be *most* useful in understanding and explaining what actually occurs certainly seems justifiable. Professor Caldwell tends to prefer the first statement; in most American universities, the second is more popular. Public administration is more commonly studied and taught in departments of political science or government than in schools or departments of "administration" or "business and public administration."

While recognizing the usefulness of both statements, I tend also to prefer the second. It seems to me that propositions of theory capable of explaining the phenomena of public administration are slightly more likely to come from the comparable phenomena of other types of politics than from attention (useful as this may also be) to the comparable phenomena of non-governmental administration. Or, in other and oversimplified words, the theoretical potential of considering administration to be a category of politics seems greater to me than that of considering politics to be a category of administration.

This last statement may be considered an objection to a proposition which Professor Caldwell did not intend to make. But it seems to me that his emphasis upon defining "public administration" as those complex social activities which affect the community certainly leads to the conclusion that he intends his revised concept of public administration to be inclusive enough to comprehend the activities of political parties and pressure groups and legislative bodies and courts and diplomats, as well as those of General Motors and the Bata Shoe Company and the Roman Catholic Church. If the suggested definition is this broad, as it appears to be, a theory of public administration becomes a theory of organized society, and an attempt to escape the constricting limits of focusing attention on a "narrowly" defined set of social phenomena leads to a proposed span of attention so wide as to baffle the student.

Led by the imperialistic urges which must be rooted very deeply in human nature, I am tempted by the brilliance and richness of opportunity suggested by a proposed definition of my own field as including all, or nearly all, of the complex organized social activities which affect the public. As many observers have begun to note, the realm of privacy in modern society is increasingly circumscribed, and nearly all of social life can properly be considered within the scope of *res publica*. If public administration be taken to include the whole realm of public policy and public matters, it includes business and economics and most of education and law and sociology. A "validated general theory of administrative behavior," which Professor Caldwell would like to seek before he begins to narrow down his theoretical endeavors, becomes, it seems to me, a general theory of social behavior, given the pervasive nature of complex organized activities in our society.

I am afraid, furthermore, that the concept "administration" does not have the psychological appeal or attractiveness to bear the weight which he wants to put upon it. I do not think that, either in the world of scholarship or in the world of professional practice, people can be led to consolidate such a sweeping array of explorations or endeavors under this particular rubric.

I am perfectly willing to agree that, in the past, the study and teaching of public administration has been too narrow. We did attempt to focus upon a fairly narrow range of phenomena, without sufficient recognition that the particular fabric which we were examining was merely a part of a seamless web of social phenomena. Part of the narrowness came from our failure to realize the great analogies and even identities between behavior in governmental agencies and behavior in nongovernmental entities. But I think we have suffered even more from our effort to concentrate upon the processes of public *administration*, as something different from public policy, values, goals, and politics. This latter shortcoming has now been publicly admitted by both academic and practicing members of the profession, and strong efforts to remedy it are being made. We now admit the value-laden policy content of administration, and try to articulate and examine both goals and means more directly and carefully.

Although its lack of discernible limits also leaves me somewhat frightened, I would submit that the concept "public affairs" is both more attractive as an image and more promising as a source of theoretical generalizations than is the generic "administration" which Professor Caldwell suggests. And, given the breadth of his attempted redefinition of "public administration," and his announced skepticism about the continued value of the traditional term, I think it not unlikely that Professor Caldwell could be converted to this position. The great problem, again, is that, in an attempt to escape the constraints of an organizing concept which may be too narrow, we substitute one so broad as to be of little definitional value.

It may seem unfortunate to many, although I must confess that I find elements of both stimulus and freedom in the fact, that we have been embarked so long upon a field of study and practice the limits of which we cannot yet precisely define. And I am not sure that this discussion has led us any closer to such a definition. But whatever the criteria for the selection of phenomena to be studied, we still have other problems in the development of theory about them. To construct or develop theories, the great problems are the identification and the measurement of the phenomena, and determination of the influence of any variable or set of variables upon these phenomena. To construct a theory of any range—general or specific—we need to find out what has happened (or is happening), how much it has happened, and what causes it to happen.

As Professor Caldwell suggests, there are gradually becoming available tools for much more careful observation of administrative behavior. We have more observers, more reported data, more precise and dependable data. With statistical and other logical techniques and with powerful calculating equipment, we can count and measure and determine mathematical and other relationships between happenings. We can, in some circumstances, test out hypotheses, either directly or by analogy or simulation. Professor Caldwell suggests that in forming our theories, or explanations, we need to make greater use of the techniques of the natural sciences, by using carefully defined data which we secure from situations as closely controlled as possible, in order that the relationships which we discover or test can be verified or modified by others.

I agree. But I am not at all certain that tightly quantified data, controlled statistical manipulation, or the arrangement of "experiments" or simulations to test articulated hypotheses—useful as they all are where they are feasible—constitute the most promising ways toward the formation of theories of public administration in the foreseeable future. As Professor Caldwell well realizes, the behavior of people in public administration—even more so if public administration be defined as broadly as he proposes to define it—is exceedingly complex behavior. While some administrative situations have many characteristics in common with other administrative situations, they also have many differences. As he so clearly suggests, differences in place and culture introduce many complicating variables. Furthermore, both patterns of behavior and organization forms change rapidly—they do not stand still to be observed. And controls to eliminate or to take into account extraneous or unanticipated or unknown variables are very difficult to devise. I think that much—probably most, for a long time—of our knowledge will continue to come from more loosely structured experiences and observations and reasoning.

We need, of course, to measure much more carefully and much more frequently than we have in the past—although measure must always be for a *purpose*, not just for the sake of measurement. We need to compare, and identify as precisely as possible, those variables in our comparisons which coincide and those which differ.

What is needed, and is gradually being secured, is much more rigor in, and much more critical examination of, our observations and descriptions and explanations. Some of these observations and descriptions can be precise; others will need to be tempered with the creative imagination of the observer in order to get anything approximating the full richness of reality. We can do much by "heuristic analogy," as we have done in the past, describing situations and happenings as carefully as possible, and suggesting the possibility that what happened in the described circumstances is likely to happen again in similar circumstances. But such analogies, to be truly heuristic, need to be made with great care, and they need to be examined and criticized by other observers. We need to be much more precise in detailing the evidence which leads to a descriptive conclusion, or to theoretical explanation. We will continue to learn much, and perhaps much more in the future than in the past, through the testing of tentative explanations against the observations (even crude and inprecise ones) made by other people. A close engagement of scholars with each other and with practitioners, each accepting or criticizing and modifying the other, will be the really productive condition for the development of useful theory. As Professor Caldwell so well stated, method is much more a way of thinking than a matter of technique.

Observations on Willbern's Comment

By Lynton K. Caldwell

1. If advancement of understanding is the objective, the only point worth debating concerning a theory is: Does it work? If a theory possesses validity, critical analysis and testing will reveal its merits and its inadequacies. Theories, including those now prevailing, are in essence impermanent. Hence I do not see that the popularity, persuasiveness, or "psychological appeal or attractiveness" of the concepts developed in the essay on "Methodology in the Theory of Public Administration" are relevant to the discussion. The essay is not an exercise in persuasion. It is an effort to explore more rewarding avenues toward understanding administrative behavior in government and in society.

2. Professor Willbern's principal objection to the macrotheory approach is that "a theory of public administration becomes a theory of organized society." This, he feels, leads to "a proposed span of attention so wide as to baffle the student." I would argue unequivocally that no theory of administration, public or otherwise, can be valid unless it is consistent with the realities of organized society. I do not, however, think that the administrative process includes all social phenomena. In my paper (paragraphs 8, 17, 21) I have identified administration as an aspect of social behavior. The process (as distinguished from technical processes) of administration embraces the policies, "values, goals, and politics" that Professor Willbern believes that its study should include. But when he proposes the concept of "public affairs" as more promising as a source of theoretical generalizations, I find myself baffled. Is the span of attention suggested by the term "public affairs" more coherent and more comprehensible than "a theory of organized society"?

3. The theory of administration, as I see it, is the theory of what makes complex human organizations work. The largest and most complex of these organizations are governments. The involvement of these governmental systems with other aspects of organized social life is exceedingly complex. *It is baffling,* or

should be, to scholar and to student alike. If we are ever to understand how better to administer public affairs, we will somehow have to learn to broaden our span of attention and to enlarge our capacity to deal with complexity.

4. With respect to the application of science to theory-building in public administration I do not disagree with Professor Willbern's remarks. But if his expressed reservations regarding "tightly quantified data and controlled statistical manipulation" are mistaken as criticism of views expressed in my essay, the reader should refer to paragraphs 30 through 32. I agree with Professor Willbern's strictures, but they are not criticism of the method that I suggest as useful; they are rather valid objections to its abuse.

5. Finally, I believe that the suggestion that I have attempted a redefinition of public administration misses the main point of my essay. My concern is not so much with the definition of a *field* of study, as with identifying an *object* of study and defining its substance in a way that will correspond to the thing studied. The breadth of the field upon which I believe that we must focus is indeed great. The task of scholarship is to sharpen the focus and to narrow it, if the course of learning indicates a narrowing of parameters. I do not think that *a priori* definitions of a "field of study and practice" are the most promising way to advance understanding or valid theory, and in this I believe that Professor Willbern and I may be in agreement.

6. I have argued that our conventional definitions of the field of public administration are not consistent with the reality of the process by which public affairs, broadly construed, are administered in America today. My concern is with this reality in which the traditional dichotomies of public and private, government and business, are rapidly becoming less relevant to the total process, or are assuming a relevance unlike that described in the case-books on government regulation of business. A consequence of the approach that I advocate would almost certainly be a redefinition of the field of study and theory. But no scholar redefines a field of study for his colleagues, and all that I have argued for here is greater realism and clarity in working concepts and hypotheses than the conventional semantics of public administration has as yet provided.

Conference Discussion on Methodology in the Theory of Public Administration

CALDWELL: The comments that were prepared by York Willbern and Homer Durham largely had to do, I think, with two ideas advanced in my paper. The *first* was the proposition that the study of public administration could be greatly strengthened by reorientation of viewpoint, seeing public administration not merely as governmental administration, as we have been accustomed to doing, but rather as essentially a public process, governmental and nongovernmental, a process, however, in which there are varying degrees of publicness. I should say parenthetically that I agree with Homer Durham that the Boeing Corporation, for example, is in no sense as public as the Department of State or the United States Post Office, but is nevertheless significantly involved in the execution of important public programs that affect public action at the governmental level. We can no longer describe or explain the whole process of public administration if we fail to include its total ramifications. I suppose if you wanted me to put a label on the kind of viewpoint that I have expressed here, it would read, "A General Systems or Ecological Approach to the Functions of Public Administration."

The objections raised were, first, that this approach to public administration, using "public" in a very broad sense, really diluted it out of all meaning and assured its being lost in a "generic sea." However, I do not see that focusing direction and control of large and complex organizations implies a need to study everything about them in equal depth. I would certainly agree that you have a more difficult problem of defining or identifying the scope of relevance when you look at public administration in its very broad sense than when you confine it to the operations of governmental institutions in a strict sense. It seems to me a matter of focus. I do not view the study of public administration as a discipline, but rather as a focus to which virtually all disciplines have some contribution.

I have used the term "macroadministration" as one means of identifying another aspect of what I believe to be the essence of public administration, that is to say, the organizational and directive processes of very large organizations and complexes of organizations. In the space and defense programs, for example, we have developed very complex phenomena that we have not really found any good way to describe. I use macroadministration as something that, I think, goes beyond what Kenneth Galbraith has in mind when he speaks of technostructure. The space program is a kind of public-policy technostructure that has evolved, in our society, into the technoscientific demands of our time in contrast to, for instance, the Soviet practice of governmentalizing the economy. So, to me at least, the problem here is not so much one of defining a field as it is one of defining a focus.

The second idea in my paper had to do with whether or not it was possible to organize all knowledge relevant to public administration, broadly construed. Homer Durham expressed doubt that it is possible to marshal systematically all knowledge relevant to an understanding of administrative behavior. But I am confident that he would agree that one should attempt to make the most of what we know or can learn about administration. The marshaling of all relevant knowledge on *any* subject selected for study is surely an ultimate goal of science. Therefore, the task of a valid public administration, as of science, cannot be fulfilled unless one does make this effort *toward* a continuing task of analysis, reinterpretation, and expansion of knowledge. Obviously, one could push this proposition to extremes, until it became an absurdity. But the practical implication is that one should take knowledge where one finds it, whether it is in social psychology, anthropology, systems theory, or history, regardless of where it may be, if it is relevant to understanding the behavior of large and complex organizations and systems of organizations. The searching out and collating of relevant knowledge, not universal knowledge, is what I have advocated.

Let me make another point or two, parenthetically, with respect to the comments. One of Homer Durham's remarks had to do with an analogy to medicine, suggesting that if we were to take medical schools and put them into some sort of generic biomedical division of the university, this might have a prejudicial effect upon medical practice. I incline toward a different conclusion. One of the difficulties, apparently, in medical education is that its objective has been to train physicians to cure people once they get sick, but not really to prepare people, including physicians, to use biomedical knowledge to maintain a high level of public health, to prevent illness in society. There is, indeed, some thinking in the field of medical education that a change in the orientation of medical schools is required. As we extend public medical care, and the cost for this increases—and as we enlarge biomedical technology—economics, scientific good sense, and public pressures will lead us to the attempt to keep people well, rather than to try to cure them after they are ill. In this event, the traditional orientation of the medical school will have to change. This change implies much closer relationship with the basic biomedical sciences.

Science and technology are forcing a reorientation of concepts of what we mean by government, and are breaking down the distinctions between public and private aspects of life as we have known them. For example, at the meeting of the American Association for the Advancement of Science this week in New York, there has been much discussion about the question of privacy and personal rights as they are affected by science and technology. We are having to redefine privacy, partly because the barriers that formerly stood between the private individual and the surveillance of his behavior are being broken down very rapidly. I would argue that the reality of public administration is pressing against the old boundaries of assumption and theory here too strongly to be withheld. If we attempt to stay with what we find more comfortable and easier to handle intellectually, we shall simply see the study of public administration carried on by other people. Yet, I see no prospect whatever of the reality of public administration as a focus for study disappearing in the universities. We have conceived its subject matter in self-imposed limiting terms for much too long. The reality of the public need and the public condition, as we see it described on the front pages of the newspapers and experience it in life, is much too insistent to permit any withering away of the study of administration in the university. It may be called something else. But I see no reason why it should not be called public administration.

I see no reason why we should not have vital and effective programs in public administration even though we, coincidentally, have schools of administration in a generic sense.

I should like to be quite clear on this point. I am not advocating the disappearance of public administration. I am not advocating or not suggesting that the generic science or study of administration should *substitute* for public administration. I have found a good deal of difficulty with the term public administration, but chiefly because of the ambiguity of the word "public." A strengthened generic study of administration as a process of social interaction will also strengthen but not necessarily displace the study of public administration in the context that I have proposed. I can therefore be optimistic about the status of public administration in the universities, if for no other reason than because I think that the condition of contemporary life, and even, perhaps, the realizations of the people who make up this life, are going to force, in various ways, a high priority for this focus, in some form in the universities.

SHERMAN: I know that your agenda calls for discussing each of these six papers separately. However, I wonder if it would be profitable at the beginning to discuss all of these papers as a whole? There are a number of themes that run through all of them. One, for example, is the definition of public administration. I do not know why we should discuss the most appropriate definition of public administration in relation only to methodology. The question of definition relates to all of the papers—whether we are concerning ourselves with whether "public" means government or more than government, or whether "administration" means only getting things done or also deciding what to do, or whether we are talking only about public administration in the United States or throughout the world. I find these differences in definition in a number of papers. Similarly, something needs to be said at the outset on the interrelationship among scope, objectives, and method, which I find difficult to keep separate and unrelated. Consequently, I wonder, in terms of our discussion, whether, somewhere, it would be effective to talk about this whole thing.

CHARLESWORTH: On the basis of our experience in previous conferences like this, we believe that it is not wise to structure the discussions rigidly. So say whatever you wish to say on whatever subject; it will be entirely in order. We are not going to call anybody to order here.

SHERMAN: I do not know how profitable it is to discuss the definition of "public administration." I suppose that we could spend a day and a half just on that. On the other hand, it seems to me that the subject is going to come up with each of these papers and I would hate to go through discussions of the definition of public administration six separate times.

CHARLESWORTH: I do not think that you will, but I think that your observation is a good one. But I still think that people ought to be encouraged to say what they wish on the subject. It does not have to be in outline order.

CALDWELL: May I add a comment. In reading the other papers, I observed that everybody was caught in the same circumstance that I was, that they really could not write about their topic until they had confronted the meaning of the subject matter. In other words, we have all had to ask: "What kind of creature is public administration?" The apparent reason for this is that no universally accepted or orthodox definition has been prescribed. I have had comparatively little to say about methodology, and part of that can be summed up in an observation that methodology really is more a matter of attitude, a way of thinking, than it is of technique. I do not know of any peculiar or special methodology that would apply to the study of administration. Generally speaking, I have suggested the techniques that are used in the behavioral sciences. I have argued for greater reliance, perhaps, on the general approach that has worked well in the physical and biological sciences, without pushing specific technique.

CHARLESWORTH: The Latins had a word for it: "Methodus est homo ipse," or the method is the man himself. You go at it one way, and he goes at it another way.

UNIDENTIFIED VOICE: I would like to comment on all the papers just a little bit here. I find them a very interesting combination of orthodoxy and innovation. I find it very stimulating. It brought to my mind the fact which Harvey Sherman just mentioned, that our field is unlike the disciplines of the universities. I am inclined to think in contrast, in order to keep from making a decision at this time. The other disciplines are conceived by what is sometimes called a ladder of knowledge, as in chemistry there was first Aristotle, then Lavoisier, and then later thinkers. In public administration, we have people in the universities who trace origins from Aristotle and Hamilton, through Wilson and Goodnow of the New York Bureau of Municipal Research, to Willoughby and White, and so on.

DURHAM: We have another group of people who appear incognito. With more than tongue in cheek, I suggest that Professor Caldwell's paper and the field would benefit from "lower" (or textual) criticism as with the biblical scholars. Before public administration can move realistically to "higher criticism," it seems to me, we must have textual criticism and arrive at some confrontation with terminology and so forth. We are attempting to engage in higher criticism before we have undertaken textual criticism. Public administration is a peculiarly American contribution to behavioral and social science. It may one day have a different name. But, at the present, it has to be called "public administration." The only alternative would be "governmental administration." But "governmental administration" would not fit the American experience as well, nor the political theory from which we derive the expression "public administration." In the history of ideas, public administration really connects John W. Burgess' idea of the sphere of government with his "sphere of liberty." Public administration in the United States is the conceptual and practical nexus between the prized sphere of the individual and the sphere of the state. Some feel that these intersecting spheres disappeared long ago, as government absorbed or penetrated the "sphere of liberty": that liberty is now found (as is civil rights) in legislation and administration. But popular notions become facts in politics. And the notion still exists in the United States that there is a distinction between "public" and private, and this distinction in the public mind derives from circumstances in the roots of political theory. We begin, therefore, with the concept "public administration." It is or should be a discipline, I believe, as well as a focus. It should be a discipline that relates to political science. To build the ladder of knowledge, we have to go back to the roots, to the relation of administration to law, and view public administration as the systematic execution of public law.

Law is the beginning of public administration. Its beginning is not the end, however. The word "public" reflects the American culture. Public administration as the expression of law is the means toward the objectives sought through the instrumentality of law. It would be unrealistic to build the discipline on any other foundation.

The effort to organize all relevant knowledge, while a very stimulating and provocative endeavor, has limits. Yet, I had the impression as I read the Caldwell paper that, really, Keith was calling for an Einsteinian, general field theory. This aspiration, proposing a general field theory for the social universe, is certainly as laudable as for the world of physics. But I felt that the paper overreached on this point. We have to recognize the challenge of incorporating available and *relevant* knowledge before we incorporate *all* of it. We have to begin with law and government and carry the concern from that point to the general field. Public administration would have rough sledding in a new university school of "macroadministration" or general administration. Concern for the governmental also means sharp analysis and concern for the "private" and the control of government. For public administration to survive and serve governmental administration, I think, the field has to be identified as public administration. The real nurture of this discipline, and I view it as a discipline, must come in the universities.

WILLBERN: Now, I shall not say very much at this stage, but I would like to say a little. Keith's paper does raise this matter of definition probably more forcefully than any other paper. To his comments, which have much that are very persuasive about them, I raised only two reservations and did not really push either of them very hard. As he saw, these comments, these reservations, are in some measure inconsistent with each other. The first reservation was that to define public administration as broadly as he proposed to define it made it embrace almost all of organized society. It would have practically no limits. It leaves out some things, but not very many. It therefore would be an extremely difficult thing to try to grasp. It is a little like the argument we had in the curriculum committee of the department of government at my university. We had many graduate courses, G-641, G-642, G-643, and many other such courses. We were talking about how these things overlapped and how you really could not do it that way. Somebody made the quasi-serious proposal that we ought to have just one graduate course called "G-600, zero to ninety hours—may be repeated indefinitely." And there is much to be said for this way of listing the curriculum. There is much to be said, also, for embracing organized society in such a broad net. But, then, his response to me was (and it is a very appropriate one) that if you have to look at all this to understand it, then you just have to look it it. And it is not too easy to respond to that. If these things are so intertwined and so interconnected and so involved with each other as to be incapable of rational separation, then you have to look at the whole thing.

I had another reservation, which he says is somewhat inconsistent with the first because it assumes the validity of the argument for an all-embracing look. That reservation turned on whether or not he had chosen the right term or organizing concept for it. If the touchstone for macroadministration is the degree to which it affects the public, then, it seems to me, the cornerstone of the concept is *public*ness, not administration. The term you choose then ought to turn on the *public*ness of what it is that you are examining. The term that you choose will, in some measure, influence the disposition of those people who are studying. These are the characteristics which they will look for. If you are going to talk about so embracing a concept as the one that Keith is talking about, it might be that the term should be *public* affairs or *public* policy and administration or some other term which leaves administration in a secondary rather than in a central place. You can postulate a definition for any word you like, but if you postulate a definition that is not the one that is commonly in the minds of people, it does not really take so well.

Of two reservations—I do not press either one of them too vigorously because I am not really confident about either—one is that this is too broad a concept. You just can not manage it with the manpower and the talents that we have available to study it. Even Keith recognizes fully the difficulty which we would have in organizing an academic environment for it, because this concept would involve, you see, all of education and economics and law and much of sociology, if you want to define it this broadly. Second, if you are going to be that broad, I am not sure that you have the right word for it.

SHERMAN: Mr. Chairman, I wonder, since Homer Durham said two or three times that he regards public administration as a discipline, whether this is an appropriate point for Dwight Waldo to say something about this subject. In his paper he insists that we should at least act as if it were a profession rather than a discipline.

CHARLESWORTH: This is very appropriate.

WALDO: The word "profession" has not as yet been introduced into a situation which is already very complicated, and I do not know whether it should be. My own position, as those of you who have read the paper know, is that it now makes no sense to talk about public administration as a subdiscipline of political science, and hardly much more to regard it as a separate discrete discipline. Searching for a next step which does not take us into an infinite void, I came to the concept of "profession": I proposed that we see what there is in the concept appropriate to our present situation. I still propose this. But my thought after reading and listening to the comments on my paper was that it might have been more strategic to have spoken in this paper only of a "professional *school* approach." This wording might not have raised all of the objections or apprehensions which the blunt statement that we ought to take a professional approach arouses, even though I put in the paper all sorts of disclaimers and reservations. Now, I shall just let it go at that for the time being.

UNIDENTIFIED VOICE: About Homer's comments about public administration as a discipline: I wonder if you were thinking, Homer, in terms of having the same kind of intellectual base, for instance, the same attraction that the other so-called disciplines in social science have. Certainly, it must have been that because it could not be in terms of the way the universities are organized. There is practically no place where it is organized as a discipline. The analogy of the medical schools seems to me to be relevant here. No one talks about discipline in medicine. What they are talking about is the way in which a number of disciplines are brought together to serve both the intellectual needs and the surgical and operative needs as well. It seems to me, that, in the proposed "administration," what we are seeking is to focus on being fair, whatever academic enterprise this is called, and somehow to link it with what happens in a real world. Now, I am not sure what that linkage word is, but "profession" may be as good a term as the one which we used before. Just as a practical matter, would you say that this is an acceptable way to proceed, or should we insist and stand on our rights, and demand that the universities recognize public administration as a discipline and organize themselves on that basis?

DURHAM: I used the word, discipline, in my comment to make a distinction from the expression, "focus" that Professor Caldwell used (when he asked if public administration were a discipline or a focus) I see it as a discipline in which a "focus approach" is useful. I think that there is a place for public administration as a discipline. I see it as a discipline in the sense that pharmaceutical chemistry is a discipline. There may be varying "administrations" and "chemistries." Pharmaceutical chemistry is the chemistry that, related to pharmacognosy and pharmacology, underlies the preparation of prescriptions, written by doctors, for the drugstore to fill. Pharmaceutical chemistry becomes a professional university discipline, within the College of Pharmacy, but also within the broad field of chemistry. The discipline of public administration, in or out of a professional school, is a subdiscipline of political science. As such, public administration exists as a relevant body of subject matter. Public administration grows out of legislative acts. It is concerned with carrying out of the mandates of the law. It is concerned with what the law will or will not permit to be carried out. In studying this area of behavior, public administration must go beyond law; it must evaluate origins, nature, character, and effects of policies. This is an increasing body of phenomena in our time. The scope and significance of the phenomena require that the discipline be recognized. "Public administration" is the best existing name. The discipline, as it develops, may be as important to the continuation of civilization as Albert Lepawsky claimed, in 1949, for "generic administration." Unless public administration is viewed as a discipline of importance, as a body of phenomena, relating to governmental administration, to political theory, to the problems of man, state, government, and politics, then I think that we have cut loose from our moorings. In this sense, I view it as a discipline.

CALDWELL: I am wondering whether or not we can link the two words "profession" and "discipline." Dwight talks about a profession. Homer talks about a discipline, and maybe we are talking about a professional discipline in two senses, in terms of its academic home (a matter of studying a number of things in order to prepare people for a profession) and the actual practice of administration by trained "professionals."

CHARLESWORTH: I can see a sharp distinction there. We ought to study public administration as a part of our total culture in America. It has an impact on everybody the same as public health or any other enveloping public activity. There is another point that I might fill out while I am talking. You know, in 1776, when Adam Smith wrote "The Wealth of a Nations," he had been a professor of moral philosophy, but what he was writing was what we call economics, more specifically, classical economics. Later, the field of economics began to embrace a lot of practice fields—transportation, finance, and the like. These fields are now all highly developed, and economics has become economic theory. So we have departments of transportation, departments of finance, and the like. Now, these finance people bridle at the notion that they are merely nuts-and-bolts people or how-to-do-it people, so they try to turn into economic theorists insofar as economic theory bears on their subject. One other point: several times it has been suggested that it is time for a split in the field of political science, that political science should deal with what we call, for want of a better word, government. Public administration should be a professional discipline, resting on its own base, not being a subordinate part or an unwanted child of political science, and, third, the general field of international relations should be segregated on the grounds that international relations has nothing whatever to do with government. It concerns the relations between whole entities. This government might be Communist, and this other one might be democratic, or two of them might be Communist. It deals with the relations between or among macrocosms, whereas government is confined to the relation between the microcosm and the macrocosm. I think it would be a wholesome thing if we did make a split, as far as our academic structure is concerned, in those three fields. Personally, I anticipate that that is what will happen.

GLADIEUX: Mr. Chairman, my question follows from your comment. Speaking as a practitioner who is, perhaps, not as intellectually oriented as some of our friends from the universities, I would like to ask the question: Are these differing concepts of the subject necessarily incompatible? I find myself at least understanding, and probably agreeing with, Keith Caldwell when he says here that public administration basically represents the focus of all the disciplines through which all human knowledge can contribute. At the same time, I find myself in agreement with the others who claim that there is something distinct, discrete, and unique about public administration in terms of legislative control, motivation, total public impact, even some techniques and procedures. My layman's question is: Are these not reconcilable? Is there such a basic gap or void here between these two concepts?

CALDWELL: I agree with you. I feel that these are not incompatible approaches. I like two things particularly that Homer said here. He used the term "phenomena," and it seems to me this may well be the key to the problem of definition. The physicist does not have the problem of definition, although you could argue that as physics studies everything, therefore you could not have a definable field of physics at all. Yet, physics prides itself, perhaps, on being the most rigorous and most specifically definable field of the sciences. The physicist studies what he calls "physical phenomena." Now, it seems to me that we are looking at phenomena, that we are looking at what happens in the process of development, translation, execution, or implementation of public policy. I also like what you said, Homer, about the way I was looking at this problem. I had not thought about the Einsteinian approach. Let me try to put into other words what I think you were saying because I think that you are right. I think that you have said much more clearly than I have said what it is that we ought to be trying to do: that is, to try to move toward a general field theory for the cybernetics of large organizational complexes that develop and implement social policy. The general field theory, or the cybernetics, of large and complex organizations, or organizational complexes, is the field of inquiry as I see it. Now, if we study that body of phenomena, no matter by what name you call it, we are trying to understand what actually happens, and I think that, within that context, you could subsume these various approaches. I agree with Homer's feeling that we ought not to neglect law, we ought not to neglect any of the things that are a part of the total function of public administration. I merely feel that we need to avoid assuming arbitrary parameters even though we cannot, at this point, define what this general field thory really may be. If we knew now, our definitional problems would be solved.

RIGGS: Are we not addressing ourselves to two related but different problems? I think it might help to separate them. The first is essentially a problem of university organization. This is a practical or expedient problem. Where do you put public administration in a university's curriculum? This has to do with the availability of students and their needs, the best way to organize academic faculties, and so on. I believe it is desirable to teach candidates for public service careers in professional schools, outside of political science departments.

Is this what Mr. Charlesworth had in mind when he suggested that we should separate public administration (and also international relations) from political science (or "government")? Or was he raising the very different theoretical problem: What is the nature of the subject? Does the inherent logic of public administration dictate its separation from political science? This question should be answered on logical grounds, without regard to how a university is organized. Clearly, theoretical analysis may produce answers quite out of line with current academic organization. But at least we would be better off if we could clarify in our own minds the discrepancies between what is logically and theoretically correct, and what is organizationally practicable in our universities.

The problem of the organization of medicine in relation to public health schools raises a similar question. Certainly, in as affluent a society as ours, the ultimate objective of medicine should be to keep everyone well, not just to cure those who have fallen ill. Yet, the way in which the practice of medicine is financed and the way in which our medical schools are organized put the emphasis on curative medicine. Public health schools tend to become appendages, whereas, ideally, medicine should, perhaps, be an appendage to public health. If we could keep most people well most of the time, the problems of treatment could be reduced drastically in scale and scope. However, we recognize the immense practical difficulties involved in any attempt to transform the practice and teaching of public health and medicine.

Similar problems apply in the academic field of public administration and related careers in government service.

There is another topic on which I would like to comment. This involves some expansion of the range of our discussion. However, I think it would throw light on the questions which I have just raised. So far, we have been talking about *"American public administration,"* although the title we have formally used is "public administration." If we broadened our outlook to include public administration in other countries outside the United States, we might reach rather different answers. I agree that many of the propositions advanced, so far, in our discussion apply very well to *American* public administration, but they apply with much less relevance to public administration in Europe, and they may be positively misleading in Asia, Africa, and Latin America. I think that you should not say "public administration" if what you mean is "American public administration." It leads to terrible confusions.

Ironically, tendencies which are still incipient in the United States often show up in magnified form overseas. This can be seen if we look at the way in which American ideas about the subject of public administration, and how it should be organized academically, have been applied abroad. Without doubt, the proliferation of institutes, schools, and departments of public administration in a great many countries overseas during the last twenty years has been largely a response to American initiatives. What has happened? One very clear result is a split, almost a complete split, between public administration and political science. It is rare to find overseas any political science department in which public administration is taught well, or even taught at all.

SAYRE: In *those* political science departments. You are talking about a different animal overseas, are you not?

RIGGS: All right, political science abroad is also different from the American variety. Let me illustrate by taking Brazil as a case in point. Both Steve Bailey and I recently attended a conference in Rio de Janeiro which happened to come two weeks before another meeting in Buenos Aires. The Rio meeting was concerned with the improvement of public administration teaching and research in Latin America; the Buenos Aires meeting was on political science. There was almost no overlap between the two, in planning or participation, yet the two subjects are not only interdependent but substantively almost indistinguishable.

The University of Minas Gerais in Brazil is building a strong political science department with very substantial American assistance, financed by a private foundation. It devotes virtually no attention to the study of bureaucracy or the problems of governance. By contrast the Vargas Foundation in Rio, with substantial assistance from the United Nations, and later from the United States government, by way of a contract with the University of Southern California, has established exceptionally strong facilities for the study of public administration, presumably not "American public administration." Only recently, and in a very small way, has the study of politics been brought into this school.

Counterparts may be found in other countries. In India, for example, which has long had departments of political science, we find the emergence of parallel departments of public administration. But the major American thrust for the strengthening of public administration in India has taken the form of support for a new and independent Institute of Public Administration in New Delhi, following lines recommended by Paul Appleby. In the University of the Philippines, similarly, there is an old political science department and a new College of Public Administration, set up since the war with American assistance. In Thailand, also, public administration was set up, with American help, as an autonomous institute at Thammasat University, although political science had been organized before the war at Chulalongkorn University. The two pursue their separate and unrelated ways.

If, on intellectual grounds, administration and politics cannot be separated here in the United States, how much more indefensible is it to make such a separation in the less developed countries? There, the public bureaucracies are deeply and unavoidably involved in politics at every level, and it makes no sense to analyze public administration except in a political context, nor does it make sense to study politics there except in an administrative context. These are two aspects of a single phenomenon. Yet this bifurcation of the study and teaching of politics and administration abroad can be directly traced to the way in which public administration is taught in the United States.

I am not only arguing that the way we have tried to solve and to teach about problems of American public administration is dysfunctional when exported to other countries. I am also arguing that, for our own good, we need to see public administration in a broader context. The comparative study of public administration (not just American public administration) will help us overcome the malaise into which the theory of public administration has fallen in the United States.

To summarize, I think that we need to see public administration as a general field, not just as an American phenomenon. We need to study it in a political context, and hence in political science departments. In addition, we need to train people for the public service in professional schools offering an interdisciplinary array of subjects, among which the study of public administration and politics is an important element.

SHERMAN: I would like to go back to Gladieux' question and to the first of the three points you made, Mr. Chairman, and then end with a question for York Willbern on his position. The first point that you raised, Jim, in your three points, was that one can learn about public administration either as a profession or practitioner, or in general, since it is a good subject to know for any citizen. That brings me to the question of whether it would be useful to use the term "public affairs" for what the citizen should know, and the term "public administration" for what the professional public administrator should know. This brings me to my question for York. You put the emphasis on "public" rather than "administration" and suggest that "public affairs" is a better term than "public administration." Therefore, you seem to eliminate public administration as a meaningful term except, perhaps, as a synonym for public affairs. It seems to me that they must be separate concepts. When a person is in a voting booth, for example, he is engaged in public affairs, but he is not engaged in public administration. There *is* something called public administration, even if there is something else called public affairs. Now, what is your position?

WILLBERN: The response I would make to that, I guess, is this. It turns on another distinction that we have argued about for years. The more you use the term, "administration," the more the hearer gets the implication that you are talking about means, not ends; the more the hearer gets the idea that you are talking about *how* to accomplish an assigned task and responsibility, the less he has the concept that the task involves defining the end as well as the means. That is the chief concern which I have about the use of the term. It has, historically and traditionally, been taken to mean those activities which are not concerned with the goals, the ends, the policies, the substantive content of public affairs.

SHERMAN: I would not so define it. But even if one defines administration that way, it exists. One might choose to have a school of public affairs because one's interests are in ends rather than just in means. But even if one defines administration as the subject which deals with the means of carrying out public policy, one can not eliminate the subject.

UNIDENTIFIED VOICE. I get the impression that there is a kind of a trauma in this program this year, or maybe chronically, symbolized by the fact that either three or four papers refer to the absence of public administration as a major category in the political science meetings next year, less than last year, and presumably indefinitely in the future.

CLEVELAND: I really agree more with Dwight's orientation on this. It is not enough for public administration to be thought of as a subdiscipline of one academic department, just as administration cannot be thought of as one bureau of a government agency in which all other people are concerned with something else. Above a certain level of responsibility, public administration is everybody's second profession, everybody's second career.

If we think of it as a second profession, yet still insist that it is a distinctive discipline, then public administration is the discipline of being interdisciplinary. In order to have standing in a faculty, you have to prove that there is some special body of phenomena that is yours, like cells or rocks or something else, and you had better be prepared vigorously to defend your own particular and limited phenomena as not belonging to anyone else outside your "discipline."

What is interesting about public administration is that you get to be relevant to everybody's field; you get to include even the sciences that pride themselves on being called "hard," simply because one of the factors common to all fields is that of putting people together in organizations to make something happen in the public interest, regardless of the subject matter involved. Obviously, the subject matter involved does deeply affect what is done and how it is done by executives; the "program" part of the process of administration just has to be learned by exposure to that subject matter. You can not really learn about running a hospital without working in a hospital. But there are some things about what goes on in a hospital that are shared in common with a Marine platoon, and it is this common factor, or factors, that we have to keep trying to identify in our administrative theory. I would defend the American orientation in this set of papers, including my own, because I think that there is a sense in which we are on the frontier. We are the most developed country, and we have played around in an extreme fashion with public-private intermixtures. If we can really figure out why we are so successful in the things in which are are successful, that may be more help than teaching Ethiopians about bells, buzzers, and girl secretaries, which is part of what goes on in "overseas public administration." I would argue against our trying to make public administration a vertical discipline, one that can fit in between the other fields, either as a subdiscipline of political science or as a major department in its own right. We need, instead, this concept of overlay and an attitude of being unembarrassed about the fact that the subject matter that we play around with is everybody else's subject matter—is physics, is political science, is economics. We need to look at public administration in a more integrated way—and perhaps also a more policy-oriented and action-oriented way—than do those academic disciplines that are comprehended in the usual sense of that term.

Methodology in the Practice of Public Administration

By Harvey Sherman

ALTHOUGH others are dealing with the "scope of public administration," it is pertinent to say a few words at the outset on the "scope of this article." Somewhat arbitrarily, I will limit myself to "methodology in the practice of public administration" in the United States, rather than world-wide; in the executive branch primarily (recognizing that there are fascinating problems in the practice of public administration in the legislative and judicial branches, as well as in the relationships among the three branches); and with emphasis on the most important current and likely future trends and developments.

Others are also dealing with the "objectives of public administration." Nevertheless, since methods are, or should be, related to objectives, let me say only that, in this article, I am assuming what has been so often pointed out by the most recent generation of knowledgeable observers—that efficiency and economy are not the only goals of public administration. Some of the other legitimate goals of the public administrator, which may often be in conflict with efficiency and economy in government operations, include service to the public, responsiveness to public opinion and to pressure groups, aid to minority groups, aid to depressed areas, maintenance of the privacy of the individual, and even the need to get re-elected.

Probably the most distinguishing characteristic of public administration in the United States, given over 80,000 separate governmental jurisdictions, is its plurality; its essential variety. Further complicating the picture is a vast proliferation of government agencies and programs, many of which are making deliberate efforts to improve the quality of life of the American people. Because of these facts, it is most hazardous to generalize about the practice of public administration—the safest generalization being that one cannot generalize. Nevertheless, one can hardly write a meaningful or useful article of this nature without generalizing, so I shall throw caution aside and take the risk.

Unquestionably, the methods *available* for practicing public administration have changed. One might even hazard the guess that they have improved. Further, it is clear that the most modern techniques are being used in some jurisdictions, although even the most "conventional wisdom" is not being utilized in many others. Unfortunately, the size, complexity, importance, and potential explosiveness of the problems facing government have increased drastically—probably to a much greater degree than the methods available (or being used) to cope with them.

Fortunately, on the other hand, there appears to be greater recognition then at any time in our history of the fact that governments are not adequately coping with their major problems and that it is imperative that effective techniques be developed and used. Consequently, there is a good deal of experimentation, ferment, and thought on how governments might more effectively deal with their problems—at least in the most progressive jurisdictions.

Recognition of the problem has gone beyond the "professional" public administrator. Take, for example, two nationally known journalists who ordinarily write about subjects with much more political sex appeal:

James Reston of the *New York Times* has written:

As President Johnson starts his fourth year in the White House, one fact is not only clear but undisputed: his Administration is poorly organized to administer the domestic programs he has introduced, and the administrative chaos of the state and local governments is even worse. . . . He [the President] has an administrative monstrosity on his hands, and even his own people are beginning to criticize it in public.[1]

And Marquis Childs, in a recent syndicated column, after discussing the rapid growth of state and local government in recent years, has stated:

Part of this reflects the upsurge in population and the inevitable growth in services. But surely some of it is also to be found in the wanton waste of a crazy structure of government that has had no real overhaul

[1] James Reston, *New York Times*, November 23, 1966.

since its inception. How long even a country as rich as the United States can afford this is the burning question.[2]

Many businessmen have also become aware of the problem. Thus, the Committee for Economic Development, in excellent recent reports on the problem of modernizing state[3] and local[4] government found these governments, for the most part, woefully inadequate to their tasks. These reports have received wide acclaim in the press and among business and civic groups.

Turning to the question of "what is new and consequential" in the methods used for practicing public administration, I will review current and likely future developments in five principal areas: government–private sector relationships; government–government relationships; science and technology; government–employee relationships; and government–citizen relationships.

Government–Private Sector Relationships

Governmental problems have become so vast and so complex that various ways of mobilizing private resources to work along with government in solving them have been developing rapidly. The result is a blurring of lines between what is "private" and what is "public." Many "private" institutions operate primarily with public (tax) dollars, are regulated by the government in almost as much detail as government uses to control its own agencies, make decisions that affect the public interest to a large degree, and perform functions identical to those found in government. Many "public" institutions operate under a net revenue (self-support) concept, utilizing business-type financial and operating methods, carry out their functions primarily through private institutions, make decisions that affect the public interest to a relatively small degree, and perform functions identical to those found in the private sector.

Government by contract

One of the most revolutionary changes in the way that government work gets done is found in the dramatic growth of govern-

[2] Marquis Childs, Bergen County (New Jersey) *Record*, December 13, 1966.

[3] Committee for Economic Development, *Modernizing State Government*, July 1967.

[4] Committee for Econonic Development, *Modernizing Local Government*, July 1966.

ment work by contract. Many "private" companies are now engaged entirely or principally in government work. In some cases, entirely new private enterprises, such as RAND Corporation and the Institute for Defense Analyses, have been created to perform government work.[5] Some private companies and some universities actually spend more federal tax dollars (through the contract device) than do some of our federal departments and agencies. It has been estimated that over 90 per cent of the funds appropriated for the government atomic energy and space programs go into private hands through hundreds of universities and thousands of contractors and subcontractors. Government is by far the biggest single customer of business, and even a single government contract can make the difference between survival or demise of a particular company.

Initial use of the contract device was primarily for procurement and for research and development. Its use is now spreading rapidly to the day-by-day operation of government programs, as in rendering technical assistance abroad, conducting training and other programs for the Office of Economic Opportunity, utilizing banks for tax collections, and operating hospitals.

The use of cost-plus-fixed-fee contracts has changed the nature of business for many concerns by eliminating the risks of the marketplace. They cannot lose, and they are using government capital to boot. Perhaps even more surprisingly, as Don K. Price has pointed out, the government contract seems to have changed the nature of the reactions of businessmen to government. In his words, "their jealousy no longer takes the form of fighting socialism, but of haggling over the administrative provisions of contracts."[6]

At best, the government contract combines the public purpose of government with the flexibility and freedom from red tape of private enterprise. At worst, it combines the private purpose

[5] For a description of the different types of organizations handling government work by contract, see U. S., Bureau of the Budget, *Report to the President on Government Contracting for Research and Development,* printed by the U. S. Senate Committee on Government Operations, Document No. 94, 87th Cong., Second Sess., 1962, especially pages 2–4.

[6] Don K. Price, "The Scientific Establishment," *Science,* June 29, 1962, p. 1104. See this article and Don K. Price, "The Future of the Public Service," *Public Personnel Review* (April 1963), for a brilliant analysis of the problems of the government contract.

of private enterprise with the inflexibility and red tape of government. The problem is to insure that we get more of the former and less of the latter. This means that major public policy decisions should still be made by government, but that governmental controls should be limited to the minimum necessary to insure that public policy is being carried out effectively. This is not easy to achieve in practice—especially since the higher salaries and less restrictive environment in the private sector attract many of the people in government most competent to handle complex value problems, and leave in government many of the routine-minded people most comfortable in the role of exercising detailed controls.

There are other problems with the contract device—for example, how to decide which programs or activities are best handled by contract and which are best handled directly by government; how to avoid conflict-of-interest situations; and how to avoid the award of contracts on the basis of "politics" or undue personal influence of highly placed people.

There is also an additional major advantage—perceptively noted by Don Price—in that the contract device provides a means of "decentralization," in the sense of avoiding monolithic, overpowering government, in the same way that the grant-in-aid was an earlier device for reducing the transfer of power from state and local government to the federal government. If the government, however, in the exercise of its control functions, makes decisions formerly made by the contractors, we may bring about further centralization rather than decentralization, and we may find contractors more concerned over satisfying government requirements than over producing the best product.

The mixed government-business enterprise

A second device for a joint attack on public problems is that of the mixed government-business enterprise such as the Communications Satellite Corporation created by Congress in 1962 to develop and operate a global commercial communications satellite system. The board of directors of this corporation consists of representatives of the government, the general public, and the communications industry. The management problems involved in joint ownership and joint management are legion.

However, this approach has been seriously proposed for a whole variety of problems ranging from feeding the world's population to eliminating poverty. If adopted, and I predict that it will be, such an approach will provide an important and fascinating new problem for study and analysis by both the public and private administrator.

Other techniques for involving the private sector

In addition to the government contract and the mixed enterprise, governments have attempted to utilize the services and skills of the private sector in a host of other more informal ways. In some cases, no government funds are involved; in others, a variety of financial arrangements such as loans, grants, and tax incentives have been used.

New York City is a good example of a jurisdiction which, in recent years, has adopted as one of its major strategies the active involvement of the private sector in the solution of city problems. Thus, it has initiated a program for using college professors from local universities to assist in solving major city problems (possibly, in return for which, the city will help the universities to meet their physical expansion needs), and has created a Citizens Summer Committee of leading business and labor leaders to work with a Summer Task Force of city officials to develop a program of action to correct conditions in the city's ghetto areas that might lead to broad-scale disruption of civil peace during the hot summer months.

Other interesting examples in New York City include:
- An Operations Research Advisory Council consisting of top Operations Research (OR) specialists to advise on the use of this technique in the city and to analyze specific city problems utilizing OR techniques.
- A Management Advisory Council, consisting of the chief executives of national corporate headquarters located in New York City, who lend experienced individuals to the city on a no-cost, full-time basis to conduct studies in such fields as electronic data-processing, organization analyses, office procedures, cost accounting, and pensions.

- An Executive Volunteer Corps consisting of successful business executives to advise small-business owners and managers at no charge.
- A Volunteer Co-ordinating Council to co-ordinate the use of volunteers to help the city in a multitude of ways.

Other jurisdictions are also finding novel ways of involving private industry in the solution of public problems. Two highly publicized examples are the use by the State of California of four aerospace firms to undertake systems-engineering studies in the fields of transportation, crime-prevention, data-handling, and waste-management; and San Francisco's Community Renewal Program through which businessmen work with government officials in developing public policies that will encourage business to invest in undertakings that will improve urban living.

Mention should also be made of two other recent and novel approaches of great potential for government-private co-operation in solving major urban problems. One is the Urban Coalition, established in 1967 to enlist the private sector (business, labor, churches, the academic community, voluntary organizations, and the leaders of disadvantaged groups) to help government solve such pressing urban problems as housing, employment, education, and economic development. The second is the National Alliance of Businessmen, created in 1968 to find jobs for the hard-core poor (often classified as "unemployables"), with government money available to offset some of the training costs involved.

The extent and nature of current problems in urban areas has awakened business to its responsibilities for helping to solve them. As the president of one giant industrial company has said: "Businessmen can no more turn their backs on urban and community problems . . . than they can ignore production and sales problems."

Government regulation of business

As has been noted, involving the private sector in the public's business—whether by contract, mixed enterprise, or other methods—has narrowed the distinction between what is public and what is private. The distinction is also narrowed in another sense for any large business—even those not significantly involved in government work. This comes about from the fact that the increased size and importance of many businesses have made it imperative for government to regulate them in the public interest. Any major industrial firm today has regular and continuing contacts with and interest in a multitude of federal, state and local agencies, resulting in a sizable relationship problem. Political and administrative decisions have become as important to business success as the play of the market. In the words of Thomas R. Reid, Civic and Governmental Affairs Manager of the Ford Motor Company:

What happens in business today is determined more and more by what happened in government yesterday. Government has an impact on business policy and planning at least as great as the impact of competition in the marketplace because government, to a large degree, determines the nature of the marketplace.[7]

GOVERNMENT–GOVERNMENT RELATIONSHIPS

While the lines between "public" and "private" enterprise have undoubtedly been blurred, those between the levels of government in our federal system—at least in the operational sense, if not the legal and structural—seem to have become so intertwined that one wonders if they ever could, or should, be untangled. In simpler times, the major question asked about our federal system concerned which governmental functions should most appropriately be assigned to local government, which to state government, and which to federal. With the growing interdependence of all segments of our society, this question is now irrelevant for most major domestic governmental functions. The real question has become how to mobilize all levels of government into effective instruments of co-operation for jointly meeting the demands of a rapidly changing society, without sacrificing other values such as pluralism, democratic control, and the dignity of the individual.

A series of factors, such as a more mobile population, urbanism, technological advances in transportation and communication,

[7] "How To Do Business With Governments," *Edison Electric Bulletin* (June–July 1962), p. 220. See also John K. Galbraith's most recent book, *The New Industrial State* (Boston: Houghton Mifflin, 1967), in which he argues forcefully and persuasively that for today's giant corporations which conduct most of the nation's economy, the demarcation between public and private has little meaning.

and critical problems such as air and water pollution, poverty, crime, and congestion, have left existing geographic and jurisdictional boundaries with little more than historical, sentimental, and perhaps employment, value. Nevertheless, these lines are written into constitutions, contracts, deeds, governing laws, and the mental and emotional outlook of the majority of our inhabitants.

The grant-in-aid

The most important innovation affecting our federal system in the past hundred years has been the federal grant-in-aid to the states. This technique has many advantages: it provides the money necessary for needed programs which would not otherwise have been undertaken at all, or at the needed scale; it allows problems which exist throughout the nation to be handled at a scale and in a way suitable to different conditions in different parts of the country; it enables funds to be allocated so that poor areas with serious problems can receive more than they pay; it provides a way, through making grants conditional on certain requirements, of effectuating basic national policies such as the merit system, nondiscrimination, and adequate planning.

As governmental programs have multiplied and grown more complex, certain problems have arisen. For example:

(1) *Number and complexity of federal aid programs.* As of January 1966 there were 162 major programs under 399 separate authorizations or subcategories of authorizations. There were 91 formula grants and 226 project grants. This proliferation and fragmentation make it difficult to know what aid exists, inhibit the development of a unified approach to the solution of community problems, reduce the control of the chief executives of state and local governments over the shape of their budgets, place a premium on "grantsmanship" as a major qualification of state and local officials, and have brought about the creation of the new job of "Washington Representative" as a powerful influence in state and local affairs. By the end of 1967, some seventeen states, twenty-four cities, and four counties had established "on the ground" representation in the nation's capitol.

Efforts are being made to minimize this problem, principally by grouping related grant programs into a single financial package

—as in the Comprehensive Health Services Act of 1966—and by providing more systematic information on available federal grants. Thus, the Office of Economic Opportunity has recently published the first comprehensive single catalogue of all federal grants and other assistance programs and services, containing information on over 450 federal aid programs. And the National League of Cities, the International City Managers' Association, and the Department of Housing and Urban Development have all established programs to assist cities by providing information on federal aid programs.

(2) *Bypassing the states.* The urgency of major urban problems, the weaknesses of some states, and political factors such as rural domination of many state governments, have led to certain federal grants being made directly to cities, and even to private organizations. This practice often only further weakens the states.

(3) *Bypassing the chief executives.* Decisions on grants have often been made by federal agencies dealing directly with their counterparts on the state or local level, thus weakening the control of elected chief executives over their own governmental programs. In an attempt to correct this situation, President Johnson recently directed that the elected chief executives of state and local governments be consulted *before* program specialists enter into binding agreements on new or revised administrative directives, rules, regulations, or standards.

(4) *Weakness in state and local government.* The inability of many state and local governments to utilize federal funds effectively, unless drastic steps are taken to correct this situation, can ultimately lead only to a larger role by the federal government in direct action to solve local problems.

Oddly enough, the grant-in-aid device may be the best available means of motivating and helping the state and local governments to improve their management and alleviate their manpower problems. Several current efforts are being made in this direction. Senator Edmund S. Muskie, for example, has introduced legislation (known as the "Intergovernmental Personnel Act") that would, among other things, extend the requirement of merit standards to more grant-in-aid programs; authorize grants to states to enable them to strengthen their systems of personnel-administration as well as those of their subdivisions; authorize co-operative recruitment and training programs by the federal government with state and local governments; establish a grant-in-aid program for in-service training of state and local employees; and provide for interchange of employees between the levels of government. Two proposed administration bills, known as the "Intergovernmental Manpower Act" and the "Education for Public Service Act," embrace, with some modifications, the proposals made by Senator Muskie and would make grants to institutions of higher education to improve teaching programs and research related to education for the public service; provide grants to assist students in preparing for the public service; and facilitate the interchange of federal, state and local employees. Even more ambitious is a proposed bill being circulated for comment by Congressman Henry S. Reuss that would provide $25 billion in federal grants over a five-year period to states which take steps to modernize state and local government.

Because of resistance to federal "strings" attached to grant programs, there has arisen a demand in many quarters for some method of out-and-out sharing of federal funds with the states. While some such plan may well be tried, I think that it would be a serious mistake. In any meaningful partnership, the federal government must be more than a banker; it must play an active role in the solution of major urban problems. Moreover, if we are to save the federal system—that is to say, avoid rapid centralization to the national government in the face of ever-increasing interdependence among the states—then it seems to me imperative that there be certain stipulations to the receipt of federal funds. Most important, heavy pressure should be put on the states to improve planning and management in their subdivisions as well as in their own operations.

As an alternative to the straight sharing of federal funds, some sort of tax credit plan against federal taxes might be adopted for those states which have an income tax. Such a plan would serve the purpose of encouraging states to adopt an income tax (or increase their rates), but it is difficult through such a plan to achieve equalization among the states on the basis of need and ability to pay. Each of these plans—that is, the unrestricted sharing of federal funds with the states, and the tax credit—assumes that the federal government has, or could readily get, surplus funds for this purpose. This is a questionable assumption.

Creative federalism

More important than the specific problems that have arisen over the administration of grant-in-aid programs is a brand new dimension in intergovernmental relations to which the name "creative federalism" has been applied. In the past, the federal government either directly conducted nationwide programs, or financed (or partially financed) programs through the grant-in-aid to states. Now, based on recent legislation attacking major social problems such as the antipoverty program, federal, state and local governments all participate directly on specific projects in particular communities as coequal partners, with shared powers, shared functions, and shared resources. Clear lines of authority from superior to subordinate do not exist. Success in this multi-jurisdictional approach can be achieved only by mutual co-operation among equals. This is always a difficult task—complicated further by the fact that more than one federal agency and more than one local government jurisdiction are often involved.

There is no one easy administrative answer to the problem of achieving effective co-ordination. Nor will the answer necessarily be the same for each state or each locality. Clearly, agreement on purpose, mutual trust and confidence by each partner in the other, and competent people at each level, are paramount. But there are administrative devices or approaches that will help. Of prime importance for any major project in a given community is the designation of one local governmental jurisdiction as the chief co-ordinating agency. Certainly, the functions of establishing goals, developing comprehensive plans, and determining priorities among grant proposals must be a local, not a federal responsibility. The creation of the Housing and Urban Development Department to co-ordinate the work of different federal agencies in urban areas is a step forward. Especially important are its "convener" authority—a more effective way for bringing the right people together at the right time to solve a specific, concrete problem than the ubiquitous but usually ineffective interdepartmental committee which has responsibility for co-ordinating "in general;" funds for assisting governments in an area to co-ordinate their planning functions; and the Model Cities Program which attempts to reduce federal and local political fragmentation in a given area.

Unfortunately, since major urban problems inevitably involve many federal departments, it is not possible to bring all "related" federal programs under one department short of creating a "Department of Everything." Further decentralization of authority to federal field offices, a better rationalization of federal regions or districts, and effective use of the Federal Executive Boards would also help, as would better and more uniform information shared among all partners through a Central Data Bank, computer centers, technical assistance services, and other techniques.

Of course, major community problems such as ghettos, slums, and racial discrimination will not be solved by better co-ordination or other administrative techniques. The solution to such problems is, first, a matter of national purpose. Given this, it would then become possible to devote the massive funds and massive talent, similar in proportion to those devoted to war or to conquering space, necessary to achieve a solution.

State-local relationships

In the area of state-local relationships, where the federal government does not play an active role, the principal development is simlar to that discussed above—that is, the two levels working together co-operatively on major problems rather than each performing separate, completely autonomous functions. One of the major consequences, as pointed out by such perceptive observers as Wallace Sayre and Luther Gulick, is the relative meaninglessness of the shibboleth of "home rule." [8]

The states can play a crucial role in improving local government through such methods as revising their constitutions to modernize the forms and powers of local government, reducing the number of local jurisdictions and modifying their boundaries

[8] See *Modernizing State Government: The New York Constitutional Convention of 1967*, Papers Delivered at the Conference Sponsored by The Academy of Political Science, January 10, 11, and 12, 1967, ed. by Sigmund Diamond and Nancy Lane (New York: Academy of Political Science, 1967), 106–116.

to allow for viable jurisdictions more closely related to today's problems, and giving local jurisdictions broader authority to levy taxes. A constructive trend is the creation of separate state units to focus on the problems of local government and the relationships of the state to them. Such units can collect and disseminate useful information, provide technical assistance to local governments, co-ordinate federal and state aid programs, and encourage improved management in local jurisdictions.

Regional problems

With the growth of urban metropolitan areas, it has become obvious that today's economic and social problems are no respecters of geographic boundaries. Perceptive observers of a generation ago foresaw this development—and predicted the creation of regional governments to cope with it. Unfortunately (or fortunately, depending on one's point of view), this approach has been used infrequently and, with few exceptions, has been of questionable value where tried. Contract services provided by one jurisdiction for another and services provided jointly by a number of different jurisdictions have proved to be more successful, but even these apparently logical approaches are still far more the exception than the rule.

Where metropolitan areas cross state lines, the interstate compact agency, such as The Port of New York Authority, has proved a viable way of solving problems in specific functional areas—especially for commercial-type, revenue-producing activities. The number of such agencies has been growing steadily. A new variation with interesting possibilities is to include the federal government as a partner as in the Delaware River Basin Compact. Uniform state laws are also an aid to solving problems that involve more than one state.

Two new joint federal-state approaches to handling regional problems are worthy of note. The Appalachian Regional Commission, created in 1965, and consisting of the governors, or their representatives, of the twelve Appalachian States, together with a federal cochairman appointed by the President, develops plans for and co-ordinates comprehensive regional economic development programs which will contribute to the growth of the region. The Economic Development Administration, created by the Secretary of Commerce in 1965, designates economic development regions, assists the states in establishing regional action-planning Commissions within designated regions, and provides continuing advice and assistance to these regional commissions on the preparation of economic development plans.

Within a state, special districts and state authorities (for example, the Metropolitan Transportation Authority in New York) which cut across local jurisdictional lines have been created to solve specific interjurisdictional problems. A basic problem is one of numbers. Even if each such special district is successful in its own field, there comes a point when their proliferation causes problems in the management of government as a whole that outweigh the advantages.

Regional or metropolitan planning agencies have been established in large numbers throughout the country. These bodies have proved to be fairly effective where federal or state grants have been made dependent on whether a specific proposed project fits into an accepted regional plan. A strong push in this direction came from Section 204 of the Demonstration Cities and Metropolitan Development Act of 1965 which requires the review and comment by an area-wide body upon certain federal grant-in-aid applications. Where federal or state involvement is lacking, such planning bodies have often proved to be relatively ineffective discussion groups—largely because the basic interests of the central city and those of the surrounding suburbs are competing and divergent.

Some observers see great potential benefit in the dramatic growth of metropolitan Councils of Government (COG's) which are voluntary organizations of local public officials in a metropolitan area. Beginning in the mid-1950's, there were over a hundred such Councils by 1968, stimulated by federal financial assistance under the 1965 Housing and Development Act. Their activities have included joint planning, exchanging views on problems of mutual concern, sponsoring legislation, providing co-operative services and co-ordinating metropolitan programs. In some cases, COG's have been designated to exercise the "review and comment" functions under the Demonstration Cities and Metropolitan Development Act. While some COG's have had notable success, many have been beset by problems ranging from the basic issue of reconciling central city interests with those of the suburbs, to attacks from both the right wing ("a Socialistic or Communistic conspiracy to abolish local government") and the left wing ("a conspiracy of the White power structure to retain dominance over minority groups").

The problem of the relationship between the central city and the suburbs is becoming rapidly more serious as the middle class rushes to the suburbs, leaving the central city with its problems of minority groups, poverty, ghettos, and slums, together with a decreasing tax base to provide the ever-increasing need for funds to solve them. I think it almost a certainty that methods will have to be found by which those who live in the suburbs help to finance the central city.

Science and Technology

The impact of science and technology on public (or private) administration has probably received more attention in recent years than any other one influencing factor. One can hardly pick up a management journal these days that does not contain one or more articles on some aspect of this subject, and any school of public or business administration that has not added a series of courses on quantitative analysis, management science, and electronic data-processing is regarded in many quarters as archaic, if not completely passé.

Rate of change

More important than any particular technique or set of techniques made possible through scientific or technological breakthroughs is the incredibly rapid *rate* of change with which the public administrator must cope. As I have pointed out in considerable detail elsewhere,[9] this phenomenon is likely to have many important implications for the practice of management including the following. Management will have to recognize its responsibility for setting a climate that will anticipate, accept, and welcome change; there will be less rigid and less spelled-out views on objectives; there will be less rigid job descriptions and

[9] Harvey Sherman, *It All Depends: A Pragmatic Approach to Organization* (University: University of Alabama Press, 1966), pp. 136–143.

less rigid definitions of responsibility; there will be more frequent use of the task force, as contrasted to the usual hierarchical organization structure; more emphasis will be given to long-range planning and to the continuing study of the external environment; and there will be more instances of the establishment of a special organization-unit whose job is to question everything, including objectives.

The new techniques

The new methods or techniques affecting the practice of public administration, made possible by scientific and technological developments, are too numerous to discuss in detail. Most important would seem to be (1) the computer and electronic data-processing; (2) a series of quantitative-oriented tools which, for want of a generally accepted name, I shall refer to as "management science" techniques; and (3) the systems (or "total systems") approach. In one way or another, all of these methods involve information-processing and attempt to provide decision-makers with more objective and more reliable information, taking into account more relevant variables than heretofore possible. All of them are powerful and valuable tools for the executive—when used properly. But like other powerful tools, they can cause great harm when used improperly. Thus, we may become so enamored with "information" that we will confuse it with "wisdom"; so immersed in "facts," that we will ignore values and morality; and so impressed with our ability to quantify that we will forget that quality also counts.

Electronic data-processing and the computer

Basically, electronic computers perform three types of operations, all at fantastic speed—scientific (as in engineering calculations), management data-processing (as in accounting or tax administration), and process control (as in traffic control). For purposes of this article, I will be talking primarily about management data-processing computers.

Since the installation of the first computer for processing management data in the early 1950's, there has been a phenomenal growth in the use of computers and electronic data-processing at all levels of government. The federal government, for example, was estimated to have over 2,600 such computers in operation at the end of fiscal year 1966. Recent estimates place over 275 computers in the states and approximately the same number in local governments—mostly in cities with over 25,000 population.

Most of the computer installations in state and local governments are general-purpose computers used for data-processing in such areas as accounting, payroll, licensing, registration of motor vehicles, inventory-control, assessment, personnel records, utility billing, and voter registration. Future installations will undoubtedly see new applications, such as for transportation or land-use planning, and central data banks, as well as more special purpose, on-line, real-time applications dealing with such problems as criminal apprehension, traffic control, and hospital care.

The earliest installations of most data-processing computers in government focused on "savings" expected to result from the replacement of people by equipment. In many cases, the expected savings did not materialize when offset by the cost of the equipment, the salaries of computer programmers and operators, and the need for new people to analyze the additional data and reports turned out. Moreover, where savings did accrue, they frequently resulted primarily from the simplification of procedures in preparing them for computer use rather than from the computer itself.

Most recent justifications have been based on the fact that the computer provides more information than was previously available, and provides it faster. Both of these advantages can be crucial under certain circumstances. On the other hand, executives have long had more information than they can handle. The essential problem is not so much how to add to this flow of information as it is to decide what information is important, how to digest it, and what to do about it. As someone has correctly noted: "What the executive needs to know is what the executive needs to know."

It would seem self-evident that information not worth having is not worth having faster and more accurately. The computer cannot take irrelevant, unimportant, or inaccurate information and change its nature. It is well to remember that the letters GIGO stand for "Garbage In—Garbage Out," and not, as some would have it, for "Garbage In—Gospel Out."

It has been predicted that the computer will make middle management obsolete. This may happen in some circumstances—particularly where the computer replaces employees on a wholesale scale. But if the manager's job is to decide what to do, to get things done through people, to motivate others, and to ask the right questions, then as long as people are part of an organization, I can see the role of the middle manager only as continuing—even growing—in importance. Rather than replacing the middle manager, the computer, in many cases, is apt to enhance his job by identifying new problems, revealing new complexities, and providing new opportunities.

Management science

"Management science" is one of the generic terms that has been applied to a broad range of techniques that have been developed to help the manager through the quantification of data, the application of sophisticated mathematical techniques to his problems, and/or the use of simulation (model-building). These techniques become feasible, in part, because of the availability of the computer to digest and manipulate large quantities of information. They include, among others, Operations Research (which itself utilizes a host of tools such as linear programming, game theory, and simulation); Planning, Programming and Budgeting Systems (PPBS); network planning and control techniques (for example, PERT, CPM); and cost-benefit analysis.

One of the currently most glamorous of these techniques is PPBS—introduced into the Defense Department by former Secretary McNamara, extended to other government agencies by the President, and being adopted, or being considered for adoption, by many of the more progressive state and municipal governments. PPBS extends the use of the program-type budget, ties budgeting and work programming more closely together, integrates long-range planning with the annual budget, and uses such mathematical tools as cost-benefit analysis to assist in the selection of programs and the allocation of funds thereto.

PPBS, like any programming or budgeting system, is essentially a method of making choices. Utilizing cost-benefit analysis and other quantitative tools, this system can be extremely valuable when operating near the means side of the means-end spectrum.

Thus, given a desired end, such techniques can help in choosing the alternative means that will achieve it most economically and effectively. A good example is the selection of a particular weapons system that will best meet a previously determined military objective. As one nears the "end" side of the means-end spectrum, however, he is making choices among values. He is making choices which are political in nature; in other words, choices that determine who gets what, when, and how. Quantitative methods no longer suffice. Politics is the name of the game, and rightly so, under our democratic form of government. Thus, PPBS can tell us which weapons system to use in Vietnam, but not whether we should be there; how to produce a more powerful atomic bomb at less cost, but not whether to use it; what kind of space system to use to reach the moon, but not whether the same amount of money is better spent on helping to clean up the slums or searching for a cure for cancer.

Moreover, while PPBS has proved its efficacy in the procurement of weapons systems or other hardware, it does not necessarily follow that it is equally useful where the human element, with its nearly infinite variety of reactions, is a major part of the problem. Thus, motivation and spirit—intangibles not subject to quantitative analysis—can well be the controlling considerations. For example, I would guess that the North Vietnamese and the Viet Cong make little use of PPBS or cost-benefit ratios, yet, as of this writing, they are doing pretty well.

Like the "scientific management" movement founded by Frederick W. Taylor, the new mathematically oriented techniques have added an important new dimension to the practice of management, and therefore to the practice of public administration. But also like the scientific management movement, especially as interpreted by a long line of Taylor's disciples known as "efficiency experts," those who promote the use of these new tools often take a mechanistic approach, either forgetting that people are part of the equation in any important management process, or assuming that people are "rational" only.

While the new management scientists generally admit that certain things cannot be quantified, they often proceed to quantify what they can, and then draw conclusions as though the intangibles and unquantifiable values no longer existed. The quantitative approach gives an aura of objectivity to the study of managerial problems, but, in the present stage of our ability to measure, it covers only a small fraction of the factors affecting important management decisions, ignoring such important considerations as informal relationships, communication patterns, and leadership styles, not to mention spirit, motivation, courage, compassion, love, and plain old individual preference. The most important problem in decision-making is not quantification of data. The basic problems are determining what factors are relevant, how relevant they are, and what basic values and assumptions are held by the decision-maker.

It is interesting to note that reputable technical experts can be found to take opposite sides on even the most technical questions when they become adversary or controversial in nature. Curiously, using the best scientific and quantitative techniques, such experts practically always come out on the side of those who pay their salary.

The systems approach

In a certain sense, there is nothing basically new about the systems approach. It is a cyclical process involving careful definition of objectives, gathering of relevant data, analysis of the data, development of alternative approaches with an analysis of the consequences of each (especially in terms of effectiveness and cost), testing the alternatives where appropriate, requestioning objectives, assumptions, and alternatives, and the like. What is new is that through the use of the computer and the available sophisticated mathematical tools, this approach can take into account more variables and analyze more interrelationships—in other words, it can look at a problem in the framework of a larger system than had been possible in the past. Often, to do this, a team of analysts drawn from different disciplines is used.

One of the important characteristics of public administration is the critical impact that decisions in one program may have on another. To the extent that the systems approach can take into account a larger number of the ramifications of a particular decision, it is valuable to the decision-maker. He should know the probable consequences of his actions.

But there are dangers in trying to look at too broad a system.

The first and most obvious is that of delay. If a needed hospital, for example, must await the adoption of a master plan in a given community, many sick people may suffer for many years. More important, perhaps, is the possible impact on creativity, innovation, invention, and risk-taking. All governments in the United States, for example, could be looked at as one system. If they were totally rationalized into the one most efficient system, I wonder whether it would be possible to get the same amount of experimentation, of new and different approaches, that is possible when looked at as a large number of different systems.

Many advocates of the systems approach talk glibly about studying a problem as a "total system." Whatever the desirability in theory of looking at problems in terms of broader and broader systems, in a fast changing world it is often simply impractical to wait until the total system can be changed to adjust to the new environment, and much more effective to make a series of improvements in various subsystems even if such changes are not related to the total picture. Charles E. Lindblom's concepts of "muddling through" and "successive limited comparisons" may often give better net results than an attempt at one big final answer. Ultimately, the question may be which is more efficient in the long run, uniformity and neat logical systems, or variety and an increased number of options.

Government–Employee Relationships

I suppose that it would be generally agreed (from the point of view of modern personnel-administration, even if not always from the point of view of political objectives), that government seeks to attract, develop, and retain high-quality employees at all levels, and to provide a climate that makes it possible for each employee to do the best job that he is capable of doing. Some of the more important changes in the methods used by governments to achieve these objectives are discussed below.

Composition of the work force

In government, as in industry, there has been a sharp trend in recent years toward more white-collar and less blue-collar employees. In the federal government during the last decade, for example, white-collar employees increased by 15 per cent while blue-collar employees decreased by 19 per cent. Most of the increase among the white-collar employees was in the professional, technical, and managerial categories (often referred to at "knowledge workers"). The same categories are growing at even greater rates in state and local government because total employment in these governments is increasing much more rapidly than in the federal government.

As a result of the growth in the number of knowledge workers, as well as the general increase in schooling in the country, the educational level of those making up the work force has been rapidly rising. The consequences for the practice of public administration are already discernible and can be expected to continue.

Better-educated employees are apt to be dissatisfied with routine, monotonous, and noncreative jobs with little responsibility and much supervision, and to place greater emphasis on democratic, as contrasted to authoritarian, values. Because knowledge workers tend to want to retain their individuality, there will have to be less emphasis on consistency of treatment and seniority—prized by manual and clerical workers—and more emphasis on the differences among individuals rather than the likenesses. I expect also that there will be fewer (or at least, different) controls, fewer layers of supervision, greater use of project teams which change membership as different projects are completed or initiated, and more freedom to undertake self-initiated work. The term "colleague control" as contrasted to "hierarchy control" is becoming popular as a description of the new type of control governing those who work primarily with their minds.

Union relationships

Probably the most volatile problem in government personnel-administration today is that of government-union relationships. It might seem at first blush that, with all the experience that industry has had in this field, government would merely have to follow suit. However, there are many differences, ranging from questions of sovereignty and the right to strike to the fact that many of the most militant unions in government, in contrast to industry, are in the professional and subprofessional fields such as social workers, teachers, nurses, police, and firemen. Another critical difference lies in the concept of separation of powers in American government. The responsible administrative head may well negotiate agreements which require legislative action to effectuate—especially where the question of money is involved. This may be another way of saying that basic decisions affecting employment in government are primarily political, whereas in industry they are primarily economic.

The trend in government is clear. Union membership is growing rapidly; unions are becoming much more militant; and more jurisdictions are adopting a formal framework for dealings between government agencies and employee organizations. These plans usually recognize the right of public employees to join or refrain from joining employee organizations, authorize collective bargaining on personnel policies and the terms and conditions of employment, authorize dues check-offs, and provide a plan for handling grievances which may include compulsory or advisory arbitration. Perhaps the first government agency to adopt a plan of this nature was the Tennessee Valley Authority. Other examples of such plans are those set up by Executive Order of the Mayor of New York City in 1958; by Presidential Executive Order for the federal government in 1962 (Executive Order 10988); and by legislation in Wisconsin (1962), Michigan (1965), and Connecticut (1965).

There may well be many advantages to this development—for example, those generally associated with employee participation in setting policies; improvement in management-employee communications; substitution of partnership for paternalism and joint for unilateral decision-making; improvement in working conditions for governmental employees (employee organizations have sometimes provided the necessary additional leverage to get legislative acceptance of particular personnel benefits that management also desired). But there are a host of problems and unanswered questions, such as the following:

(1) *Right to strike.* Rigid antistrike laws have frequently not been enforceable (or, at least, enforced). Quasi-strike methods have arisen—for example, work-ins, "blue-flu" (police calling in sick), and mass resignations. There is some question over whether government employees performing the same kind of

work as those in private industry should be treated differently on this score. Some believe that true collective bargaining is not possible without the right to strike; others, that collective bargaining can be an effective method for avoiding strikes.

(2) *Compulsory arbitration.* Compulsory arbitration may be one answer to the question of the right to strike. But is it compatible with governmental sovereignty? Might it not weaken the process of collective bargaining? And what evidence is there that employees will not strike if they do not like the decision of the arbitrator?

(3) *Bargainable issues.* If wages are bargainable, how does this affect the budget process and to what extent can appropriating (legislative) bodies be committed through the collective bargaining process? One of the critical issues in the recent strike of social workers in New York City was whether the question of allowances to welfare clients was subject to negotiation.

(4) *Effect on classification and compensation plans.* If wages are set by negotiation, what happens to the customary job-classification and compensation plan which follows a policy of "equal pay for equal work" rather than the strength of a particular employee organization?

(5) *Effect on the merit system.* With traditional union emphasis on seniority, work rules, and production quotas, can a personnel system based on selection and promotion by merit be maintained?

(6) *Effect on Civil Service Commissions.* If personnel rules and regulations are set by collective bargaining and policed by the unions, what will happen to the traditional government civil service commission?

(7) *Bargaining units.* There are many questions as to the appropriate bargaining unit for both the employer and the employee. For example, should bargaining be done on an agency basis or government-wide? Should it be on a craft or industrial basis? How can small communities hold their own in bargaining with unions that are affiliated with national or international organizations?

Despite the problems, I think it is safe to predict that government unions will continue to grow and flourish, that they add a powerful force to the decision-making process in government, and that it behooves management in government to increase rapidly the number and expertise of managers and personnel-administrators with skills and experience in collective bargaining. There is much that can be learned from experience in some other countries, notably Canada.

Executive development, training, and placement

The Government Employees Training Act of 1958 was undoubtedly one of the major landmarks in federal personnel legislation. It opened to federal civilian employees training opportunities that had been available to military and industrial employees for many years. And it set a pattern for state and local governments to follow, although as yet only some of the more progressive jurisdictions have done so. Executive Order 11,348, of April 20, 1967, supplements the 1958 Act by providing a new charter for affirmative action on training and education of career employees.

Prior to 1958, there were virtually no federal training courses for civilian executives operated by the government, and only a handful attended university courses. Less than ten years later, in fiscal year 1966, some 22,000 federal employees from 65 departments and agencies attended 545 Civil Service Commission courses, and some 65,000 employees attended nearly 2,000 interagency courses. In 1968, a Federal Executive Institute was being established, to be operated by the United States Civil Service Commission. Through a series of eight-week courses, the new Institute will train some 360 top federal executives a year. Emphasis will be on broad constitutional, policy, and program issues; on the major problems facing our society and what government is doing or can do about them; on the interrelatedness of government programs; and on building a sense of common purpose and common loyalty to the government as a whole.

The Institute will be based on experience gained in a number of programs initiated in the previous decade—including two Executive Seminar Centers for mid-career training located at the United States Merchant Marine Academy at Kings Point, New York, and at Berkeley, California; a series of conferences for federal executives run by the Brookings Institution; and university-based courses through the National Institute of Public Affairs, the Princeton Fellows program, and others.

At all levels of government, there has been a rapid increase in the number of internship programs and part-time jobs for college students. Such jobs serve a number of purposes—they help students get a college education; they expose students to a better knowledge of government; they interest students in public employment; and they give a particular agency and a particular student a chance to "size each other up" for possible later employment.

The more effective assignment and utilization of top federal executives should be facilitated by the recent establishment of the Executive Assignment System. Over the years a series of different studies and reports, including those of the two Hoover Commissions, the American Assembly, the Brookings Institution, and the Committee for Economic Development, have recommended changes in the senior civil service, generally along the lines of basing compensation on rank in the man rather than in the job to which he is assigned, and building primary identification with the government as a whole rather than with one agency or function.

The new Executive Assignment System does not go this far. However, it does provide an executive inventory of some 26,000 executives in grades GS 15-18 and equivalent, so that the appointing officer can select the most capable person available from the entire government (provision is also made for consideration of outside talent), rather than confining his search to his own particular agency, which has been the usual case in the past. The aims of the new system are to systematize the location, development and utilization of the best executive talent available for key federal posts; provide executives with more opportunity to use their talents where they are most needed; and build loyalty to the federal service as a whole.

Mobility within the federal Establishment is relatively simple when compared with attempts to achieve mobility between governmental jurisdictions and between government and the private sector. The obstacles are great—separate retirement systems, differences in pay structure, residence requirements, and personal problems, to mention a few. Nevertheless, the subject of mobility is receiving a great deal of attention, and I look for considerable progress in this area in the years to come.

Motivation

One of the most crucial problems in government is how to make rewards commensurate with performance. Great strides have been made in recent years in adopting a great variety of incentive awards (monetary and nonmonetary) to recognize outstanding individuals and units. But this is the icing on the cake. Drastic changes are needed in the more basic methods of rewarding and motivating the effective employee. For example:

(1) *Salary.* Government salaries, especially at the federal level, have improved significantly in recent years. But this affects all employees in a given grade. The exceptional employee needs additional monetary recognition. One way is to adopt a merit increase system under which an employee's periodic within-grade increase is based on performance rather than merely on putting in time.

(2) *Promotions.* This is perhaps the most important motivating force of all. Yet promotions are often based on the ability to take examinations rather than on performance. Also, promotions are frequently handicapped by requirements that a person spend a certain number of years in grade before becoming eligible for the next grade. Such restrictions should be eliminated. Further, no matter how excellent an employee may be, he generally cannot be promoted until there is a vacancy. In many professional areas, a new concept is needed—that is, that a person should be promoted when he is ready, not when the job is ready. The use of "maturity curves" rather than standard classification methods for certain types of professional jobs is one method of at least partially accomplishing this objective.

(3) *Management climate.* A management climate that allows for freedom of expression, acceptance of responsibility, risk-taking, the chance of doing something important that does not require a multitude of clearances, and acceptance of the non-conforming personality, is highly important. All too often in government, the opposite is the case.

Equal opportunity

Over the years, governmental jurisdictions with effective merit systems have shown little overt discrimination against minority groups. As a result, a relatively large proportion of the members of such groups have gravitated to government work. At the same time, the very nature of a merit system which uses testing (especially written or other verbal tests) for filling vacancies penalizes disadvantaged groups, whose members are largely from minority groups, since they lack the education and middle-class values important to scoring well in such tests. As a result, at least until the very recent past, we have had a system that does not "discriminate" but that does not at the same time achieve a sufficient measure of "equal opportunity."

Much can be done to correct this situation where there is a will to do so, as evidenced by the impressive record of the federal government and some states and municipalities in increasing Negro employment in recent years. The techniques for accomplishing this objective, however, are not yet adequately developed or understood.

By and large, the search for "culture-free" tests has not proved to be very effective. Better results can probably be achieved by a reduction in the use of written and other verbal-type tests and an increased use of performance-type tests, interest inventories, simulation, and measures of past performance, as well as by a return to that much maligned testing device, the employment interview.

Also, the straight addition of a certain number of points to the test score of "disadvantaged" or nonwhite persons, or setting a lower passing score for them, presents numerous serious pitfalls, not least of which is the danger of perpetuating the idea that such persons are somehow inferior. However, it might be possible to develop a scoring technique that measures a person's achievement *in terms of his own background* rather than in comparison with the scores of others of different backgrounds. In college recruiting, for example, we frequently make some allowance for a somewhat lower grade-point average by the student who has worked his way through school. Why not give a similar credit to the person who has achieved a measure of success relative to his cultural and educational background?

Because of the lack of education and skills among the disadvantaged, efforts must be concentrated on providing the types of jobs they can handle—with on-the-job training to enable them to progress. Along these lines, the federal government's MUST (Maximum Utilization of Skills and Training) Program inaugurated in 1966 is a good example. Under this program, jobs are redesigned to separate nonprofessional tasks from professional, and routine tasks from technical, in order to combine lower-skill tasks into new jobs at low grades.

Equal opportunity is a concept that applies to more than minority groups—it also applies to women and the physically or mentally handicapped. The federal government has made especially great strides in the hiring of women in recent years—principally by drastically limiting the right of appointing officials to specify sex when considering appointments or promotions, and by aggressive recruiting for talented women wherever they can be found. Most states and local jurisdictions have done little in this area. Several states (for example, Minnesota, New York, and Pennsylvania) and a number of municipalities have adopted constructive and imaginative programs for hiring the physically handicapped and mentally retarded.

Behavioral sciences and the search for excellence

It is impossible to assess the extent to which over a million government supervisors, managers, and executives are applying the findings of the behavioral sciences in the day-to-day management of government affairs. One perceptive observer of the federal scene bemoans the relatively little use made of psychologists in the federal service, notes the increased use of economists, and believes that there is a growing recognition of the fact that organizations are social systems.[10]

The one fact that appears clear to me is that there has been far too little research and experimentation concerning the application of behavioral science findings to the management of government agencies. An exception is the major attempt by the United States Department of State to increase its effectiveness by using a team of advisors consisting of Department officials, behavioral scientists, business leaders, and other specialists. Resultant changes, according to one observer, have included the

[10] Roger W. Jones, "Developments in Government Manpower: A Federal Perspective," *Public Administration Review* (June 1967), pp. 139–140.

adoption of the "program manager" concept, the elimination of several layers of supervision, the use of "sensitivity" (or "laboratory") training and off-site problem-solving conferences, the adoption of improvements in information-processing, and the use of a variety of methods for encouraging innovation.[11]

While the findings of the behavioral sciences are sometimes too general, and sometimes too specific, to be useful, and often seem to be internally inconsistent, nevertheless, I think that by now we have learned enough from them (especially in such areas as motivation, creativity, interpersonal relationships, group dynamics, mental health, and the management of conflict) to give some real clues on the kind of organizational climate needed in government to help achieve excellence in the public service.

Too often in the past, government agencies have adopted bureaucratic values featuring ritualism, discipline and excessive conformity. Under this system, authority becomes vested in the office rather than in the person, and an organizational structure is created which tends to eliminate personalized relationships and nonrational considerations and to foster precision, reliability, and efficiency. The demand for reliability of response and strict devotion to regulations interferes with appropriate action in situations not provided for in the regulations. The personality pattern of the bureaucrat becomes focused around impersonality, and work loses any sense of personal fulfillment. At work, men play it safe, seek security, and cultivate smooth human relations. The innovator, upon whom society depends for a steady flow of new ideas and actions, is overwhelmed. The group—the team—becomes supreme, and woe betide the individual member of the team who does not "fit in." The over-all result is a consistently low level of predictable, organized mediocrity.

A new atmosphere is needed. We must begin by assuming that healthy, mature people do not see themselves as mere passive lumps of clay, helplessly being acted upon by forces from outside; rather, they see themselves as active, autonomous, and self-governing. For the most part, they wish to be movers and choosers and individual centers of their own lives. If we wish

[11] For an account of this program, see Alfred J. Marrow, "Managerial Revolution in the State Department," *Personnel* (November–December, 1966), pp. 8–18.

them to perform in an "excellent" manner, we must create a climate of openness and freedom in our governmental agencies.

For this type of organizational environment, we need a new type of executive, one who is creative, enterprising, dynamic, flexible and goal-oriented, with a high tolerance for ambiguity, ability to live with stress, and a restless desire for improvement and progress. Under the view that the executive is the overseer of the agency, we have too often in the past developed a leadership that is based upon power and the authority of office. Frequently, therefore, the final product has turned out to be a status-oriented, inflexible, conservative, cautious and procedurally minded person. This type of leader exists to preserve the status quo. The master of the bureaucratic system, he succeeds in producing mediocrity and conformity, carefully dressed up in the trappings of impartiality, rationality, and equality.

Government–Citizen Relationships

Ultimately, under our form of government, the citizen must retain control over his government through his elected representatives and, where appropriate, through the courts. Nevertheless, elections are frequently based on personalities, or on one or two major issues. And resort to the courts is expensive and time-consuming.

The citizen's day-to-day contacts are largely with the executive bureaus and agencies. We need to devise the best methods possible within the executive branch to prevent arbitrary action by civil servants, to ascertain the desires and reactions of the citizen to particular government programs, to maintain his participation and interest in government, and to insure that he receives fast, courteous and responsive service.

Redress of grievances

The most talked-about new device for handling citizen complaints is the "Ombudsman"—an institution first established in Sweden to protect the public and the citizen against abuse of administration authority, arrogance and maladministration. The Ombudsman plays a role somewhat similar to the Inspector General of the United States Army. His value has been more often in "thorough explanation" than in achieving changed decisions. The first such office in the United States was established by Nassau County, New York, although the Complaint Bureau established by Mayor LaGuardia in the New York City Department of Investigations many years earlier fulfilled many of the functions of the Ombudsman.

Although the Ombudsman has worked well in parliamentary governments, it is not yet clear whether he could work as effectively under our separation-of-powers system—even whether he should be appointed by, or report to, the legislative or the executive branch, or be independent of both. Also, we do not yet have sufficient experience to know whether, in a country our size, the Ombudsman would be an effective device at all levels of government (federal, state and local) or only at one or two levels.

Another device for handling complaints is the civilian review board composed of private citizens who review the actions of government employees—most frequently, police officers. Such a police review board seems to have worked well in Philadelphia, but was established and then abolished, by a special ballot in New York City. Proposals for review boards have raised strong emotions on both sides. Again, we still have too little experience to determine under what circumstances they can work most effectively.

The citizen demonstration—peaceful or otherwise—has had a long (and relatively successful) history in the United States as a method of trying to get government to take action, or to change previous decisions. While no established government can tolerate demonstrations which involve violence, there is much government can learn from them—if it systematically attempts to do so.

In order to make it convenient for citizens to express grievances or complaints, New York City has established a variety of methods in addition to the normal means of contacting the Mayor, Commissioners, City Council members, or particular departments. These include a Department of Investigation, Box 100 (written communications may be unsigned), Night Owl Mayors (responsible officials serving as "duty officer" throughout the night seven days a week), a Mayor's Action Center, and a central telephone number for all complaints on housing and building matters.

Determination of public desires and reactions

It seems to me that government agencies at all levels, with relatively few exceptions, have failed to make effective use of scientific polling techniques and other modern marketing research tools in determining the desires of citizens for services or their reactions to existing programs. Local government agencies, in particular, are prone to assume that a telephone call from an individual friend or influential citizen expresses the feelings of a large segment of the community.

An effective device, too rarely used, is the establishment of a specific organizational unit within an agency with the responsibility of systematically obtaining the views of the citizens its agency services. The Port of New York Authority, for example, has established a Patron Services Unit which, through an analysis of all patron correspondence and the use of a great number of questionnaires and selected depth interviews, continuously obtains the views of the patrons that use its various facilities.

Much attention has been given in the last few years to another method of obtaining citizen views—that is, involving citizen representatives directly in policy-formulation and operations. This interest has developed because of the requirement that representatives of the poor be directly involved in some phases of the antipoverty program. The advantages of utilizing the poor in programs aimed at helping themselves are obvious. But the mechanics for making this approach work effectively are not clear. Much more experimentation is needed to avoid the many pitfalls involved. To mention just one—people at the poverty level in policy-making positions may well not appreciate the need to pay adequate salaries (when measured in relation to their own income) to obtain competent staff.

As government grows bigger, more complex, and more technical, the natural tendency for the average citizen is to feel that he does not understand it, that he has no control over it, and that he can have no effective impact on it. The result can easily be apathy with respect to government policies and operations, and bewilderment in knowing how to deal with it. Whether democratic government can survive under these conditions—unless solutions can be found—is certainly debatable.

Improving service to the citizen

It is easy for public employees to forget that they are first and always "public servants." Strenuous and continuous efforts must be made to insure that this concept does not get lost.

The federal government inaugurated a systematic program to insure fast, efficient, and courteous service to the individual citizen in November 1965. This program is aimed at providing faster and more responsive communications to the citizen, improving the courtesy and general attitude of employees who deal with the public, and improving the accessibility of government. In attempting to achieve the first two aims, use is made of training courses, special publications, incentive awards and better controls. The third aim is to be achieved through such means as more convenient office hours, better building-directory boards, better location of offices, and "one-stop" service. The first Federal Information Center providing information on all federal activities was opened July 11, 1966, in Atlanta, Georgia on a pilot basis. In addition, in order to provide more convenient information on all federal jobs, some sixty-five full-time Interagency Boards of Examiners have been established to replace 546 single-agency boards, many of which were part-time.

A similar example can be found in the Service Center Program of the State of California. In 1966, the state authorized the establishment of thirteen such centers to bring together in convenient localities the services of all state, county, and municipal agencies engaged in helping the poor. Hopefully, federal and private services will also be added.

A similar approach, appropriate to large cities, is the establishment of "Little City Halls," representing the chief executive, where a citizen can conveniently go for immediate action or to find out where he can get action.

Another way to help achieve better service would be for the "public relations" or "information" office to broaden its concept of the function from the typical one of issuing press releases and answering specific inquiries to a much broader one which would include all the modern techniques of community relations used in progressive industrial firms, responsibility for helping to insure courteous and fair treatment of the citizen by employees in the agency, and responsibility for furnishing policy advice *in advance* to top decision-makers on the public relations implications of major policy and operating decisions.

Maintaining the privacy of the individual

As government influences and controls a bigger part of our life, it becomes all the more important that the individual maintain a certain amount of personal privacy. The courts and legislative bodies are currently trying to define this area with respect to wire-tapping, electronic eavesdropping, and the lie detector. The use of personality tests for employment and the detailed scrutiny of the private lives of people receiving welfare funds add to the problem.

Various proposals are currently being made to consolidate into one National Data Center the information which is now scattered among many different governmental agencies. The "logic" of efficiency and effectiveness will undoubtedly bring this about in the not too distant future. But, certainly, ways of insuring that this information is used for legitimate purposes only must be found.

A related question—and one of the fuzziest areas in government today—has to do with accessibility to government files. The recent federal "Right to Know" Act lays down a general policy of access to government information, puts the burden on the agency to justify denial of access, and gives the citizen a speedy method for determination of the issue. This can be a two-edged sword. The citizen may have much to gain by the right to know what is in his own files in the government. But he has much to lose if such information is open to others who may use it for mischievous or improper purposes.

In a broader context than information in government files about a particular citizen is the question, too big to treat here, of the right of the public and the communications media to know what is going on in government versus the need for the public employee to be able to put his honest beliefs on paper without worrying that he may some day have to answer for them in a political or personal context.

Conclusion

Another way to have approached this article would have been on a program-by-program basis. Looked at this way, one could describe many drastic changes that have taken place, or are likely to take place, in particular program areas. For example, if the present system of social welfare should give way to one which focuses on the negative income tax, the family allowance, or some form of guaranteed annual income, the whole methodology for practicing public administration in this area would be revolutionized. Could any two approaches be more different than those of the social worker and the internal revenue agent?

Whatever the methods or the techniques that are used in public administration, they are less important to successful public administration in the long run than the caliber of the people that make up our government (the executive branch, in the context of this article, although it may be even more true for the legislative and judicial branches). This is especially true at the top levels. Technique is no substitute for leadership. John W. Gardner, in a brilliant speech entitled "The Antileadership Vaccine," expressed this point eloquently. He comments caustically on leaders who "put through a series of clearances . . . or take a public opinion poll . . . or devise elaborate statistical systems, cost-accounting systems, information-processing systems, hoping that out of them will come unassailable support for one course of action rather than another," or who feel that all "kinds of problems can be solved by expert technical advice or action." He goes on to state that these notions are based "upon a false conception of the leader's function. The supplying of technically correct solutions is the least of his responsibilities. . . . Leaders worthy of the name . . . contribute to the continuing definition and articulation of the most cherished values of our society. They offer, in short, moral leadership."[12]

[12] Published in the Annual Report of the Carnegie Corporation of New York, 1965, pp. 3–12.

Comment on Sherman's Paper

By John W. Macy, Jr.

THE grand sweep and conceptualization of Harvey Sherman's paper on "Methodology in the Practice of Public Administration" is so satisfying that it leaves room for very little to say except "amen." But, with the usual persistence of the commentator to have *something* to say, I should like to use Sherman's exemplary piece, first, as a springboard for elaboration of some very important points and, second, to supplement it with a few observations of perhaps lesser significance.

Complementary Observations

There are a number of well-taken statements, conclusions, or predictions by Sherman that, in my judgment, deserve major attention and which I should like to reinforce briefly.

(1) Quite properly, he devoted considerable space to the most inadequately studied facet of modern public administration: government by contract. Although the total impact of this post-World War-II phenomenon is not presented in the paper, the thread of significance comes through.

It always strikes me as curious that one of the invariable purposes ascribed to contracting for certain services with private organizations is the need for "flexibility and freedom from red tape." Yet the very inflexibilities and red tape that are cited have been imposed by representatives of the people through their elected officers or legislative bodies precisely for the purpose of *control* of public administration. Therefore, it behooves one to speculate whether the act of contracting does not suggest either of two circumstances: (a) it is an evasion of public accountability; or (b) it demonstrates that controls on public administration that already exist are outmoded and too rigid.

Clearly, if it is the first condition, then the whole process of contracting deserves searching re-examination. And, if it is the second, the situation provides a powerful argument for administrative reform of the public service. In neither case does contracting appear as the inevitable, or necessarily the most favorable, solution for getting much of the government's work done. It is interesting to observe, as an aside, that by comparison with the federal government's dealings with state and local governments through the device of grants-in-aid, the requirements and controls on contractors appear to be minimal.

When the generalizations are swept aside and one gets down to specifics, the public service limitations that appear to create the greatest red tape are such things as competitive bidding, audits, open competition for personnel, veteran preference, discipline, and salaries. On salaries alone, to take one example, if the taxpayers and the voters are justified in setting certain restraints on the establishment of public salaries, then by what rationalization should these restraints be absolute and constraining for the regular public service but rather relaxed and loose for government contractor personnel? This issue alone deserves more than passing scrutiny of the scholars and statesmen who are evaluating American public administration.

It might have been useful—assuming it could not have been accomplished within the scope of Sherman's paper—to have had at least one dissertation in this volume on the contracting subject, including analysis of one very significant and often overlooked factor: the point that controls on public administration are usually prescribed by administrators and politicians (presumably representing the people) and that controls on contractors are usually prescribed by contracting officers (whose relationships are with special interest groups and ordinarily not the general public).

(2) I was especially impressed with Sherman's recognition of the scope and importance of public manpower problems. Because it has been my special area of concern for many years, I may be accused of ignoring other equally important issues, but Olympian as I may try to be, I cannot refrain from being distressed by the sheer magnitude of the administrative, professional, and technical manpower needs, particularly of our states and cities, and, even more so, the general lack of sensitivity to and interest in this subject on the part of legislative bodies, professional groups, and the general public.

Two measures now pending in Congress, the proposed Intergovernmental Manpower Act and Education for Public Service Act, are receiving by no means the urgent attention that they deserve, in spite of valiant efforts by a single legislator, Senator Muskie of Maine. Yet, in my judgment, the problems which these measures seek to treat rank alongside, and, indeed, are inextricably intertwined with, the great issues of our society— with urban blight, poverty, water supply, transportation, education, employment, health care, and all the others.

(3) I was pleased that Sherman emphasized the need to find ways for suburbs to help "finance the central city." Here the incongruities of our governmental structure and the artificiality of political boundaries plague us as they have never plagued us before. Creative federalism, regional compacts, and all the other adaptations that are innovative and fruitful will do their part, but I suggest that we are nowhere near the end of this problem and that we are far from an adequate solution for the long-range future.

(4) It is reassuring to have a distinguished student and practitioner of public administration warn us of the dangers of over-reliance on quantitative techniques. The old scientific management school of a half-century ago appears to be blossoming forth all about us in a kind of *nouveau riche* of automatic data-processing, operations research, systems approach, and cost-benefits analysis. Like Sherman, I do not disparage the value of any of these. But I am suspicious that some devotees of such tools look upon them as panaceas and elevate them almost to a place of worship.

Just as Frederick Taylor's sycophants of some decades ago fell into the error of overlooking the importance of the individuality of human beings, of the role and forms of communication, of the fact that workers and managers have wills of their own, so we may be in danger in the 1960's of overlooking that all administrative needs are *not* adequately dealt with through economic quantification and through information storage and retrieval.

(5) This automatically leads to my applause for another Sherman contention—his stress of the need for a personnel system to be based on the differences among people instead of on a concept of mass uniformity. It is perhaps this stumbling block of insistence on uniformity and on an impossible level of

egalitarianism on which so many of our legislators, and, I fear, even the representatives of our public employee unions, have tripped. In efforts to insure against favoritism, political manipulation, or other unholy operations, laws and regulations have too often moved in the direction of stultifying recognition of unique talent and handicapping full utilization of individual capacities. Old-fashioned as it may sound, I am still partisan to the need to recognize human differences, to reward extraordinary achievement and effort (and even "above ordinary" achievement and effort!). I cannot accept the idea that modern technology or the size of public enterprises necessitates standardization, seniority, and protectionism in our public services.

(6) I am pleased that Sherman calls attention to the importance of executive training and placement in modern government. We take pride in the advances that have been made in training programs in recent years and in the establishment of the new Executive Assignment System in the federal service. Recognition of the impact of executive behavior and performance in an organization has finally come into its own. It is gratifying that progress in this area, progress that seemed so remote thirty years ago, is so real and genuine in the 1960's. I hope that the same can be said a decade from now about some of the other aspects of public administration that are still lagging.

(7) Finally, it is good to see a public administration expert bring out the importance of service-mindedness on the part of public officials and employees. Sheer size will continue to make this a troublesome area, and such escapes as contracting or emphasis on protectionism of civil servants will contribute nothing to its solution. Hence it is all the more important that eternal vigilance be exercised to keep public servants alert and receptive to their ultimate responsibilities to the people.

By comparison with the foregoing, my supplementary observations, that is, points which Sherman did not touch upon or on which I would offer some amendment or modification to his views, seem to be of lesser magnitude. I shall refer to each of them very briefly.

Supplementary Observations

(1) In the discussion of grants-in-aid, I note that Sherman resists the temptation to support a no-strings-attached grant pro-

gram. He suggests that the federal government "must be more than a banker." I support the thrust of his contention, but would only add that even a banker requires of his debtors a considerable amount of adherence to standards of good practice and performance. Ranging from the investors for the great insurance companies to the International Bank for Reconstruction and Development, the compelling necessity of this approach is clearly evidenced by the staffs that banking institutions build up to insure compliance with proper administrative and technical requirements. Like private contractors, public servants in state and local governments should not escape accountability for *how* they get the public's work done through the technique of federal grants which require no such accountability; the taxpayer in Wisconsin has a right to some assurance as to how his money is being spent in Alabama.

(2) Sherman interprets "creative federalism" more narrowly than I understand the phrase is intended. I believe it embraces new techniques in grant programs, administrative and manpower improvements, regionalization programs, and a host of other intergovernmental relationship areas—not just the joint-partnership ventures in the programs treating poverty and urban blight.

(3) I would question the implicit criticism of job classification expressed in Sherman's discussion of promotions and "maturity curves." I detect some attraction to rank-in-man systems, some faith that they are superior to the traditional reliance on the assignment itself, developed through job evaluation, as the controlling factor in promotion and pay. I must confess to some past leanings in this direction myself, but I am becoming less and less enchanted with the rank-in-man system—with over-promotion, with building up overexpectation, and with the disillusionment that takes place when not enough VIP-size duties are available for the number of VIP ranks that get filled. Too often, it creates a waste of talent and a failure to recognize not only that continuous promotability is not the only virtue that motivates competent people to do their best work but that a frenetic drive to be promoted is not shared by all workers. In my experience a sensible use of job-classification systems, fully recognizing the variations that can and should be established as a result of the "impact of the man" on what would otherwise be

similar jobs, still stands out as preferable to the closed, "up-or-out" career systems that invariably accompany rank-in-the-man personnel policies.

(4) Sherman's stabs at testing are too broad. Accepting the fact that, in many instances, written tests have been used when they should not have been used, that very often invalid or wrong tests have been used where others should have been used, that some tests have indeed been culturally biased, it does not follow that all written tests, even those with emphasis on verbal facility, must go by the board in order to insure true equal opportunity in the public service. We must, in my judgment, continue in a number of areas to test not only for the immediate job, but for the promise and potential beyond. And, most important, we cannot escape the fact that, for many jobs and many careers, no other selection device has yet been contrived that is anywhere within hailing distance of the degree of validity and assurance of equal opportunity that is provided by sound written tests professionally developed and applied.

In spite of these few reservations and caveats of mine, Harvey Sherman deserves the commendation of the public administration profession for the practicality and the insight demonstrated by his excellent treatise on administrative methodology in the public arena.

Comment on Sherman's Paper

By Bernard L. Gladieux

I FIRST scanned Harvey Sherman's paper at the end of a long workday simply to get the force and thrust of his message. My immediate reaction was: "Well, Harvey has written another very savvy treatise on the current state of the art." More mature study confirms this initial highly favorable impression.

His mission is to discuss "what is new and consequential" in the methods used for the practice of public administration. He introduces the topic by recognizing the plurality of government jurisdictions, agencies, and programs, as well as the diversity of the goals of public administration, ranging from efficiency to public-opinion responsivity. He concludes that the methods available for the conduct of public administration are changing in many jurisdictions and that there is greater recognition today of the need for a more hospitable environment within public management circles for innovative methodology and highly motivated productivity. Nevertheless, Mr. Sherman points out that many advanced methods basically remain in an experimental stage, and even those that have progressed beyond this trial status are, by no means, in common use in American government.

Mr. Sherman's statement represents a sophisticated panorama of the whole field of current technology and practice in government. His outlook is scholarly, but his pragmatism is reflected in acute delineation of current concepts and practices. He exposes some of the myths of certain new management schemes but appraises their contribution with balance and perception. His analysis of forces and trends which are operating as determinants of the future of our profession I found to be accurate and instructive.

The increased blurring of lines between what is private and what is public is a phenomenon of our times which Mr. Sherman elucidates in one of the best passages of this paper. I agree with his thesis that this represents a desirable as well as an inexorable trend. Nevertheless, I would underline a reservation or two which he treats. First, great care must be exercised that government control in the public interest remains paramount through processes whereby massive amounts of federal funds are allocated to private interests for the performance of specific functions. Private-sector agencies are and must remain agents of the government and subject to its transcendent control. Something less than optimum control sometimes now prevails. Excessive rigidity on the minutiae of contract-administration in no way substitutes for oversight of program effectiveness.

Secondly, I have the impression that some contracts with private entities are engaged in, not because the service is more appropriate to the private sector or that it will be done better, or even necessarily that the avoidance of red-tape requirements is so compelling. Rather, this procedure has been too often followed for the simple reason that government pay-scales are so noncompetitive that the numbers and quality of personnel required for the performance of the function are simply not available in government. In my judgment, this circumstance is to be deplored and can only be rectified by genuine implementation of the concept of pay comparability.

With respect to federal-state relations and the whole concept of the new federalism, the most controversial aspect has to do with the sharing of federal funds. Many proposals are being made for some form of block grants or outright sharing of federal tax revenues with the states. I agree wholly with Mr. Sherman, who claims it is imperative that there be certain stipulations to the receipt of federal funds. While we would all hope that the number and complexity of federal programs could be considerably simplified, it seems axiomatic that federal criteria must prevail if we are to be certain that federal funds are to play a positive role in the general national uplift effort.

While all of us appreciate the advance in decision-making which can be provided by more objective and reliable information supplied by computer processes, enthusiasts for these new techniques need constantly to be reminded of Mr. Sherman's caution that we should not become so enamored with information that it is confused with wisdom, or so immersed in facts that we ignore values and morality. The field of public affairs is uniquely concerned with human welfare, involving a whole spectrum of factors and forces which have to be reconciled and accommodated in the decision-making process. Computer information can facilitate, but in no way will it be a substitute for, legislative and executive judgment. As the article properly points out, selectivity is much more important than the massive flow of data no matter how fast or accurately generated.

I am impressed with Mr. Sherman's sophisticated treatment of Planning, Programming and Budgeting Systems (PPBS). There is no question but that this system, so spectacularly employed by Secretary McNamara in the Department of Defense, has joined program-budgeting and cost-benefit analysis as a constructive aid to the selection of programs and the allocation of funds. PPBS is particularly suited to decision-making in the field of logistics or where other quantitative measurements are of paramount force. But, again, it cannot substitute for decision-making in terms of strategic human values, where choices have to be made as to who gets the benefit, when, and how. With its great virtues, we simply need to understand and emphasize the limitations implicit in a PPBS approach. Mr. Sherman has done exactly this.

I agree with Mr. Sherman that the most volatile problem in government personnel-administration is that of government-union relationships. But I wish that he had both amplified the subject and been more definitive on this transcendent issue of public employment. I am convinced that the effort to transpose the practices of militant unionism from business to government is destructive of the merit principles we have cherished so long. Furthermore, I fear that rising union demands for decisional participation on policy and program matters, as well as with respect to administrative subjects, threaten to impair the foundations of representative government by compromising the authority of legislators and responsible government executives. How we can assure equitable treatment for public servants while guaranteeing dependable protection to the public from the paralyzing consequences of strikes is a question which could well merit more extensive treatment. No viable formula has been found by anyone, so Mr. Sherman cannot be faulted here.

Mr. Sherman's treatment of the behavioral sciences in the

search for excellence represents a brilliant description of government organizations as, essentially, social systems requiring a new type of executive whose leadership is less based on the authority of office but who is creative with a "high tolerance for ambiguity," ability to live with stress, and a restless desire for improvement and progress. Traditional leadership techniques which tend to tolerate mediocrity and conformity are grossly inadequate for the flexible and fast-moving demands of modern government staffed by increased numbers of "knowledge workers." Mr. Sherman is at his best on this subject.

There is, of course, room for disagreement with or modification of some of his observations and emphases. Necessarily, the paper raises more issues and dilemmas than it purports to settle. One frequently wishes that Mr. Sherman had presented stronger conclusions or made more explicit recommendations on some of the issues he raises. Some might also claim that the paper does not adequately reflect the dynamics of society and politics as determinants in administrative methodology. I think also that Mr. Sherman might have given more emphasis to the vast gulf between the advanced concepts and practices, which he describes as available, and their infrequent adoption and implementation, particularly by state and local governments. I wish he had "deplored" a little more. We know a lot more than we practice, and we, as professionals, need to place a great deal more stress on adoption of manifest reform by both political and executive leaders. Admittedly, however, these subjects were not within the scope of his subject or purpose.

In sum, he offers new perspectives and aspirations for the future practice of public administration. The paper is skillfully organized, articulate, trenchant, and marked by acuity of observation. It may well endure as a landmark in taking stock of the current state of public administration practice; certainly it is the best overview of trends and forces shaping the public management of the future that this reader has encountered in recent times. Unqualifiedly, I recommend its thoughtful study by all of those interested in advancing the case of good governmental management.

Conference Discussion on Methodology in the Practice of Public Administration

SHERMAN: I guess I ought to start by saying that since my paper contains over twice as many words as I was asked to write (and that is cut down to half of my original draft), I did not spend too much time arguing about what public administration is. I did make certain arbitrary assumptions. One is that I am talking only about United States public administration, not on the logical and philosophical grounds that Harlan Cleveland just gave, but on the very practical grounds that my paper was already too long, and would have to be longer if I talked about what was being done in practice elsewhere in the world. Another is that I am talking primarily about the executive branch, ignoring other elements that I would consider theoretically to be included in public administration, that is, administration of the legislative and judicial branches and the interrelationships among the three branches. Incidentally, Jim, I object to the third point that you made about taking international relations out of political science on the grounds that present-day theory talks about a "total systems" approach. Looking at government only "down" and "intra" rather than "up" and "inter" gives much too limited a view.

It seems to me that the commentaries written by Gladieux and Macy, by and large, do two things. They elaborate on some of the points that I made, and they disagree, in part, with some of them. Where they elaborate, I think that they have contributed useful additions. Where they disagree, I am willing to let it rest. I think that their points are well taken. I do not necessarily agree with their disagreements, but I am glad to have them on the record. I would like to say a word on one point that Gladieux makes. He says that he wishes that I would have "deplored" a little more: deplored in the sense that a large number of jurisdictions, mostly at the state and local level, are not anywhere near following what would be considered advanced practices. I guess my only justification is that part of what I took out of my first draft tried to do that very thing. I am now ready to hear any comments on the paper that anybody chooses to make.

MACY: I would like to start off the commentary, and hopefully the discussion, on the point that Harvey makes in his paper with respect to the relationship of the public and private sectors through the contract, or what Don Price called the new federalism, because I think there has not been a degree of intellectual analysis on just what this new federalism represents. I do not cite this with any series of value judgments in mind but only to really see what this does mean in terms of a new methodology of administration. This is a widespread and diversified practice at the present time. It covers a wide range of the involvement of nongovernmental entities in the practice of government, and the inference is made and offered in Harvey's paper that much of the motivation and use of the contract is to avoid the inflexibilities and inhibitions that exist in public structure. My view is that the motivation is substantially broader and more subtle than that, that it is an effort to bring into play resources that exist throughout the national society in the accomplishment of public objectives.

The problem that we faced in the Bell Report of 1962, the problem that we merely touch on in both Harvey's paper and our comments, is what criteria should be applied by public decision-makers in determining which processes or functions or services should actually be performed under contract and which should be retained as governmental activities in order to exercise essential control in response to the will of the legislature and the expectation of the people. We have a variety of patterns that have emerged, largely in the course of the last twenty-five years. And I think that we can deplore, on the one hand, and on the other hand, commend these patterns that have existed.

We have tended to build certain political forces within the contracts which have given them a political role to play. Their continuance in the public business has become a part of corporate policies. You have varying degrees of involvement all the way from virtually total involvement in some of the aerospace industries to relatively marginal involvement in some of the universities. I think that we have been deficient both in government and in the academic world in dealing with the full implications of this particular issue, and I would urge for this a prominent place on the agenda of research and discussion in that period ahead.

I think there are some very fascinating case studies that are emerging in a number of different categories of public operation, and that the existence of those combinations and partnerships, through contract and through grants, establishes some wider and broader dimensions of public policy which, I believe, fall within the scope of public administration, in a nontraditional sense. As deeply as I have been immersed as a practitioner during the last twenty years, I am still unable to find any set of reasonable criteria which can serve as guidance. I think that in some instances, there has been excessive utilization of what I would view to be nonaccountable private agencies without an adequate degree of supervision. I am sure, on the other hand, that there has been a degree of political supervision which has made the conduct of public business an enormous chore to the private authority. But this gets more into details of technique. So my comment is by way of urging further exploration and study in the area. I am gratified that it was pointed up as fully as it was.

SHERMAN: May I make a minor comment on that? Some of you may know that Harold Seidman is the first Fellow of the National Academy of Public Administration. In this capacity, he is going to be writing a book on federal organization. This is the man who probably knows more about the subject of contracting than anybody else and I would like, maybe through Don Bowen, to urge him to make this contract problem an essential part of his study.

MACY: Harvey, I also want to comment on your reference to the intergovernmental relationships. I have felt for a long time that the profession of public administration provided an ideal arena for the interchange in views, the conduct of research, the development of training programs without regard to the individual public jurisdictions. The urgency for that kind of intercommunication, interstimulation, is everywhere apparent at the present time. The myriad of problems that are involved in carrying out national programs through a number of different jurisdictions is far beyond the comprehension or intent of those who designed the original grants in aid. And as experience has been accumulated, instead of adjusting the previous pattern to these new needs, we tended to perpetuate existing methods whereby federal-state or federal-city relations have been carried on. At the same time we have added new forms almost with the view that if we had enough different patterns, we would eventually hit the target. This has been wasteful. It has really reached the point now where, in the world of the practitioner, public administration is seriously on trial. It is on trial in terms of its capacity to translate public policy, in the form of public social objectives expressed in legislation, into the reality of dealing with problems in human terms at the local level.

This urgency is very fresh in my mind because I had a frustrating day yesterday trying to see if we could work out patterns of interplay among federal agencies at the city level, so that even some of the most fundamental and simple objectives of the Administration could be accomplished. Such a need as a common information system in order to ascertain the import of federal resources into a given municipality appears unavailable. There is no known central means for achieving that at the present time. Nor is there a common pattern of delegations so that all federal agencies dealing with interrelated programs at the local level could have the same degree of decision-making authority.

I could go on with a long list of these very fundamental problems which are faced within the federal portion of the house without even being sufficiently sophisticated to cover the problems that emerge when you inject the state or local government, and all its various elements, nurtured by federal funds. This is a very fundamental part of the field of public administration and one which really demands far more attention than it is receiving at the present time.

And the third item—and I can only give three or my comments will be as long as Harvey's paper—the third one is to concentrate on the whole matter of union-management relations with the public sector. I think that, in a very real sense, this is an area of public administration which has been sorely neglected in our considerations. The easy tendency now is to call in a labor economist and have him give you a plan for labor relations at the local level, assuming that you can very largely adapt in full to what has existed in the industrial sector. This is only partially so, because it also involves many facets of public administration. It will tell us some things, as Harvey has indicated, about the evolution of the merit system as a means of bringing staff into governmental appointment. It tells us things about the attitude and behavior in the public context. It tells us things about the application of law as the control of behavior in the public sector. This is further complicated by this interplay between public and private sector in carrying out the public work. We had many instances where, in a federal installation, we have private contractors who have a contractual relationship under law with a union, and we might have, as well, government activities within the structure with a different setting, with different groups. My comment is that I think Harvey did a remarkable job in providing for us a smorgasbord of appetizing items that really call for exploration in depth and can be an action agenda for the public administration profession.

UNIDENTIFIED VOICE: May I react to one minor point. On your second point, government relations, I think that I would quarrel only with one thing that I thought I heard you say, and that is that you seem to assume that there ought to be uniform delegations to federal agencies in a particular locality. I would question that statement. It seems to me that maybe the Department of Defense and the FAA in a particular area might have to have different degrees of delegation for different reasons.

MACY: Allow me to clarify my shorthand. I am really referring to the agencies that are involved in administering or approving programs that represent action at the local level, by the local government.

I say they are. I say that when the Defense Department closes a plant in a local area, this has tremendous significance but I do not necessarily say that, therefore, some Defense Department official is going to make that decision. This has so many congressional implications, so many defense implications that it is a completely different thing.

UNIDENTIFIED VOICE: That is beyond my example. My example would be six federal agencies that make grants that have something to do with water or sewers. My view would be that there ought to be some degree of consistency in the delegation of authority among those agencies in dealing with that particular area of public works at the local level.

GLADIEUX: Mr. Chairman, there is little that I can add to what I have already expressed in my comments applauding Harvey's paper, which can well stand as a landmark, at least at this time, concerning the status of public administration. Before going on, I would like to salute the response of the Chairman of the United States Civil Service Commission to Harvey's paper, in confirming that a sound personnel system must be based on the differences among people instead of on the concept of mass uniformity. Also worth noting is the Chairman's statement: "I cannot accept that modern technology or the size of public enterprises necessitates standardization, seniority, and protectionism in our public service system." I welcome such perception from leadership in the federal establishment.

Harvey has raised a wide spectrum of issues and problems, ranging all the way from public service unions to Planning-Programming-Budgeting Systems (PPBS) and the contract problem. I wish that we had time to discuss them all. There is one matter I would like to put on the table, however, perhaps because I have a peculiar interest in it. Harvey, in one very brilliant part of his paper, echoed the thesis that was expressed in more amplified form by Harlan Cleveland in his excellent paper, "The American Public Executive: New Functions, New Style, New Purpose." This line of thought was expressed also by Herb Emmerich and others, namely, that modern government requires a new type of executive, someone with a soft voice but an iron will who relishes working in a horizontal frame of reference. This modern public executive must have the creative urge for innovation and change. In accepting that concept of the style of the modern public administrator, my question is: From what sources are we likely to get such an executive paragon? Are we not likely, in view of this trend of phenomena, to find more of these types of people coming out of the senior career service of our government than, perhaps, has been true in times past? We are now witnessing in the federal establishment a distinct trend in this direction. I happen to be one of those who have applauded this policy, within reason, of course. My own conclusion would be that we are likely in the years ahead to witness an increasing reliance upon people who are accustomed to working in a confused environment, who understand how to work with the legislative body, and who can reconcile divergent public interests. We may find increasing numbers of these among government careerists.

SAYRE: I hope that everybody felt the thud or the swoosh as we descended, or ascended, whichever it was, from Caldwell's imperial general theory to Sherman's more specific problems. I am reminded of a comment by a physics colleague of mine that the trouble with physics these days is that it is running out of mysteries; it has only problems left. I think we have to settle for middle ground here, between preoccupation with specific problems and the search for what I regard as a premature search—general theory. Let me illustrate what I mean by talking about government by contract. The problem-solver tends to exaggerate the short frame characteristics. On the contract phenomenon, I would remind you that this is the way Elizabeth I defeated the Spanish Armada; this is the way we built our transcontinental railroads, using land instead of money; and this is the history of the Army Engineers, quite a long one, and that of the Bureau of Public Roads. We ought to be able to learn something, it seems to me, from our long history of contracts between the public and private sector, and we ought to be quite certain as to whether we are really confronted now by something new. Perhaps, we are confronted by something new in terms of either magnitude or function. I remain unpersuaded, even by the eloquence of Don Price, that we are here confronted by what Jim called the "new federalism," particularly if you italicize the word, "new." But this is simply an attempt to bring the discussion back to some point halfway between general theory and specific managerial problems.

LEPAWSKY: I do not want to divert us from the general issue raised just now by my colleague, but I would like to address myself to the question raised by him, namely: "Where shall we recruit this new type of professional administrator, grounded in the science and disciplined by the kind of public administration with which we are concerned, and which we shall discuss further here. Shall we restrict ourselves to, or shall we emphasize, the senior or middle-level civil servant who is philosophically grown up enough to do this job and certainly most ready to combine his iron fist and silk glove? I would not neglect the presently antagonistic generation of young people at the universities, particularly, who are interested in finding their way back into the midstream of public service. I do not have to speak for this group here, some of whom themselves are graduates of this tradition in an earlier generation. I would warn you that what you see superficially today is a hostile attitude towards bureaucracy in administration and Establishmentarianism of all kinds. In my judgment, it is hiding a good deal of enthusiasm and potential at this level of our society, so that I would add that we must keep the newer recruits, the younger men, especially the universities' by-products. We must not forget that we are presently moving from a situation in which 50 to 60 per cent of our high school graduates are entering a university and becoming college graduates, and in increasing numbers, products of our graduate schools and placement schools, but we are moving towards a percentage which, by 1975 or 1980, may be closer to 75 per cent of our total high school graduates entering a university. So, you are talking about a very practical matter here. What are you going to do with your population, your educated population, your upgraded intellectualism which we have in this country, if you want to call it that, and let us not forget that they are a tremendous reservoir and potential, and at the very level on which we are discussing this problem. Despite the fact that some of us may have differences, principally with our most articulate students and with radical students, when it comes to having the intellectual capacity to analyze problems at the interdisciplinary level, I think that this generation, not the coming generation but the current one with which we are dealing, is most facile and is not limited merely to articulation in words, but, I think, has behind it the desire for action. I hope that there will be comments by others who are engaged in teaching graduate students at the present time. I do not want to go into the broader aspects of the problem right at present.

DURHAM: I venture the opinion that we do not have a better field theory yet than the one advanced by Frank J. Goodnow. We forget that Goodnow was seeking a new theory to describe the process of government. He called his work, *Politics and*

Administration, a *new theory* of the separation of powers. He argued that the process of government is best understood by looking at it from the standpoint of policy-formulation and policy-administration. John Macy's comments about the contract describe the cutting edge of current phenomena in policy-formulation and administration, where the discipline needs attention. Remember the studies of grants-in-aid, done by V. O. Key, Leonard White, and others, thirty years ago. A great opportunity for classic research, investigation, and descriptive analysis beckons where policy-formulation and its execution meet in contemporary contracts. What is the nature of the process when Boeing sits down with the Defense Department? Professors in the departments of political science and public administration have been chasing behavioral rainbows when they might have been looking at some very concrete, significant phenomena, namely, the government contract. This important segment of the political process *is yet terra incognita*. The application of Goodnow's "field theory" to this phenomenon would still yield results.

NAFTALIN: I think that many of the comments that have been made, including what Homer just said, make me very eager to get to Steve's paper, because it seems to me that in our discussions this morning and in the papers that we are talking about oranges and apples, and pears and bananas, all under a broad rubric called administration or public administration. Some are concerned with recruitment of personnel and manpower problems. Others are concerned with John Macy's case of large questions of public policy and how this affects the course of government. I would put it this way: all of the social sciences, and for that matter the natural and physical sciences, are nothing more than arbitrary constructs. Along the way, somebody got the idea of looking at social phenomena in terms of some of our social institutions, regarding this as a handy way to put together a mass of material and, over time, this has proved to be handy and worth-while. So they revert to a discipline called sociology, where the limitations and the barometers are undefined and unknown except that people generally have a notion, when they talk about sociology, that they are communicating about something and, by and large, they are. By and by, we get other disciplines that are emerging in pretty much the same way, and I might say that this relates to what Harlan was saying earlier; that it is apparent that each of the disciplines, in its turn, regarded itself as the integrated discipline and still does. There is a natural tendency for every social science discipline, for every natural science discipline, to be ultimately imperialistic, to embrace the entire universe, and to say that this is a central explanation which offers, ultimately, a full encompassing of all the related phenomena. Everything is related to everything else, so, in fact, everything is related. Then it remains for identification or definition of what is the central point of integrated approach, and this is something, I think, that we have just simply not done in administration.

I think that in Steve Bailey's paper there is, at least, a beginning, and I anticipate really what Steve will do when he takes up his paper, but at least here is the beginning of some effort to define the theoretical construct that relates to administration in terms of our practice, in terms of administration both as a discipline, if it is that, and in terms of its being a teaching effort. One further point that I would like to make here is: whether it is political science or the social sciences generally or just the intellectual effort to gather central notions, we are in the same relationship between basic information, basic intellectual views and constructs, and the practice of public administration. Sociology has social work. In almost all of the disciplines this kind of problem appears. What do you do with the outcropping which is forced upon modern higher education in the form of professionalism, in the form of vocationalism, in the form of some kind of service? Every discipline has to face this problem. There is nothing new or unique in the relationship between political science and public administration, and I would say that we ought to face this pretty much in the same way as sociology faces its relationship with social welfare, as something that may be exploited, something that may be used to build a budget in the institution of higher education so that there are enough people around to do the work that has to be done. But this is not relevant to our problem. We still need to know what the field of administration is, whether there really is one field of public administration which is distinctively different from the other fields of administration, and, if so, how it can be reduced to communicable ideas, or ideas communicable to a definition which defines it. I think that in some of these papers there is a beginning. I think that Keith has phrases there that begin to build into something that tells us about the character of public administration, but I do not know. I know that the comments which I have made here are somewhat disjointed, but I feel that all of our discussions here are disjointed. I am not sure at this point what we mean in this discussion about what is methodology. I am not sure that John Macy's view of methodology at all matches what I would think methodology would mean or what I think is implicit in the proper use of methodology in scientific terms. I think that we do need to define it. I think I understand what objectives are, and yet I am not quite sure what the objectives are in public administration. If I say to you, "What are the objectives of sociology?" "What are the objectives of history as a discipline?" "What are the objectives of physics?" You could say that these are just not comparable notions. That tells us something, does it not? It tells us that public administration, then, really is not a discipline. In other words, I would like to know: "What do we mean by methodology?" "What are objectives and what are scope in the terms that we are using this?" And, I do not think that we can just gloss over the confusion between terms such as discipline, profession, and focus. If public administration is all three, then all that we have got to deal with are apples and oranges and bananas. If it is a profession, then we ought to define what that profession is. I have been away myself, just for a personal note here, from the formal discussions on political science and public administration for several years, and I have really been so busy with the kinds of problems with which John Macy is concerned that I have not really thought in these terms very much. I was rather surprised —it is a kind of Rip Van Winkle experience—to come back after these years and find that the same old unresolved dilemmas are there, the same lack of definition, the same mixture of categories. I find that I have a vague unease about the disjointed relationship among these statements. Maybe I should have waited and made these statements last.

LEPAWSKY: Regarding Arthur's comment about our definitional confusion, it is true that we have lacked a certain conceptual rigorousness. But as to his point that public administration's relationship to political science or the policy sciences, or possibly the social sciences, is comparable to social welfare's relationship to sociology, and I presume one might add business administration's relationship to economics, I would raise some question about that. Not only do some of our academic specialists tend to be as broad, and sometimes, insofar as organizational theory is concerned, broader than the parent discipline of political science, but I would question the comparison as a matter of historical description of what most of us have done or thought in public administration.

Under the pressure of current political and public policy developments themselves, it is true that social work has broadened its sceintific base, just as business administration has been increasingly interested in the economic fundamentals. But it seems to me that there has for a longer time been a basic approach to the subject matter of public administration. The contrary position is something of a myth fostered in part by our own colleagues in political science, justly critical of some of our so-called "sewer-counting" techniques and of some of our other unrelevant, but also untypical, researches.

NAFTALIN: Mr. Chairman, let me just refer to this rather quickly. I only meant to suggest that I do not regard as terribly relevant to establishing and identifying a body of theoretical principles to the field of administration the question of what its relationship is to any any particular social science, whether it is political science or history or sociology. I regard the relationship between economics and business administration as nothing more than just a kind of recruiting ground, an entry point, because the world of business does bear a relationship to economics but it is not any much greater or much less than its relationship to sociology or political science or history or physiology or chemistry. As a matter of fact, in some respects, modern business today has a closer relationship to chemistry than it has to economics. So I just say that almost every major discipline has this kind of problem, but the fact that economics graduates, or those who major in economics, go into business administration, does not in any fundamental way, affect the character of economics as a discipline. This happens to be a social fact. And that is how I see the relationship between public administration and political science as a social fact.

RIGGS: I would like to raise a point of order. We have been talking a lot about objectives, but I remain confused and disturbed about the objectives of this conference. Are the things we have been discussing relevant to the purposes of the conference? Would the Chairman or Vice-Chairman help us to clarify our thinking on this matter?

Let me state my own image of why we are here. As I understood the invitation and preliminary program, there is a widespread feeling that the general theory and scope of public administration (and not just American public administration) as an academic subject in our universities was in serious trouble. It was thought that a conference on public administration would clarify the nature of this difficulty and help us to revive or invigorate public administration as a creative and rigorous subject of study. It would point us along the way to a brighter future.

Now, I am greatly impressed with Harvey Sherman's paper. It makes a major contribution by outlining an astonishing array of current administrative problems faced by the American federal and state governments. Certainly, these are among the practical problems with which scholars of public administration should concern themselves. However, I do not think that the paper deals at all with the theoretical question of defining public administration as a field or helping universities decide how to handle this field.

CHARLESWORTH: I shall try to answer that very briefly. The three people who formulated this conference were not thinking about the curriculum of the universities or whether there ought to be separate schools of public administration. They were thinking about public administration in American society, not in African or Latin-American society, but in American society, and what kind of person the administrator should be and what body of knowledge he should possess. This was not a procedural effort to advise the universities' curriculum committees on how to organize their courses. That is secondary. At the present time, I detect a disposition on the part of political scientists to cast us off, as if we were a foreign organ in the common body. My personal view is that we ought to welcome that and get ourselves out. When the Quebecians wish to get out, the Ontarians try to persuade them to stay in. It might be a wholesome thing for the Ontarians to say, "This is good. You go." Well, anyhow, as a political scientist, which I am primarily, and having been chairman of curriculum committees for many years, I can assure you that there is an inhospitable attitude toward public administration in most departments of political science. But that is not what this conference is about. This conference is about the state of public administration in the United States. Or, that is what we thought it was to be about. It does not have to be about that. It can be about whatever we gentlemen decide it to be.

SHERMAN: One of the most useful things I have found in these papers, in thinking about what public administration is, is York Willbern's two propositions: one, that you can think of "administration" as the generic field and break it down into public, private, military, and the like; or two, that you can think of "public" (that is, government) as the generic field and break it down into administration, legislation, adjudication, and the like. York's feeling, apparently, is that it makes a difference which way you do it. I am inclined to think that it does not make much difference, and that, either way, it is joining two things, politics and administration. But, to me, at least, this is a useful focus for a discussion of what we mean by public administration.

WILLBERN: Well, not to pursue that point—that is not what I had in mind when I held my hand up—but to speak to both Fred's and Art's points, I think, together, to me, this meeting is concerned with what public administration is about. What is it? What is it concerned with? One way that you could look at what it is concerned with is to look at its relationship to other concerns: that is, you define a thing by comparing it to other things. One attractive kind of definition of public administration is to say, as Dwight does in some measure, that it is a field of applied professional activity. The analogies are frequent in the university and in life. Medicine is the professionally applied aspect of human biology. Engineering is the applied or practical aspect of physics and mechanics. Social work is the applied or practical aspect of sociology. Education is the applied or professional aspect of human psychology. The woods are full of instances of this kind, but that does not then take you easily to the step of saying that public administration is the professional aspect of some academic discipline. Business is not just precisely applied economics, by any means. It is also applied sociology and applied this, that, and the other. But all these—engineering, business administration, social work, engineering, medicine, and education—are professions which people have to perform in increasing measure in our society.

Public administration is also a profession, an activity, a tremendously important area of human endeavor, which people must perform and for which good people must be recruited. And they must have some kind of background in what it is that they are doing, learned either on the job or in universities. Certainly, the universities, therefore, have an obligation, I think, to be concerned with what it is that these people ought to know. But to define, within the universities, those branches of knowledge which are carried out in this profession, is very difficult. One of the problems, which Dwight points out in his paper, is that the people who are actually practicing public administration come from every background under the sun. After all, medical people do not monopolize, but they do dominate, the applied activity of keeping people healthy. They are the central core of the professional operation. The Public Administrators, defined with a capital *P* and a capital *A*, are not the central core of the people who actually perform public administration. They are a relatively small minority and mostly concerned with, as Harlan suggested, in passing, awhile ago, little bureaus which include the accountants and the personnel people and the budget analysts, and the like. We know and sense and feel that public administrators (without the capital letters) are concerned with much bigger things—the determination of social goals and purposes, as well as the mechanical means of getting there. And how you define an intellectual background for the practice of this kind of occupation is an extremely difficult matter. It is not easy.

CALDWELL: May I just take this idea one step farther, referring also to what Fred said a little earlier about the national versus the international focus? I agree, York, with the way you put the task of understanding the business of public administration, essentially the development and implementation of public policy. In whatever way one understands and defines public policy, it seems to me that, while it is perfectly appropriate to focus on the American experience, if we really want to learn something that is true generally, we are going to have to examine the phenomenon generally. That is to say, if we wish to distinguish between those variants on the American scene that are unique to our historical tradition and experience and factors that are common to public administration generically, we are going to have to take into account the way in which administrative phenomena occur in other contexts.

And increasingly, it seems to me, this is so, for the very practical reason that international business administration and the administration of international organizations are bringing these cultural variants into confrontation with one another. And while I think it is quite appropriate for the individual papers and our discussions here to focus on the particular status of the subject in the United States, I would enter a strong second to the plea that Fred Riggs made, that we keep in mind that we are dealing here with a universal phenomenon and that whatever is really true of public administration in the American context cannot be really contradictory of it as a general phenomenon, although perhaps the American experience may present us with exceptions to the "norms" of human experience (if, indeed, there are such "norms").

WILLBERN: May I just add one other point to that, too, because I think it brings in Harvey's paper. Harvey's paper is an excellent summary—though, I am sure he would agree, not completely comprehensive (it could not be)—of what public administrators are actually concerned with now, and it is highly relevant to the discussion.

SHERMAN: This was what I assumed from the topic assigned to me. But, as Jim Charlesworth knows, I wrote him a letter when he asked me to write this paper, saying the same thing that Keith Caldwell says in the first part of his paper—to wit, that the subject is not self-defining and that it is practically impossible to discuss "methods" unrelated to "objectives" and "scope." Nevertheless, I tried to stick to the subject of methods and to stay away from objectives and scope as much as I could.

UNIDENTIFIED VOICE: Well, I think Steve does go quite a way in relating what happens in the real world and in the universities. There really is a difference. He does focus on the level of what it is that we are talking about here. What I really wanted to deal with is what I take as an interest in the observation about the elevating of the problems And, in some measure, I think that what we are grappling with will be reflected in how we go back and try to relate to public administration and what happens to it in the universities. It is clear that, even if we should, we certainly are not making much progress now in matching, equating, on any kind of a one-to-one basis, the profession of public administration, the discipline of public administration. It would be nice to know more about how the discipline is invented, if you assume it is invented, how you stake out the claim, but the fact is that, in the state in which public administration is now, it has no claim. It is just there. The political science departments maintain custody of it, but it has been a Chinese-foot-binding kind of custody. They have not been willing to give it its head, nor have they been able to develop it, and it has scratched around for some loophole which will enable it to break through the walls of what I believe is referred to as the complete inner discipline. I wondered if picking up whatever is relevant on public administration, whether it is a dignified discipline or not, is not the most practical way of doing something about what needs to be done now in building the kind of intellectual base that would give public administration in the universities the full legitimacy that everyone wishes it would get.

SAYRE: I would like to comment on something said earlier and just repeated. Public administration, as a label in the university curriculum, is about forty years old. Political science is not much older, so what we are dealing with, in the American terms at least, is fairly recent. My impression is that public administration may have lost its pristine identity, but it has made a conquest. I am a member of a fairly large political science department. I do not know any part of that department where the things with which public administration is concerned are not a salient part of the teaching and research. If we take, for example, the largest single group of our graduate students, who are majors in comparative politics, you do not very often in that section of the curriculum, or in their dissertations, encounter the phrase "public administration"—but you do encounter a primary concern with bureaucracy and its significance as a part of the political system. No one, to my knowledge, teaches comparative politics today without being concerned with the ideas of Fred Riggs and others about bureaucracy. This seems to me to be the obviously true field of American politics. It seem to me to be increasingly true of the field of international relations. It seems to me to be making its point even in the political-theory wing of most political science departments. So I do not know what the complaint is about. It may be that the specific phrase "public administration" has ceased to have glamour, but these changes in vocabulary are familiar changes in fashion. I do not understand the feeling that there is an inhospitality on the part of political science toward public administration, unless it is just toward the formal label, because the concerns which the public administration people have emphasized have made a deep penetration. It is public law, for example, which has suffered more, if you want to find somebody to sympathize with, and classical political theory as compared to the new emphasis called empirical political theory. These political science departments that I am describing export quite a few people into political science departments all around the country. Thus, I think the reading of the situation is wrong. Public administration, as we have known the subject matter for years, has made a conquest, not lost it. The training of practitioners in schools of public administration, it is true, may represent a specialized problem, with some conflict between liberal-arts objectives and professional-school objectives, but these issues are not special to public administration.

CHARLESWORTH: Well, that is what I was thinking about. But, you see, I think that this has really got very little to do with what the typical political science department is doing in this country. I see this bifurcation as a specialized phenomenon. A political scientist has to take cognizance of public administration if he's going to teach government because public administration is such an important part of government. As Goodnow and the others say, first you make up your mind what you want to do, then you do it, and that is the whole process. We get into difficulty because we do not have the right terms; we do not have communication. I have not communicated with you. I do not propose to throw out the public aspects of public administration that cannot be separated from government. When I talk about inhospitality, I am talking about the professional training of administrators as distinguished from the education of political scientists.

SAYRE: Well, this takes us back to a very old dilemma. We are not going to train the engineers, or the public health people, or other similar groups. A public-administration-profession definition is our main difficulty. This question of profession, if you push the point too far, defining the purpose of the schools of public administration as training civil servants, pushes the schools back to a very narrow range of what the government is concerned with in the carrying out of public business. Since you simply cannot take the whole field away from the doctors or the engineers, or the lawyers, or the accountants, and the like, you will be back to the staff offices as the career targets of the schools.

RIGGS: May I comment on the alleged inhospitality of political science to public administration? I think there is both a yes and a no answer. Wally, as I see it, political science departments are, very widely, inhospitable to the training of candidates for the public service, inhospitable to the offering of a Master in Public Administration (MPA) degree. The MPA is offered primarily to students planning to enter government employment. They do not expect to become scholars and teachers in this field.

By contrast, however, I think political science departments are, or may well become, hospitable to the teaching of public administration as an academic field for those planning to become scholars and teachers in our universities. They see it as a relevant specialty for the Ph.D. candidate, in other words, but not as an important subject for undergraduates or M.A. candidates.

If one of the objectives of this conference is to find ways of improving the preparation of candidates for the public service, then we ought to discuss the curricula of training programs in professional schools, including not only schools of public administration, or just "administration," but also schools of law, education, public health, agriculture, and the like. From this point of view, I think that a point that Wally makes is very important, and we ought to grapple with it seriously. He asks whether a school of public administration can train people to become professionals in "public administration." Is this a meaningful professional field? Alternatively, do we want to think of people in the public service as practitioners of a variety of professions, each of which has an administrative component or aspect? If we take the latter view, we might pay more attention to the teaching of administration in the professional schools of law, of medicine, of agriculture, of social work, of education, of engineering, and the like. We might also pay more attention to the need for career-development training programs, designed to enhance the administrative competence of people already established in a variety of professions, none of whom think of themselves as primarily "public administrators." A related approach would be to offer an MPA designed explicitly for persons who already hold a professional degree, just as a public health degree is often offered only for MD's.

Sherman: I would like to push this idea a little farther. I agree with Wally Sayre, but not for the reasons he gave. I do not agree that a student with a degree in public administration will necessarily have been educated only in the staff functions. There are a great many ways of teaching public administration. Al Lepawsky says that he is from the University of California, which he is, but he is also from the University of Chicago. At least in the days of Robert Maynard Hutchins, one may have believed that the "hundred best books" was the best way to train public administrators, or anybody else for that matter. There are a lot of ways of training public administrators, whether you use the term "public administration" or not. Given where we are in public administration in this country today, together with the size of the country, a pluralistic approach makes the most sense. I would like to see many "Universities of Chicago" with emphasis on the classics, many other universities with emphasis on the mechanics of public administration, and still others with a variety of other approaches. Whether we call such education "public administration" or something else does not matter to me, especially with so many people moving from private industry to government or vice versa. I think that the average person in his early twenties does not know whether he is going to end up in public administration or private industry. He may go into private industry from college but may, in five or ten years, find himself in government. So, as far as I am concerned, I think that the universities should provide a variety of approaches and that we ought not to say, "This is *the* way." I do not think we are ready to say: "This is *the* curriculum; this is *the* method that should be used to train people for the profession of public administration."

CHARLESWORTH: On behalf of the Academy, I want to thank you gentlemen for your trouble in coming here, for your care in preparing your papers, and for the earnestness of your participation. We are adjourned.

A Report, and also Some Projections, Relating to the Present Dimensions and Directions of the Discipline of Public Administration

By James C. Charlesworth

ONE of the points of agreement among the participants in the conference seemed to be that the convener, who also is editor of this monograph, should contribute a kind of concluding article, with a title something like that above.

It was not intended that I should act as a *rapporteur*, or that I should produce a *precis*. Nor was I to be an interpreter of the conference, since the sophisticated reader can readily make his own interpretation of the lucid prose provided by the participants. Rather was I to contribute a statement which would fill the place of the concluding article in the monograph titled *A Design for Political Science: Scope, Objectives, and Methods*, published by this Academy in December 1966. The purpose of that article was "to pose a number of questions which came out of the conference and the thinking that led up to it." Most of the quotations in this article are from the concluding article in the political science monograph. A few are from papers contributed by participants in the public administration conference. In the political science article, I said that "in putting these questions I hope I shall not be considered offensive if I exercise my academic right to suggest answers." It is my hope—and my expectation—that my colleagues in the public administration conference will entertain these suggestions in the same spirit of sweet reasonableness which they displayed in abundance when we were together.

What Is Public Administration?

Public administration is an academic discipline, but, of course, it also is a field exercise and an area of professional expertise. The participants in this conference were deliberately selected to represent these two aspects of the subject, and they attended in almost equal numbers. Consequently, the discussion moved from one area to the other, and the discussants had the advantage of a reciprocal perspective.

Some of the participants attempted to define "public administration," but others said it could not be done.

These are representative views of the more sanguine members of the conference:

"Administration" is generic; "public administration" is one of its aspects. Since no new legislation is unconstitutional any more, the role of public administration is expanding. Public administration is any kind of administration in the public interest, and the word "public" should be emphasized over the word "administration" (since we have administration in many private enterprises). Or, public administration may simply be governmental administration. Public administration is now so wide that it is coterminous with social behavior, but our study of it is too narrow; we must include in it values and public policy. Nevertheless, it does not cover private endeavors even if they deal with the public, for example, railroads and telephones, although it covers government corporations and independent regulating agencies. Another view, more metaphysical and precise, was that public administration is an "attempt through government to harness natural human resources for the purpose of approximating politically legitimated goals by constitutionally mandated means."[1] But the consensus was that man as an administrative animal has not been described and classified, whereas references to the basic nature of man in ethical, military, economic, and other contexts abound in literature and theology. Another view was that public administration is the organized effort to realize the intent of recognized public policy-makers.

The nay-sayers, after pronouncing flatly that no one is able to define public administration, made some elaborations, saying that public administration does not have discernible boundaries, and that it is traumatically confronted by a crisis of identity. Another source recommended that we should leave "public" out of "public administration," and perhaps substitute "macro." Still another view was that in the absence of a validated general theory of administration, a theory of public administration is impossible.

[1] Bailey.

Also, we must recognize that public administration as a discipline is basically different from political science or sociology. Moreover, the difference between public administration and private administration is diminishing; many private agencies perform public functions, and many public agencies perform private functions.

On the relationship of public administraiton to political science, it was stated, on the one hand, that it would be disadvantageous for public administration and political science to separate and, on the other hand, that it is no longer realistic or fruitful to consider them as parts of a single discipline. This second view was fortified by the pronouncement that public administration is too big to be a part of anything, which doubtless was what influenced the American Political Science Association to leave the subject entirely out of its 1967 national conference.

Another problem in identity had to do with the word "bureaucracy." Once a word with a bad connotation, being used by political philosophers to refer to a governmental system in which public policy was formulated and enforced by desk workers (civil servants) and hence in the same dark cellar with plutocracy, oligarchy, timocracy, ochlocracy, theocracy, and the like, it has now been shriven and made respectable, and refers merely to the mass of functionaries in the executive branch. In its transformation, its etymology is flouted and it is pronounced "burocracy." One participant in the conference persisted, however, in denigrating the word, and said that it meant "bureau pathology."

Points of Consensus Revealed or Indicated in the Papers and Discussions

The difference between this section of my article and the following section, titled "Nonconsensual Opinions Appearing in the Papers and Discussions," is one of degree, for there was little or no unanimous agreement discernible, nor was any participant completely alone in holding a view. I shall have to take the blame if I at times misread the mood of the conference, for I am not about to undertake the timeless task of trying to persuade all of the conferees to agree to a single text of a summary article.

Just as it was difficult to formulate a definition of public administration, so it was hard to fix the scope of public administration. Admonished by the Chairman that the members of the conference had not assembled merely to redesign university curricula and that more was involved than the structure of academic departments, the group initially agreed that the scope of public administration cannot be determined apart from the scope of the whole political system. It was not held, however, that this coterminous relationship extended to the whole social system. It was agreed that public administration agencies (above an easily recognized level) help to make public policy, and that the old bifurcation of government and public affairs into policy and implementation is erroneous. Also, if government by contract is nevertheless government, should we not increase governmental controls over the contracting private organizations, for instance, in salaries, security, and the like? (Great Britain and Russia exert less control over their public corporations than does the United States over private corporations which do not have contracts with the government.) It was also agreed that the discipline of American public administration should deal restrictively with public administration in America. Also, the bureaucracy is to be described, analyzed, and controlled, functionally as well as structurally.

On the subject of cognate disciplines, it was recognized that public administration and business administration resemble each other only in their relatively unimportant aspects, and that training in the two subjects should not be combined, despite the strident claims of the business management people. Also, the professional side of public administration must be separated from the academic and professional sides of political science. (This should not be difficult, for academic political scientists are inhospitable to public administration as an academic subject.)

Since the objectives of public administrators are determined in large part by the administrators themselves, it is distressing to recognize that normative administrative theory is in disarray. It may deal with the ultimate dignity of man, or may confine itself to publicly agreed upon objectives, like education, or it may deal with instrumental values like clientele participation. Normativism, if it is anything, is synoptic, and therefore requires a bold and comprehensive philosophic statement.

Descriptive-analytic theory also is in disarray, for old concepts of legalism and monism are lacking in reality; we need more studies of administrative ecology.

We have had administration for special groups in society, for example, bankers, and farmers, and also administration by special groups, for example, physicians, industrialists, and parents of pupils. It is anticipated that administration by ostensibly private agencies will grow, hence public administrators must restate their objectives accordingly.

Since the day of the public administration generalist is waning, and since administrators like to associate themselves with a professional program, like public health or conservation, we must set about to make public administration training available to administrators who have been trained in such professional specialties.

In training the administrator, we can use the analogy of medicine or engineering, which are the applied parts of physiology and physics. Physiology and physics should be taught in colleges of liberal arts, and medicine and engineering, in professional schools. Likewise, the teaching of government and of public administration should have a separated residence.

As to administrative methods, it was generally agreed that administrative authority and responses are no longer hierarchical, if they ever were; many nonhierarchical agents play in the game, so the manager is a broker as well as a director. Pyramidal organization is now recognized as no longer apropos. The executive is not so much on top as he is in the center, being affected by "subordinates" who surround him, hence the wise executive must "consult" before taking action. Because of this and other determinants, there is a great deal of difference between the behavioral outlook of an elected as distinguished from an appointed official.

Except at modest levels, the executive deals with people whom he cannot order around—with co-ordinates, not subordinates; "colleague control" is challenging "hierarchical control". Moreover, federal-state-local relations are getting more heavily intertwined every year; constitutional law and practical administration are ever more divergent, and lines of command are obscured, especially by the grant-in-aid programs, of which there are now more than four hundred.

How does the executive get to know what he needs to know? Computerization is all the rage now, but computerized information is not good simply because it is computerized. Nor does PPBS (a Planning-Programming-Budgeting System) give political answers. Quantification and cost analysis create an aura of objectivity about our study of management, but they cover only a small part of the total factors in a decision. Consequently, emphasis on management ability in public administrators is now yielding to preoccupation with policy and political considerations. Indeed, we cannot separate normativism from public administration.

How should public administration be studied? Future administrators should be familiar not only with administrative organization and procedures, but with the psychological, financial, sociological, and anthropological envelopments of the subject. For instance, there is still too much emphasis on managerial and staff functions, and not enough stress laid on functions as distinguished from structures. Also, we should notice the differences between public and private administration less, and break the subject down into subdivisions resembling those in political science.

Certain professional skills are needed, hence administrators should be trained in a professional school, whether or not they have been educated in a political science department. For example, since government unions will continue to grow, administrators should get more training in employee relations and personnel management. Since Ombudsmen and review boards will become more numerous and more powerful, and since courts will become more obtrusive, administrators should know more than they do about administrative law. (And this does not mean only the study of court cases.)

NONCONSENSUAL OPINIONS APPEARING IN THE PAPERS AND DISCUSSIONS

The "scope" and "objectives" of public administration, although not coterminous, widely overlap. But public administration theory has not caught up with emerging problems, like the huge military-industrial complex, riots, labor unions and strikes, public school conflicts, slums, the impingement of science, and developing countries. We are too preoccupied with academic definitions, with identification, meanings, semantics, and boundaries.

We would do better if we confined ourselves to the implementary side of administration. "The process of administration should be sharply differentiated from the process of policy-formation, even when carried on by the same persons,"[2] although there are strong opinions that public administration cannot be separated from the formulation of public policy, and that, in most cases, public administration can be equated with government. It is stated that public administration is, in fact, bound by presumptions of law and culture, and these are the data which permit a comprehensive approach. But this draws the rejoinder that public administration should not be broadened into public affairs or public policy.

Moreover, public administration scholars are too preoccupied with the highest strata of government, and with administrators who are policy-makers more than they are administrators. If we are to become engrossed in the processes of policy-making, we should bring into public administration the operations of local government, legislatures, courts, political parties, interest groups, professional associations, and also governmentally initiated private operations, called by one scholar the "new federalism."

Public administration has reached the nadir in relationship to political and other social sciences. Political science is making motions to embrace social psychology, epistemology, philosophy, and mathematics. but public administration is still parochial. But since public administration is essentially a profession, it cannot be a subdiscipline of political science, although there is a place for it as a discipline on its own. But if it stands alone, if it is made discrete, it will be much less attractive to students.

The governmental role of our society is being upgraded; there is more participation by citizens, and professionals are being bypassed. Indeed, the closer public administration is to the people (as in small units of local government) the greater the number of Ombudsmen. Even the role of the politician is attenuated.

With respect to the study of public administration in developing countries, and the growing prominence of studies of comparative administration, we are in need of a much more comprehensive and versatile methodology, and we need a separate

[2] Moak.

statement of the scope, objectives, and methods of public administration in non-Western countries. But there is dissent from this view; it is stated that administrative analysis in primitive societies should be left to anthropologists.

In turbulent or unstable societies, the public administration scholars and practitioners need not, and sometimes cannot, follow conventional political science methodology and standards; they find themselves dealing with coups, as in Greece in 1967. Political scientists recognize and treat coups and revolutions, of course, but public administration has a smoother continuum in constitutional crises than do sovereignty and legitimacy. Consequently, in these countries, the theory and practice of public administration are more certain and predictable than the theory and practice of public law, political parties, and constitutional processes.

The administrator has been thought of as being provided with "givens," or clearly defined objectives. But what he does is really determined by himself; for the first time in history, the administrator sets his own tasks. New applications of decisions have multiplied by several hundred in this century. Other voices caution us, however, to distinguish between the political public executive and the administrative public executive; the great majority of administrators (those not at the top) have been told exactly what they are supposed to accomplish. And in examining the administrator's area of decision-making, we must distinguish between the normative and the pseudo-normative.

Meanwhile, the articulateness of the public in government and administration is improving; and, just as the administrator is becoming more of a policy-maker, so the political officer is becoming more of an administrator.

Since an agency can be both a political and an administrative unit, accepting direction from above and giving direction below, we must study the whole of government, and be careful to distinguish between structures and functions. Accordingly, public administration as a discipline must take the initiative in codifying cross-disciplinary theories.

The professionalization of public administration is an area of contention. Some say public administration is every public servant's second profession; some say it cannot be professionalized, and, anyway, no one knows what a profession is. Technical training in a service field should come first, and schools of public administration should provide the second career or overlay. And it is more important to identify a focus for the study of public administration than to define the field of study.

But the objectives of public administration cannot be pursued or realized unless we do something different with the human material making up the administrative machine. First off, we should recognize that no IQ or general-ability test has been or can be devised which separates a person's innate ability from his learning and experience. But we can go much farther in the direction of "culture-free" tests than we have gone. In so doing, we shall get better recruits and also reduce discrimination against minority groups. Moreover, persons should be promoted when they are promotable, and should not be required to serve a particular period of time in a particular grade and should not be required to wait for a job vacancy into which to be promoted. And we need a system of financial rewards of individual employees, apart from rises for a whole grade.

The discipline of political science is bogged down in a methodological quagmire; we should keep away from it. Also, public administration is broader than political science in many respects.

To put administrative theory in order, we need four methods; the descriptive-explanatory, the normative, the assumptive, and the instrumental. There is a paucity of instrumental theories, because things are so contextual. Instrumental theory is a principal goal, but can you have a theory about how to do things? It is difficult, but if you cannot get something done, all other theory is pedantry.

But we must not insist on a "total systems approach"; if you wait until a grand design is completed, you will not get started. It is better to err on the side of muddling through. Since the public administrator generates group interactions, and is not merely affected by them, government public policy and administrative agencies are so unrelated and fragmented that a good administrator must use his own talents to put them together. This in itself is a kind of public policy.

But here are some of the difficulties in the way of formulating a general method in public administration: The phenomena of public administration are unique, hence comparative study and general theory are impracticable. Also, technologies and sciences are breaking apart. Another reason we cannot get a good view of government is because of "reductionism," that is, preoccupation with fragments. Also, someone should show us how to design a structural-functional layout which will show co-ordinate authority and processes, to take the place of the classical pyramid. In this connection, the heuristic analogy contributes directly to the realistic study of the dynamic processes of administration.

In tailoring methods to officials, it may be observed that in sophisticated societies, the administrator tends to subordinate his personal background and status, whereas in primitive ecologies, he functions as a personalized individual. It is regrettable that, for the most part, administrators are semi-illiterate; they do not read, they cannot write, and they do not even communicate with their pertinent public. There is a difference of opinion concerning the temperament of the official, some holding that he should be calm and operate on a low key, with a soft touch and an iron hand, and that he should be adept at working in confused situations. But others hold opposite views. Thirty years ago, the cry for the generalist was heard in the land. It is no longer, and we have stopped drawing precise distinctions between the professional and the scientific roles of the administrator.

Social scientists, as a class, should take more interest in problem-solving studies and research; they seem to be getting farther and farther away from the realities of the world.

On the subject of mechanical aids in administrative methods, we were warned that there is danger in the increased use of data-processing, computerization, and the like, for we are likely to confuse information with wisdom. The computer will not make middle management obsolete. Apart from machines, we need to devise a newly conceived kind of administrative machinery for the new scientific developments. Examples of new challenges are international weather forecasting, Comsats, moon shots, and the like.

ONE PARTICULAR POINT OF VIEW WITH RESPECT TO CERTAIN UNRESOLVED QUESTIONS IN THE THEORY AND PRACTICE OF PUBLIC ADMINISTRATION

We need both professional public administration and academic public administration.

We all recognize that public administration is a huge and obtrusive factor in our present culture, and that therefore anyone seeking a liberal arts education must learn about the nature and importance of public administration in his way of life. The presentation of this aspect of the subject has nothing whatever to do with the training of public administrators, however. They should be trained as surgeons are trained, that is, by showing them how to remove an appendix, and the like. The difference is the same as the difference between teaching the piano and teaching music appreciation by playing records and giving lectures.[3]

Another parallel is military training at West Point and the study by historians of Napoleon's campaigns.

In academic institutions, public administration should be separated from political science. At a typical meeting of the American Political Science Association (not the 1967 conference, to be sure):

We see in the same hotel an expert on sixteenth-century monarchomachism in dubious rapport with an expert on municipal refuse disposal. Also, there are authorities on public finance, international government, corrupt-practices acts, American constitutional law, village life in India, regional planning, nationalism and international power politics, methodology in general political research, community power structure—these make up only part of the list. Yet these professionals are all called political scientists, and they all have the same merchantable Ph.D. If this is what a political scientist is supposed to be, how can one train him? Is any other subject so extended, even sociology?

At one time economics suffered from a similar spread, but that discipline has now been made tenable and viable by a process of fissiparation. Economics proper embraces the history and mathematics of economics, comparative systems, economic theory, and the like, and separate departments and faculties have been created for business law, finance, marketing, accounting, industry and management, private and social insurance, and transportation.

There is much to be said for a division of our discipline into three disciplines—government, administration, and international relations. "Government" would embrace theory, American and comparative government, political development, planning, parties, constitutional law

[3] James C. Charlesworth (ed.), *A Design for Political Science: Scope, Objectives, and Methods* (Philadelphia: American Academy of Political and Social Science, December 1966).

and civil liberties, and cognate subjects. "Administration" would include public administration, public personnel administration, local and metropolitan government, most of state government, comparative administration, and the like. "International relations" would cover diplomacy, international law and government, power politics, and their related history, demography, and economics.[4]

Public Administration Should Not Be Absorbed into Business Administration

It is well known that a number of business management professors hold that administration is administration, and that there is no valid reason for special applications of special administrative methods to schools, hospitals, armies, churches, factories, department stores, cities, government bureaus, legislative branches, and the like. Many of these professors are arrogant, and contend that the administration which is administration is business administration, and that they are presently prepared to teach or train practitioners in all of the fields mentioned.

But it is recognized by competent students and practitioners of public administration that practices and skills in business and government become progressively less transferable the higher one goes in the organization. Thus, there need be no difference between a typing pool in Macy's store and in the New York City Hall, but different types of persons altogether are needed as the manager of Macy's and as the managing director of the city.

In governmental administration, as contrasted with business administration, the scope of the mission is different, the objectives of the organization are different, and methods (above the level of routine operations) are different. Internal controls and responses are different; external controls and responses are different. Nothing important is comparable. It is true that certain gifted men had been leaders in business and have become leaders in government and administration; there are exceptions to every generalization, but do we want to adopt a policy based on exceptions?

The training of public administrators should emphasize administrative methods rather than public policy. In considering this statement, one should distinguish among legislative policy, executive policy, and administrative policy. Let us use a new

[4] *Ibid.*

state sales tax for an example. The governor and the legislature must initially settle upon a sales tax, instead of an income tax on persons or a capital stock tax on corporations. The enacted law says that it will not apply to food and clothing, but it does not contain a bill of particulars. So the governor must decide whether umbrellas and canes are clothing and whether marshmallows are candy or "food." Finally the state revenue department must, among other preparations, lay out districts and, in so doing, must decide whether they should be smaller and more numerous or larger and fewer. I believe that only this last kind of policy should be part of the curriculum of a professional training school for public administrators, but that all three elements should be part of liberal arts courses in public administration.

The members of the conference of which this monograph is a report stressed consistently the role of the administrator as a policy-maker. But, whether for good or ill, the men I brought together were high-level operators, including the ranks of mayor, ambassador, university president, departmental secretary, director, dean, bureau chief, commissioner, and eminent professor. I still believe that it was most fruitful for men at these levels to look down at the administrative scene below than for middlings to look upward and try to see what they had never seen. Nevertheless, the conferees were not a mathematical sample of the vast mass of administrators in America. Moreover, they were quite correct in not dwelling on the routines of prescribed administrative methods.

It is only the highly placed executive who sets his own tasks. In so doing, he is not acting as an administrator but as a policy-maker. As mentioned above, the great bulk of administrators do what they are told to do.

In teaching public administration, cases should be illustrative and adjectival, not substantive and basic.

It is well known that we have case books of law, corporation finance, public administration, business management, and the like, and that we do not have case books in jurisprudence, Keynesian economics, and the anatomy of governmental and business leadership. In the field of constitutional law the case method becomes less and less apropos as the string of cases lengthens and the reversals accumulate. In the field of public administration the cases collected a few years ago were too few, too long in text, and too simple. The business of training a public administrator calls for written and oral messages with many subtle nuances, whereas the few large items in the case books create a configuration like that of separated boulders on a beach.[5]

The literature in public administration should be exoteric, not esoteric. Mature teachers in the fields of political science and public administration are presently able to perceive that the younger men in both fields have a disposition to adopt neologisms, to conceptualize concepts, to reify abstractions, and to make unclear what could readily be made clear. It would be easy to conclude that this disposition is part of a general feeling of insecurity, itself resulting from a lack of field experience in the discipline and a confidence-generating record of having recognized and solved a string of difficult problems.

If the teacher of professional public administration has not been an administrator of some kind, he should not pretend to teach the subject. "He should act as a football player, not as a spectator at a football game."[6] He should deal in exercises, problems, and methods to achieve administrative objectives, and his teaching materials should be rigidly practical and useful.

Only small parts of the discipline of public administration can be made scientific.

The more abstract, the more diffuse, the more normativistic, the more historical, and the more philosophical we are the less we can ape the real sciences and the less we can lay claim to being scientific. We can be scientific, if we severely limit the scope of our discipline, but if we did would we not excise its most valuable parts? And we are scientific, in some corners of our subject, but in other corners our subject is heavy with values and prescriptions, which can never be scientific. Why must we be scientific, anyway? Art, literature, religion, and philosophy are not scientific, and their professors and expositors render a service and enjoy a prestige at least equal to ours.[7]

Method in public administration cannot be standardized and prescribed; method is the man himself. In the "innovative, the creative, the controversial, and the influential parts of our literature, there are no appropriate rules of methodology. In the

[5] *Ibid.*
[6] *Ibid.*
[7] *Ibid.*

minuscule, the pedestrian, the predictable, and the common-pattern type of writing, it is clear that procedure governs both matter and form. If this is true, it would seem that we should divide our students into the inner- and outer-directed, and encourage the one group to be themselves and the other to learn a routine.[8]

Behavioralism in public administration gives us the "what" but not the "how" and the "why." Herpetologists learn to love rattlesnakes; social workers would be distressed if slums were abolished; physicians do not really want all people to be well; mathematical economists scorn "literary" economists. It is only human to become engrossed in one's subject, especially if it is a new departure. Presently we are hearing from a recently generated group of zealots that if you cannot count it, weigh it, or measure it, ignore it. We also hear that all we know about a person is what we learn from his behavior. That men, in the Jamesian sense, are free to think what they wish, when they wish, and that therefore they are free to be something different and separate from what their behavior might indicate, is lost on the Watsons, who make us willy-nilly responders, like rats in an electrified cage.

What is this doing to the discipline of public administration?

The present growing emphasis on quantification, observation, and behavioral recordation threatens to determine the scope of our subject. As a prominent commentator on mass communications said recently, "The medium is the message." If our medium, or vehicle, is to be confined to methods dictated by the physical laboratories, the face of our discipline will indeed be altered. I am afraid that some of our confraternity think that because the scientific method is good in some quarters of our subject, no other method is good in any other quarter. We must not be like the Christian Scientist who believes that because his therapy is good for psychosomatic diseases, no other treatment is good for cancer.[9]

[8] *Ibid.*
[9] *Ibid.*